the Romance *of* Risk

Why Teenagers Do the Things They Do

LYNN E. PONTON, M.D.

BASIC
BOOKS

A Member of the Perseus Books Group

Published by Basic Books,
A Member of the Perseus Books Group.

Designed by Elliott Beard.

Library of Congress Cataloging-in-Publication-Data

Ponton, Lynn E.
    The romance of risk : why teenagers do the things they do / by
Lynn E. Ponton. — 1st ed.
        p.   cm.
    Includes bibliographical references and index.
    ISBN 0-465-07075-2 (cloth)
    ISBN 0-465-07076-0 (paper)
        1. Teenagers—United States—Case studies.   2. Adolescent
psychology—United States—Case studies.   3. Risk-taking
(Psychology) in adolescence—United States—Case studies.
4. Adolescent pyschotherapy—United States—Case studies.
I. Title.
HQ796.P625   1997
305.235—dc21   97-12138
                                                                          CIP

98 99 00 01 ❖/RRD 9 8 7 6 5 4 3 2 1

For my parents, Bill and Elizabeth Ponton,
and all adolescents and their parents

Contents

Acknowledgments

I am grateful to my husband, Fred Waldman, for his support and encouragement of both my writing and clinical work with patients; to my daughter Sarah Waldman, for being extremely honest with me and helping me better understand what teenagers think and feel; and to my daughter Anne Waldman, for sharing with me her love of passion and romance.

I thank my assistant and friend, Amy Wilner, for her willingness to discuss this book at any moment during our workday, and for her sensitive editing and sharing of ideas around patients and the process of writing. Nancy Wilner offered encouragement to begin this effort, important words during a period when I had many doubts.

Gail Winston, my editor at Basic Books, recognized the importance of this project and shared with me her love of and curiosity about adolescents. My agent, Carol Mann, skillfully guided this book to Basic.

I would like to thank my present and former colleagues at the University of California for their interest in and support of this project and for hours of discussion about why and how adolescents take risks—Drs. Ralph DiClemente, Charles Irwin, Nancy Adler, Mary Ann Shafer, Mary Crittendon, Suzanne Bender, Jonathan Ellen, Sally Payson-Hayes, Barbara Moscicki, Nancy Reade, Mark

Lodico, and Enid Gruber; also David Knopf, Lisa Niver, Christine McGill, Elizabeth Ozer, Marsha Parker, and Debra Skidmore.

Learning about the process of writing a book has been a challenging experience. Drs. Judy Wallerstein, Peter Kramer, Jean Bolen, and Lenore Terr shared their knowledge about agents and editors, and my cousin, Barbara Loos, guided me to the title and to New York City. I would also like to thank Marie Claire Cloutier for her careful reading of the initial chapters, and Katherine Olney-Bell and Nell Bernstein for their comments. Many fellow child and adolescent psychiatrists, including Drs. Richard Searles, John Dunne, Alvin Rosenfeld, and Larry Brown, read early versions of the chapters and were tirelessly willing to discuss clinical issues.

A mother of adolescents doesn't see patients, teach, and write without skillful support at home—a special thanks to Felicity Winterbach and to my support group of women psychiatrists, Drs. Madeline Meyer, Ruth Noel, Lyn Gracie, Nancy Kaltreider, Marlene Mills, and Barbara McDonald.

For me, writing this book was an example of positive risk-taking, an effort supported by my teachers, especially Alan Skolnikoff, and, much earlier, my brother Bill Ponton and my sister Patricia Ponton Barratt, both of whom believed in the editor of *The Ponton Paper*.

I want to thank the adolescents and parents who lived these stories and later read and gave their blessings to my versions.

Finally, these are true stories, but I have had to make many changes to protect the identities of the patients and their parents. I have often made symbolically equivalent substitutes for aspects of a patient's or parent's identity and life circumstances; occasionally I have grafted parts of other patients' or parents' identities onto those I have written about. Often dialogue is fictional, and my personal reflections post hoc. If the disguises are penetrable, it is only by the patients and parents themselves. Any readers who believe they recognize any of the patients or parents in this volume will, I am certain, be mistaken.

Introduction

For the past fifteen years I've worked as an adolescent psychiatrist in San Francisco, spending each day seeing teenagers and their parents in varied settings. On a busy day I might begin by visiting a school to talk with teachers and parents about an adolescent in trouble, a teen perhaps ostracized by his or her peers, feared by teachers, struggling with grades, or in the midst of some other difficulty. Whether the parents and teachers are aware of it initially, such adolescents are almost always involved in unhealthy risk-taking. Their behavior can range from mild to severe, from shoplifting candy bars to stealing cars, from scapegoating a peer in the schoolyard to abusing others physically, from smoking marijuana to engaging in severe substance abuse, from body piercing to life-threatening dieting, from getting into physical fights to having unprotected sex, and more. Sometimes adolescents are involved in several of these behaviors at once. Teachers are concerned and sometimes angry, pointing out that if things don't change soon this young person, "a bad influence on others," won't remain in their school. The teenager in trouble is often quiet and angry but speaks up enough to demand, "Why are all these adults talking about my private business?" The parents in these conferences are also angry, but more often they're scared: "How did my child get involved in this dangerous situation?" Their most common questions focus on

1

their fears about their teenager's risk-taking: "What is it? What does it mean? What can I do?" Despite working hard to understand teens, parents are bewildered, concerned, and frightened.

In my work two things have remained absolutely clear over the years: adolescents are going to take risks, and most parents of adolescents are terrified about this. In 1995, when the Carnegie Institute published its findings on youth and risk, its report suggested that American youths today are at greater risk because they take more risks and are exposed to even more opportunities for dangerous risks than at any other time in American history.[1] The report called attention to an important and neglected issue, but it also sent a message to the culture—to parents, educators, politicians, policy makers, sociologists, psychologists, health care professionals, probation officers, juvenile justice system workers, officers of the courts, police officers, and to all those who work with and/or care about young people: there is something inherently dangerous about being an adolescent. If the dangers to adolescents are inevitable, then there is nothing any of us can do but hold our collective breath and pray as the children we love and care for approach this treacherous time. But how much of this fear is justified? How dangerous *is* adolescence? What are the appropriate areas for concern, and what are the commonly held myths and misconceptions?

Changing Our Culture's Mind: The American Dream as Nightmare

American culture is defined at least in part by risk-taking—westward expansion and the settling of the western frontier were all about risk, and the successful pursuit of the American Dream virtually requires taking risks. We are not a culture that has ever been informed by the idea of carefully assessing risks before taking them; after all, risk assessment seeks to limit a certain kind of unbridled behavior and so runs counter to many of our myths about ourselves and our history. Had the settlers known what kinds of dangers awaited them in the terrain ahead, would they have been able or willing to move forward? Today our media promote risk-taking for young people almost as sport, and it is no accident that our society has the highest percentages of risk-taking among adolescents; teens in the United States consume media almost without chewing, and despite the increasing numbers of dangerous risks available to young people, we still do not teach risk assessment.

In a country overflowing with opportunities for dangerous risk behavior, it is also not surprising that the myth of adolescent turmoil as somehow normal is perpetuated, but again, if we expect or consider chaos and disruption to be unavoidable in adolescence, then we are assuming that little can be done to interfere with the process, however disturbing it might be. This attitude of acceptance has delayed investigation and acknowledgment of the more complicated reasons behind adolescent risk-taking behaviors. It has also delayed *preventative* efforts of individual parents and society at large.

The problem is that our culture has come to believe that adolescence is naturally a tumultuous time and thus has blurred the lines between normal, exploratory behavior and behavior that is dangerous. Compounding this myth are others, including the idea that self-injurious behavior is normal rather than pathological; the notion of the "generation gap," whereby parents and teenagers are destined never to understand each other; and the perception of adolescents as fearsome creatures who don't want to be guided. All of these myths compound and validate parents' fears around their adolescent children.

For many adults, memories of their own adolescence contribute to these fears. They remember their teenage years as a time of upset and confusion. Recollections of their own personal search for identity as well as the physical development that occurs in adolescence — including such biological landmarks as wet dreams, changes in breast or penis size, and dramatic changes in height and weight — can bring back the feelings of anxiety that accompanied these discoveries and changes. And although years later adults may tell very explicit, funny stories about the shock of these physical and emotional changes, their laughter is often accompanied by other emotions they experienced at the time, such as sadness, fear, or despair.

Parents who believe that they just barely survived their own adolescence may be frightened to death that their teenager will not. And no matter how big a risk-taker a parent was, he or she is scared by the new risk behaviors available to their child's generation. Risk behaviors commonly found among adolescents now include: drinking; smoking; reckless driving of motor vehicles; reckless participation in inherently dangerous sports activities such as diving and boating; using an extremely wide variety of legal and illegal drugs; sexual activity without protection from pregnancy or sexually transmitted diseases, such as HIV; withdrawal from school; eating behaviors such as harmful dieting, vomiting, or laxative abuse; mutilating the body in various ways, including cutting and piercing; violent activities such as rape, robbery, or murder; suicidal thoughts and behaviors; and placing themselves in positions where they can be victimized, including running away from home.

For the adolescents themselves, popular myths perpetuated in movies, videos, and advertising reinforce the culture's romanticized perception of risky behavior as sexy and exciting. This perception was as true for today's parents when they were young as it is for their children now. The 1950s saw James Dean literally embody his persona in *Rebel Without a Cause*; the 1990s saw Kurt Cobain of the band Nirvana move from a worshiped cult figure to a near-god following his suicide. Both of these young men took unhealthy risks that were eventually fatal; both of them were glorified in their lifetimes and then deified following their deaths. And while adolescence is a confusing time and it is absolutely natural for an adolescent to feel misunderstood by adults, the notion of the generation gap that is put forward in the media, and perhaps even reinforced in the home, doesn't help. After all, adults don't need to share in teens' confusion, and they certainly don't need to contribute to it.

Moving Away from Myth: Adolescence Is Not Dangerous

The fields of psychology and psychiatry are not immune to the perpetuation of myths about adolescence. From G. Stanley Hall to Anna Freud, Erik Erikson, and others, the idea that adolescence is an inherently tumultuous period of Sturm und Drang has lived on in the literature and teachings of my profession.

G. Stanley Hall was a professor of psychology, president of Clark University, and a friend and colleague of Sigmund Freud's; the Viennese psychiatrist visited Hall at Clark in 1909. In 1904 Hall had published a lengthy work on adolescence entitled *Adolescence and Its Relation to Psychology, Anthropology, Sociology, Sex, Crime, Religion, and Education.*[2] Hall's tome immortalized adolescents as tempest-tossed, impulsive individuals easily swept away by emotion. In the nineteenth-century Romantic tradition, Professor Hall saw individuals as developing through predetermined stages from primitiveness to civilized behavior in a manner that reflected the evolution of the human race. His vivid descriptions and highly emotional language leave little doubt as to where he placed the period of adolescence along this developmental continuum.

Hall's meeting with Freud in 1909 was important for several reasons. First, Freud also wrote on the topic of adolescence and, like Hall, viewed it as a period of turbulence. Perhaps more important, however, Freud was accompanied to this meeting by several of his younger followers who had also been exposed to Hall's ideas about adolescence.[3] Ernest Jones, a British psychoanalyst best known as Freud's biographer, wrote a paper incorporating and expanding on Hall's ideas about the universally troubled adolescent: it was first published in 1922 and then again almost thirty years later.[4] Jones's paper spearheaded a period of tremendous interest in adolescents within the field of psychoanalysis.

In 1950 Erik Erikson published his seminal volume, *Childhood and Society,* followed by *Identity and the Life Cycle* (1959), which reflects some of Hall's ideas and adds the useful concept of adolescent identity formation.[5] Although Anna Freud (Sigmund Freud's daughter and Erik Erikson's analyst) had written about child and adolescent development as early as the 1930s, it was her paper published in 1958 that had the greatest impact. In "Adolescence," she characterizes the adolescent period as "an interruption of peaceful growth" and notes that "a steady equilibrium during the adolescent process is in itself abnormal."[6] This article further contributed to the myths about adolescence, which Anna Freud described as a period of conflict, when teens move toward independence and yet also feel a regressive pull back toward family. This push-pull dynamic is borne out clinically but does not have to be turbulent.

While Erikson did not actively dispel his teachers' myth of the inherently turbulent adolescent, his idea that there is a task for every developmental period in a person's life changed the profession's perspective on adolescence: once young adulthood was no longer seen as the end point, after which individuals are developmentally static, then adolescence could be viewed as one developmental phase among many (eight, for Erikson) over the course of a lifetime. Erikson defined the crucial developmental task of adolescence as building and shaping an identity, and he suggested that adolescents need unique tools to master the challenge of identity formation.

Myths are usually extremely difficult to get rid of and become so deeply embedded in the culture that new versions spring up when old ones are debunked and set aside.[7] Another idea that unfortunately has limited our understanding of adolescent behavior is the concept of "acting out"; initially a very useful idea, it lost its meaning when it became broadly applied to much of the behavior of all teens. As defined by Peter Blos, a colleague and friend of Erikson's, "acting out" refers to adolescents participating in and repeating activities in ways that represent significant themes from their past.[8] This chimerical term is used today in several other capacities, but primarily to understand patients' behaviors around transference feelings toward their therapists in both psychoanalysis and psychoanalytically oriented psychotherapy. "Acting out" has also been specifically applied to behaviors that occur after traumatic events. Initially those behaviors were seen as ways for the adolescent to avoid remembering; they were not believed to be specifically associated with trauma. "Acting out" has been used more recently—and again, unfortunately—as a general term for most of the risky behavior that teenagers engage in, so much so that the adjective *acting-out* frequently modifies *teenager* or *adolescent*.

Current thinking is beginning to acknowledge that adolescence is a time of risk-taking, that it is not solely harmful, and, in fact, that *frequent risk-taking is a normative, healthy, developmental behavior for adolescents*. It is during adolescence that young people experiment with many aspects of life, taking on new challenges, testing out how things fit together, and using this process to define and shape both their identities and their knowledge of the world. Adolescence is a time when, quite literally, young people are learning how to think and how to act. Their increasing cognitive skills play a significant role as they take risks and learn to understand and appreciate the consequences of their behavior. In turn, experimenting with new behaviors and feelings can promote more complex thinking, increase confidence, and help develop a young person's ability to assess and undertake risks in the future. This experimentation greatly affects adolescents' relationships with parents and other important adults in their lives. As they struggle to define themselves as separate individuals, they want to be recognized by adults for the unique people they are and will become. Their struggle is not all adolescent rebellion, then, but a much more complicated and fascinating process.

Armed with a number of clinical and epidemiological studies, Dr. Daniel Offer and his colleagues at Northwestern University have undertaken the task of dispelling some of the myths about adolescence—including the myths that normal adolescence is a difficult, stormy time; that puberty (the term for the biological development that occurs during the teen years) is a uniformly negative event for adolescents; and that adolescents are more likely to commit suicide than are children or adults. In contrast, Offer's studies indicate that 80 percent of all adolescents, including urban youth, do *not* experience turmoil but manage to negotiate the developmental period without significant difficulty.[9]

Dr. Charles Irwin, my friend and colleague at the University of California's San Francisco Adolescent Medicine Clinic and a pediatrician who has specialized in adolescent risk-taking, underscores that it's important for adolescents and adults to distinguish between behaviors that are enhancing to the adolescent and those that present not only no gains but a significant risk of danger. He notes that the outcome of adolescent risk-taking is always uncertain, that consequences may or may not be harmful.[10] Sexual activity provides a clear example: it can yield genuine pleasure and a healthy intimacy, but it may also result in unplanned pregnancy and/or sexually transmitted diseases.

Irwin defines risk-taking among adolescents as young people with limited experience engaging in potentially destructive behaviors with or without understanding the consequences of their actions.[11] Recognizing that most risk-taking is a normal, developmentally appropriate part of adolescence has not been easy for professionals or parents, at least in part because the more negative and dangerous *risk behaviors*—patterns of risk-taking with predominantly negative consequences—overshadow normal adolescent risk-taking, frightening everyone. There is a difference, after all, between turbulence and danger. It is vital to understand the spectrum of risk-taking that can appear in adolescence.

Certain teenagers—and by association, their parents—are at higher risk. A recent study I conducted with Ralph DiClemente, a professor at the University of Alabama, focused on risk behaviors among adolescents. We found that adolescents with mental health problems, specifically adolescents placed in a San Francisco psychiatric hospital, showed significantly more risk-taking behaviors than a comparative population of adolescents chosen from San Francisco's high schools. For example, the hospitalized adolescents were almost twice as likely to be sexually active and almost twice as likely to report not using condoms during intercourse. The psychologically impaired population were also significantly more likely to engage in substance abuse, to self-mutilate, and to seek out situations that carried increased risk for victimization. In short, teenagers with psychological problems are more likely to engage in risk-taking with serious negative consequences. Problems such as depression and substance abuse play several roles in adolescent risk-taking; while they can be the results of dangerous and continued risk behaviors, they can also be an additional risk factor for increased risk behavior. A better understanding of the connections between risk behavior and psychological disturbance will help parents identify the signs of psychological disturbance that adolescents might show before they engage in risky behavior, thus allowing parents and professionals an opportunity to address it.[12]

Taking the Journey: My Own Path to Discovery

I've been searching for answers to my questions about adolescents for almost twenty-five years, beginning with my first patients in medical school—one a sixteen-year-old Wisconsin farm girl who had lost thirty pounds in two months, starving herself so that she could look like the models in New York City, another a runaway teenager from another part of the country whom my roommates and I tried to help by letting her live with us for several weeks. These two and others like them were my first great teachers, letting me know that teens can put themselves in life-threatening situations with little knowledge about how they got there or how to help themselves out of it. At that point it became clear to me that young people cannot manage by themselves the more dangerous situations that they get into.

Another important teacher for me in medical school was a family therapist named Carl Whitaker. After seeing him work with a difficult adolescent from an equally difficult family, I asked to work with him for a summer. Skillfully gathering members of a family together in order to help an adolescent who is in serious trouble is a powerful tool of child and adolescent psychiatrists and other therapists trained in family therapy. I consider it to be one of the most effective ways of helping a teenager. Carl Whitaker brought families together, often from distant parts of the Midwest, more successfully than any therapist I have ever known. That summer working with him, I learned that families play a powerful role in how adolescents do or don't take risks, that parents and teens have much to learn from each other about risk-taking, and that teens suffer severely if their parents don't participate in this process.

After medical school, I went to New York City for pediatric training and found myself spending a lot of time in emergency rooms. This was another good place to learn about what can go wrong when teens don't know how to take risks in a healthy way. The results were frightening: teens experimenting with illegal drugs they knew nothing about, coming close to killing themselves; adolescent gang members challenging each other in life-threatening ways; and adolescents haunted by self-doubt and depression who attempted to end their own lives. Sometimes their parents were there, too, dazed and overwhelmed by guilt, frustration, and lack of knowledge about what was happening to their kids. In emergency rooms I quickly learned that teens and parents need a lot of help when an adolescent's risk-taking goes awry, and that the emergency room is not the place to get that help; at best it is just an unfortunate—or sometimes lucky—place to begin.

Still fascinated by adolescents and eager to learn more about how they could be helped, I next went to Philadelphia for my residency training in psychiatry at the University of Pennsylvania; that work included training at the Philadelphia Child Guidance Institute, a program dominated in the 1970s by family therapists such as Salvador Minuchin and Braulio Montalvo. I confess that I was initially confounded by the personal style of Salvador Minuchin, a rigid, often dogmatic teacher who promoted a "structural" style of family therapy that definitely left me hungering for the greater flexibility I had seen with Carl Whitaker. I was also put off by the training method—hidden mirrors and overpowering supervisors who either phoned in commands or magically appeared in my session, both dazzling and disrupting the work I was attempting with families. Nevertheless, I learned something—from the Philadelphia families, from home visits into housing and domestic situations of every imaginable description, from teenagers who were taking all kinds of dangerous risks, from parents who were hanging on, and from parents who were ready to give up. I also learned from my supervisors that there are many ways to teach the difficult subject of families, and that learning about it takes both time and a lot of practice. More than twenty years later, with both time and practice behind me, the power of family work still amazes me.

It was during my residency training at the University of Pennsylvania that I worked on my first adolescent inpatient psychiatric unit. Most of the adolescents I worked with were urban teens, many without parents—in fact, many had no families at all. Gertrude Hite, the director of the adolescent unit, was also fascinated with how adolescents take risks. She described much of adolescent risk-taking as healthy behavior that helps teens grow by allowing them to try new things and test themselves and their abilities. Normal adolescent testing can go awry, however, when an adolescent becomes locked into risk behaviors. Dr. Hite also helped me understand how important it is for adolescents to be able to see their behavior patterns as something they are capable of modifying, however slowly, rather than as something unchangeable, fueled by hormones outside of their control. She stressed the importance of adults taking an interest in this process, talking with teens in a straightforward manner, and not shying away from difficult topics.

After studying in Philadelphia, I moved to San Francisco and the Langley Porter Psychiatric Institute to complete my training in adult psychiatry and begin a fellowship specializing in child and adolescent psychiatry. The fellowship was a highly structured two-year program that helped me to see adolescent problems from a developmental perspective. How do physical, psychological, social, cultural, and intellectual factors interplay in a child's life? I was specifically interested in how these factors affect risk-taking. I was also curious about how risk-taking changes as a child develops. What skills do adolescents need to acquire to take risks in a healthier way? How can parents and other adults help them with that process? What unhealthy patterns do adults get locked into with teens that prevent them from being able to help? I learned, and now teach, that looking at risk-taking from a developmental perspective promotes an understanding of it as a normative *process* through which adolescents can learn about themselves.

After I finished my fellowship, I became the assistant director of the adolescent inpatient psychiatric unit at UCSF and worked there for seven years, eventually becoming director. Things were changing dramatically in psychiatry as medications such as antidepressants (Elavil and Prozac), mood stabilizers (lithium and Tegretol), and antipsychotic medications (Trilafon and Navane) became a part of the work with psychologically disturbed adolescents. I was particularly curious about how these drugs would affect adolescent risk-taking. It was on this psychiatric unit that I began to see so clearly that teens with very serious mental illness take dangerous risks much more frequently than "normal" kids. Treating their psychological problems was helpful in improving their risk-taking patterns, but it was clear that medications were only part of the answer to the issue of dangerous risk-taking. Only some of the dangerous risk-takers are teens with psychological problems; many adolescents with no serious mental illness also become entrenched in risk behaviors.

At the same time that I was learning how to use medications with adolescents, I was studying psychoanalysis, a method of treatment that focuses on eliciting from patients an idea of their past emotional experiences and other characteristics of their mental life in order to better understand and assist them with their psychological problems. Psychoanalysis uses free association, dream analysis, and interpretation of transference and resistance, phenomena routinely observed in psychotherapy as well as psychoanalysis. It has been much maligned during the past twenty years for many reasons. Some criticize, for instance, the length of time an analytic treatment can take; others claim that its inflexible and antiquated theoretical perspectives fail to take new ideas into account. Still, training in psychoanalysis offers the best opportunities for in-depth examination and understanding of a patient's motivations and behaviors, many of them unconscious. The psychoanalytical perspective is also useful in working with adolescents on risk-taking issues when behavioral patterns are affected by unconscious factors—for example, "forgotten" trauma from the past, or identification with a negative figure.

Following this period of intensive training, I worked on research projects that explored how teens take risks, and helped develop prevention programs to alter their patterns of dangerous risk-taking. One of the most crucial lessons I have learned from the research is the importance of identifying adolescents at risk for dangerous behavior.

Getting It Straight: Positive Risk Is a Positive Step

In truth, most teens are *not* at high risk to get locked into patterns of unhealthy behavior. When we assume that all risk-taking is dangerous, we betray our teenagers. Teens need risks in order to grow; they need parental support in order to take those risks. If the risk-taking becomes dangerous, then, of course, parents must act. *But when we assume that all adolescent risk-taking is bad, we fail to recognize both the very real dangers some risks pose and the tremendous benefits that others can yield.* This understanding requires nothing less than a radical shift in attitude—about risk, about adolescents, and about parenting. It is my hope that this book will guide the way.

Certainly American youth today have more access to more dangerous activities than did earlier generations, and violence has increased exponentially. But it is because today's parents have many legitimate reasons to be frightened *for* their children that it is especially important that they work to not be frightened *by* their children. Rather, parents must work to understand what teens are grappling with.[13]

Risk-taking behavior among adolescents is not random, uncontrollable, or inevitable. And many of the factors, both individual and social, that contribute to an adolescent's propensity to engage in high-risk behavior are modifiable. Parents need to be aware of how and where they can intervene. To develop teens' capacity for risk assessment, adults and teenagers alike need to be well informed about the risks themselves and about how young people currently look at risks and make decisions. Parents, teachers, and other adults need to develop a comfort level for talking with teenagers about these matters. It's not an easy process, and many shy away from it, but it is an absolutely imperative step in helping young people to develop in healthy ways.

More than any other age group, adolescents are attempting new things for the first time, no longer protected or limited by parents. It's important that adults remember the positive aspects of risk-taking. Adults also need to be willing to examine their own risk-taking behaviors.

Another part of the story lies in this country's attitude and response to its teenagers. A simple comparison between the number of books addressing the development and behavior of young children and the number focused on adolescent behavior and development tells us that energy and money are not yet invested in teens, who make up 20 percent of the population. Not only have problems in adolescence been neglected because they are viewed as normal, but overall commitment to the age group has been lacking.

Teenagers are not little, they're not cute, and they fight back. Parents routinely tell me that not only do they feel less gratified raising their teenagers than their younger children, but often they feel attacked by their adolescents. Adolescents fight with their parents. This is natural. Yet parents need to know that they cannot simply throw in the towel when the conflict starts. The fighting is not meant as a personal attack on parents, and parents have to understand this and respond rather than react. This fighting signals a desire for greater independence, yes, but not for total autonomy. Adolescents want to be treated with respect, they want their new maturity to be recognized, and they want to be seen as separate people, but they also don't want to be abandoned by their parents. They need to know that they're still cared for, and that they can make mistakes. They need to be left alone to make certain choices for themselves, and they need to know that their parents are available to offer opinions when asked. They need to know that they can try new experiences, and they need to know that there are limits, that they aren't allowed to do anything and everything they want. They still need to feel the presence of a supportive, guiding adult, one who can accept the changing roles in the family.

In other words, different parenting skills are required to care for adolescents than for younger children, and parents must also operate from a different knowledge base. Being able to change those skills is a special task for parents of adolescents, and it's not easy. After all, learning new skills when you feel like you're under attack is, at best, difficult. But just as we take care of and protect our children when they're small, holding them close and keeping them safe, we must learn how to guide them in adolescence, loosening our hold in order to let them explore the world and themselves in it. This is the challenge that parents face when their children become adolescents.

The multiple challenges of these years are highlighted by the stories of the teenagers and parents living through them. The sixteen stories in this book offer a glimpse into the lives of adolescents who take unhealthy risks. Some of these young people experienced violence or other trauma. Some of them inflicted trauma on others. Some came from wealthy homes and lives of privilege. One came from the streets. Some had been abandoned by their parents, and by society at large. Some came into my office for the first time in their parents' arms. When I first started to work with them, all were suffering. And for all of them, no matter what their childhood was like, adolescence brought a new kind of pain.

Their stories reflect a range of causes for dangerous risk-taking: developmental issues such as puberty and identity formation, gender issues and other environmental factors that place undue pressures on both boys and girls, unconscious thoughts and feelings that motivate behaviors. Jill sought out risk to provide more excitement in her "boring" life; Ariel found risk as she repeated deeply troubling and traumatic patterns from her childhood. The parents in these stories also reflect a range of experiences and feelings. The reader will come across parents who can't cope at all, parents who are tremendously supportive and understanding of their kids, and other parents who are simply struggling to learn how to parent their growing children.

This book is not about myths. It does not seek to glamorize or romanticize the world of dangerous behaviors. My hope instead is to provide a new understanding of why and how adolescents take unhealthy risks, and to suggest how parents and others who care about young people can encourage healthy risk-taking as a preventive

measure against unhealthy risk behaviors and as worthwhile activities in their own right. The stories in this book are about real adolescents, real parents, and the real reasons why adolescents take
dangerous risks with their lives. They also describe what parents
sometimes do wrong in response to risk behavior, and what parents
can do to help their adolescents change that behavior. I hope, too,
that this book can provide readers with some good ideas about how
to prevent risk behavior from being an option for younger children
who have not yet become dangerous to themselves or to others.

In learning how to assess risks and make reasonable choices,
young people begin to realize just how powerful they can be, how
much control over their own lives they do have, and what promise
their futures hold. Risk-taking becomes more than romance then; it
becomes a vital tool that adolescents can use to shape their lives.

Part I

It's My Life:
Risk-taking and the
Adolescent

Chapter One

The Romance of Risk

It was the most amazing experience.
Finally, I felt like I really belonged.

— Jill

Jill's parents, Celeste and Dan, were confused and frightened when they decided to seek help for their family. Their daughter was taking dangerous risks, which she thought were exciting and romantic, a way out of her "boring" life with her parents and school friends. Together we worked to understand how taking risks as a way of testing out and developing an identity is appropriate behavior for all healthy adolescents. However, "risk behavior"—risk-taking that is dangerous, has negative results, and becomes a pattern rather than an isolated event—is not healthy.

An alert fourteen-year-old with a sculpted cap of dark hair and large brown eyes, Jill sat in my office with tears running down her cheeks. She had been brought home by the police after spending five days on the streets with friends she had made after running away. These friends were avowed members of the Rainbow Family of Living Light, which sprang up in the early 1970s and has grown and flourished over the past twenty years. Beginning as gatherings of young people "celebrating life" and camping on public lands, the Rainbow Family today holds an annual national meeting that attracts up to thirty thousand people. Although many "members"

19

pledge to abstain from drugs and alcohol at the gatherings and intend to focus on spiritual and communal activities, there are still a considerable number who use LSD and other hallucinogens. Electricity is banned at these communal gatherings, but acoustic music is encouraged; there is nightly drumming and dancing under the stars in the woods. Not surprisingly, many teens searching for meaning, identity, and adventure are drawn to these events.[1]

The days Jill had spent with members of the Rainbow Family after running away from her "boring" home were apparently the most pleasurable she had ever experienced. At least they were until she was discovered by the police to be underage and was carted away. In my office Jill described her lost friends as "more than family" and recalled the blissful days she had spent with them.

"You can't imagine it. Now I don't even believe that it happened to me. It was the most amazing experience. Finally, I felt like I really belonged. Then it all had to end when the police came. I'll never see my friends again."

By this time Jill was openly sobbing, clutching a small piece of paper on which she had written the names of the friends from whom she had been torn. The whole group had been camping in the Presidio, part of the now-inactive army base located at the northernmost tip of San Francisco, overlooking the water. Several police and their eager dogs discovered the group's hidden campsite in a small wooded glen overlooking the Golden Gate Bridge on a cold, foggy morning. Jill's friends—one young woman and three young men, all older than eighteen—had been planning to leave the city and begin their pilgrimage to the annual Rainbow Family council meeting in Arizona the following day. But as she described it to me, when the police discovered that Jill didn't have identification to prove that she was eighteen, she was pushed face down against the police car door and never saw her friends again. Jill punctuated this story with more tears and lines of poetry.

This wasn't the first time Jill had run away. A year earlier she'd said that she was bored with her home, her school, and her parents and had impulsively decided to run away, abruptly disappearing with a girlfriend. I had worked with Jill and her parents, Celeste and Dan, for the first time around that period, and it had been rough. Celeste and Dan had been both heartbroken and confused.

Jill talked at length about how boring it was at her house in South San Francisco, a middle-class community of families from diverse ethnic backgrounds living in rows of almost identical houses. For the first six months we worked together, Jill had managed to fit this complaint into every session. It was clear that her comments pointed to a deeper discontent. We had all worked together to get Jill into an alternative middle school that seemed to be a better fit for her, with a program tailored to her scholastic pace and artistic abilities. Once she was enrolled at this new school, she no longer complained about her boring neighborhood.

Still, knowing that one episode of unhealthy risk-taking can lead an adolescent into a pattern of risk behavior, I had worried about Jill after the first runaway episode. Now, after the second, more dramatic episode, and all of the seemingly smaller risks that Jill had taken in the meantime, my worries increased.

Signs of Jill's ongoing discontent were pretty obvious. She told me that if she could find her Rainbow Family friends, she was planning to run a third time. She also let me know that she wasn't looking forward to school in the fall, even in the alternative setting, and hadn't contacted her school friends since she had been back home. They were "too boring . . . too young." They paled in comparison to the "family" that she had met camping out in the park. She knew she was bored, but she didn't know much else about why she'd run away twice.

"Dr. Ponton, I don't even understand why I run. My parents are wonderful. It's not them. It's something inside of me."

A few days after these words, Jerry Garcia, the beloved guitarist of the Grateful Dead, died suddenly. Jill was tearful during the session following his death and curled her body into a tight little ball in her chair. She mentioned her unhappiness about Garcia's death, and then there was a long silence. I restrained myself from expressing condolences, thinking that it might interrupt a channel of communication from Jill and that she and I both needed to understand these feelings of hers better.

Finally, she spoke, her voice quivering and her eyes flashing anger. "No adult can understand what it's like to lose Jerry. He was so special. No one will ever replace him as a member of my family." Here again I resisted saying what I was thinking, this time something about my own appreciation for the music of the Grateful Dead, and decided to sit with her anger a while. I tried to remember what connection, if any, the Rainbow Family had with the Grateful Dead. I thought it was significant that she referred to both Jerry Garcia, a man whom she'd never met, and the Rainbow Family friends, whom she'd known for only three days, as "family." I knew that, reminiscent of the 1960s, thousands of "Dead Heads" traveling in trailers, in vans, and on foot followed the band when they were on tour, buying and selling brownies, red roses, tie-dyed clothing, and drugs among themselves. I also knew that a lot of young people mourning Garcia were arriving in San Francisco from across the country. Several of them, hallucinating after sampling a salad bar of illegal drugs, had already visited the emergency room at the University of California, where I work as an attending adolescent psychiatrist. Would Jill's Rainbow Family friends be in this group of arrivals? Would she run away again? Her drug use up until this point had been minimal. Would she get more involved now?

As I sat silently with these concerns, Jill began to talk again. "It is so boring. The life, you, my parents, I feel like I could scream. When I'm with them," she said, meaning her special friends, "it's the only time I feel alive. I feel like I'm part of something special then."

At this point certain pieces began to fit together better. For a long time Jill had expressed vague longings for a different life. Her parents both worked, and she, an only child, had felt lonely after the death of her grandmother, who had lived with them. Jill had long before described to me with yearning the families she watched on television. One particularly poignant moment had been her description of the idyllic *Full House* family: two biological fathers who are also uncles to their respective nieces and nephews, one young mother who is also a mother figure to her nieces, and five children, all living together in a crowded Victorian in San Francisco, talking about all their problems and hugging in every episode. Jill's home wasn't like that. With no brothers or sisters, it was particularly quiet. And all the houses did look alike. No doubt, certain aspects of being there were very boring.

I worry about the impact of the fantasy families that Jill and other kids watch on television. Many of the kids I work with think that their families should be exactly like those on television, and even though they understand at some level that TV families are made-up, larger-than-life versions of the real thing, at another level their childish fantasies persist. Teenagers have always felt attracted to television families—many of my high school classmates wished that Robert Young or Ozzie Nelson had been their father—but one thing that is different now is that today's teens have many fewer adults in their world. Mothers are at work when the kids arrive home after school. Grandparents live in other states. Neighbors are often gone, too. For a girl who had already taken the risks Jill had, life on television's *Full House* seemed pretty tame. None of the daughters in that family have tried half the things Jill had. But if a deep loneliness was at the heart of Jill's risk behavior, it was easy to understand why a house so crowded with love might attract her. Loneliness can haunt the life of the unsupervised teenager after school. The idealized world portrayed on television and elsewhere can easily become part of the teen's fantasy world, and then a very real part of their lives as they search for people with whom they can make it real, as Jill did with her friends from the Rainbow Family.

Pressed by me, Jill began to talk about the "family" times she had experienced with her Rainbow Family friends when they camped out at the army base. For a few minutes I stopped focusing on the potential for rape, HIV, pregnancy, and drug overdose and tried to see it from her perspective. I listened to her words and heard "family" over and over again. "Someone was always there, Lynn. We were always doing everything together. I didn't feel so alone anymore."

I held on to her words when I met with her parents.

Celeste and Dan: The Family Left Behind

Parenting a teenager is an almost entirely different task from parenting a younger child. For example, when young children "run away," they often go no farther than the basement or a neighbor's house. Most parents understand that this is a benign behavior that gives the child a way of expressing hurt feelings or anger, and they know how to respond. On the other hand, when parents of a teenager are confronted with a relationship of three days' duration, like Jill's friendship with the members of the Rainbow Family, they may fail to grasp its significance to their adolescent. Parents of adolescents must shift and grow to be able to meet the specific challenges involved in guiding a developing teen who is searching for his or her identity.

Some parents are able to manage these shifts much more easily than others. With a fourteen-year-old as their only child, Celeste and Dan were just at the beginning of this process. And their daughter tended toward the implosion or trial-by-fire model. A slightly shell-shocked look registered in their eyes during our first family meeting after the second runaway episode—in which Jill had gone many miles away, to the other end of the San Francisco peninsula, camped out on an army base with strangers, and quite possibly taken quite a few other risks none of us had heard about. All of us were afraid she might have used drugs or had unprotected sex. Jill had experimented with Ecstasy and a few other drugs in the past. She had also experimented with "cutting," a self-mutilating behavior that adolescents often engage in for very serious reasons having to do with a history of sexual abuse and/or serious depression (see chapter 8). Jill had cut because she "just wanted to try it" and then had discovered that it helped her feel better. (Adolescents who engage in this dangerous behavior often describe the soothing feeling that results.) Although she had been lucky so far, there might come a time when her experimental curiosity had terrible results. Her parents and I understood this. How could we make Jill understand?

Dan was a man of few words. When he spoke of Jill's episode at the Presidio, he kept it brief. It was clear he was troubled, though. "This time wasn't as bad as the first in some ways. At least we knew what to do in terms of contacting the police, registering her as a runaway, and all that, but you never stop worrying." Jill looked miserable seeing the worry on her father's face, and said, "Oh, Dad, it's got nothing to do with you."

"Jill," said Celeste, "you say that, and I believe that you would like it to be that way, but it does affect us—a lot—every time you run. It's dangerous for runaways on the streets. It's so scary."

In prior sessions I had recounted the dangers for runaway teens, including higher rates of HIV, sexual abuse, and coercive sex. When I share this information with teens and their families, I try to do it in a matter-of-fact way with the goal of helping them make the wisest choices. But Jill was a teen who had put her life in serious jeopardy more than once now. Was it time to use scare tactics? More to the point, would such tactics do anything to stop her?

"Jill, you have responsibility for your own actions. You may not have meant to hurt your parents by running away, but you have. You have your own reasons for choosing to do it, but you have to think very carefully about this," I said.

Jill apologized to her parents for worrying them but was unable, even with my prompting, to tell them much about why she had run. Many teenagers have difficulty articulating all the motivations behind their behavior. We spent the last part of that session tightening rules, restricting curfew even further, limiting Jill's access to cash, and agreeing to have her parents monitor phone calls so that she wouldn't be able to make plans to run with her friends. We arranged frequent check-ins with me and her parents now that she was confined to her house. I also mentioned my concern about the growing Jerry Garcia entourage that was arriving in San Francisco daily. I carefully outlined the steps I go through with all families of returned runaways. It is a very serious risk behavior I place in a category with suicide attempts, IV drug use, and high-risk unprotected sex — all of which have life-threatening consequences. It's important for parents to know that once a teenager has begun to participate in these risk behaviors, it won't stop overnight. Generally it has taken time for a teen to get to such a serious point, and learning how to help him or her make better decisions and figure out the perplexing problems that go along with the behavior is a challenge that also takes time. Celeste and Dan understood this, but all of us were concerned that Jill would run again, and that next time life on the streets wouldn't just be something to celebrate.

Street Life

Nationally five hundred thousand teenagers are estimated to be on the streets.[2] San Francisco is the destination for five thousand of them.[3] Homeless youth have been a serious problem for the past fifteen years; because of a variety of problems gathering accurate data, it is unknown whether the numbers are increasing. "Runaway" adolescents are generally divided into at least three categories: those kids who choose to leave home; those kids who are forced to leave home by their families (sometimes called "throwaway" kids); and those kids whose entire families are homeless.[4] Although shelters make serious efforts to get the families in, many live on the streets or in parks, vacant lots, vacant apartments, doorways, or almost any other unoccupied space.

During the past seven years I've had the privilege of being the adolescent psychiatrist on a national grant funded by the Institute of Maternal and Child Health and Welfare. The grant's services are targeted toward high-risk youth, a category that includes runaways. This grant enables young people in the city to use a number of facilities, including shelters, day programs, clinics, and hospitals, by linking them together. This opportunity has helped me to develop expertise in working with this unique population. Many of the runaway teens are first brought to my office or clinic by social workers, but with some encouragement they eventually come on their own. When I first began to work with this group of young people, I had many prejudices and since then have experienced more than a few surprises.

First, most of the kids are *not* actual runaways but rather fall into the category of "throwaways." Their options are often very limited. Many cannot "just go home" because they were sexually or physically abused by family members. For some teens the "home" still exists, but their parents are unable or don't want to have them back. Certainly not all parents are in this category, and I've worked with many whose concern would take them over great distances to track down their child. I recently worked with a father who flew to Los Angeles and spent five nights searching Hollywood Boulevard until he found his twelve-year-old daughter — tired, dirty, and glad to see him.[5] She had wanted to be a scriptwriter, but a few days on the streets in the film capital convinced her that everything wasn't golden there. She was all too ready to come home when he found her. I encourage parents of runaways to look for their children and to be prepared for what they might find.

Second, many runaway youth struggle to maintain structure and organization in their lives. I've had patients pull out carefully preserved notes on prescriptions that they have saved from doctors on the other side of the country, a sort of portable medical record. Along that line, many take a responsible role in their own health, asking me thoughtful questions and often carefully following up on my advice. However, many young people acquire health problems on the streets that they would not have had at home. Again, one important reason to get a young person off the streets is that running away, itself a dangerous risk behavior, is a gateway to other dangerous risk-taking activities with serious health consequences. For example, unprotected sex puts adolescents at much higher risk for HIV and other sexually transmitted diseases, and, for girls, pregnancy. Drug and alcohol use is also very high in this population.

Parents should also be aware that children who are questioning their sexual orientation are more likely to run away. Many of the runaways I've worked with fell into this category. The teen, either correctly or incorrectly, believes that he or she would no longer fit into the family as a homosexual or bisexual, and so leaves. Many times the family remains unaware of their child's dilemma even after he or she has been on the streets for a while. Children with mental disturbances are also much more likely to end up in the runaway group. One study showed a threefold greater diagnosis of psychiatric problems in runaway youth.[6] Certainly these young people live under conditions of high stress that contribute to the development of mental problems, but a more accurate understanding of the huge numbers may be that children stigmatized by society, such as homosexuals and the mentally ill, are much more likely to be represented in the runaway population. It's very important for parents to be aware of this possibility and to have a plan for follow-up and evaluation when they make contact with their runaway child.

Although most runaway programs are "teen-centered" and really don't function as detention facilities, which are legally obliged to return kids to their parents, they do encourage runaways to evaluate their options, helping them learn how to assess the risky situation they are in. Jill visited at least two such youth facilities on her runaway trips. She was surprised that the staff suggested that one of her best options was to return home; they let her know that their programs were targeted for teens who were abused and really had no other choices available.

Real Risks, Real Challenges

From the time of my first visit with a teen, I look at specific risk behaviors, such as running away, but I am also interested in the pattern of a teen's risk-taking. Because risk behaviors among adolescents are increasing, a parent's or clinician's ability to understand such patterns is becoming increasingly important. Experience has taught me that behaviors may cluster together, or they may follow each other in rapid succession. Even adolescents who have taken dangerous risks in the past are not constantly participating in risky behaviors. The same teens may also experience long periods when they take no risks or participate solely in positive risk-taking. Many factors affect how adolescents take risks, including their genetic makeup and temperament; their social environment, including friends and family; their perception of their immediate environment; personality factors, including self-esteem; how they visualize their future; their innate propensity for risk-taking; their values related to health and achievement; and lastly, other behavior related to risk such as patterns of drinking or school attendance.[7]

In my work with Jill I was carefully examining her pattern of risk. When did she first take dangerous risks? Were friends involved? Did her parents directly contribute to the process? Did other risk behaviors precede the running-away episodes? Were there times when she stopped negative risk behavior and engaged in positive risk-taking? And if so, how could Jill, her parents, and I work together to make positive risk-taking happen more often?

Jill fit into the category of adolescents who take unhealthy risks as part of a pattern of testing, not only their parents' limits, but their own identities. Jill loved the idea of risk, the romance of it. She felt that her life—like her parents' lives, in her view—was mostly boring, and said that she felt most alive when she was trying out these exciting and dangerous activities. The feeling of excitement when she was taking a risk fit well with the identity she was trying to shape for herself as an adventurous person who did exciting things. Erik Erikson wrote about adolescents "trying on" identities, searching to find the best fit for themselves.[8] More often than not, these trials don't represent what adults think of as "identity" but are experimental, exotic, and transitory and often involve risk-taking, the

vital tool that adolescents use to shape their identities and, ultimately, themselves.

Between Jill's two episodes of running away, she developed a serious infection in her lungs—coccidiomycosis. The infection, caused
by a fungus, spread throughout her body, leading to a rash and joint
pain besides the disturbingly large cystic lesions in her lungs. This is
a serious illness, and potentially fatal if untreated. Jill's treatment
required that she be hospitalized and given the powerful antifungal
agent amphotericin B intravenously. Although she was in severe
pain from the illness and the treatment itself was painful and difficult, Jill had withstood the diagnosis and the hospital regimen
extremely well. Most interestingly, her risky behavior stopped completely for several months. No longer did she want to run away.
She'd told me that she felt a whole lot closer to her parents. They
were standing by her, physically assisting with the treatments, holding her hand, and providing a great deal of moral support. Their assistance was vital, but perhaps equally significant, Jill didn't see her
life as boring during her illness.

With determination and a confident smile, she'd reported to me
that her life had "more meaning" to her now. "It's special. Pretty
weird, I know, but that's how I feel about it."

Her pulmonologist had called me, worried that a kid who had
taken the kind of risks Jill had would be noncompliant and refuse to
take her medicines. He'd wondered whether he should keep her in
the hospital longer to make sure she got them, and he asked me how
she appeared to be doing with the painful, difficult treatment. I'd
told him that, curiously, she looked better than ever, at least from
the perspective of a psychiatrist. Her spirits were good, and she had
an optimistic attitude that she was going to "beat" the illness. Not
only had she been compliant, but she was organized about taking
her medicines and visiting the doctor, a characteristic she hadn't
shown before. She'd also been curious about her illness. One day I
found her taking detailed notes from one of my textbooks on internal medicine, determined to understand her illness.

Jill experienced this event in her life as a challenge. No longer
was she just another teen from a monotonous neighborhood in
"Middle America," as she put it. This was an exotic illness, and her
life became exciting in her eyes. Jill was right—the illness had

brought more mystery to her life. No one knew how she'd con-
tracted this unusual illness, which is more common in the south-
western states and almost unheard of in San Francisco. It took
several weeks to diagnose, the treatments and clinic visits were
time-consuming and painful, yet Jill was happier. She'd told me that
she no longer had to search for excitement—it was there in her life.

Jill's story illustrates dramatically how a teen taking dangerous
risks can change her behavior when faced with a real challenge, but
I've seen similar responses on a much wider scale. Working as a disaster consultant after both the San Francisco earthquake and the
midwestern floods, I made some interesting observations. Teens in
the disaster-affected areas who were allowed, even encouraged, to
participate in the exhausting, yet at times exhilarating, disaster
work were less likely to get involved in risky behavior. Even teens
who are not directly exposed to a natural catastrophe hunger for the
challenge and experience of such an event.[9] A group of Armenian-
born teens who were living in Los Angeles at the time of the massive
earthquake in then-Soviet Armenia expressed a strong desire to return to their native land and assist with the relief effort. Once they
realized that was impossible, they marshaled their energies into developing a relief effort in Los Angeles.[10] Teenagers need to have positive challenges. They need to feel that they are important
participants in life. Until the time of her illness, Jill had not been
able to feel that way. But after she got well, life became, once again,
too dull, without challenge or any apparent significance.

Risk: The First Phase of Adulthood

Celeste and Dan had also done well when Jill was ill with the coccidiomycosis. Partly, they were relieved that they finally knew
where their daughter was at night. They also frankly admired how
she handled her illness and were able to be genuinely supportive. I
had continued to meet with them in family sessions, although less
frequently, during this tranquil period, and we'd talked about the
possibility that Jill might run away again. Even with all our prepa-
rations, we were not really ready for the day when Jill left to camp
out at the Presidio.

After our first family session following Jill's second return, I kept thinking about the wide scope of feelings in this family. Celeste, who was more articulate than her husband, talked about the panic she experienced when she knew that her fourteen-year-old daughter was on the streets.

"I know it's only happened twice, and we've always gotten her back, but I really feel for the families who don't get their children back. I lived in a constant state of terror when she was gone, and those other parents are stuck in that world forever," Celeste said eloquently.

Dan again cut right to the heart of the matter when he said, "It's like your gut is ripped out."

The terror that Jill's parents—and to some degree, I, too—had experienced when she was gone contrasted sharply with Jill's elated mood after she returned. I could feel her excitement when she described her life on the streets. Besides feeling a part of the Rainbow Family, she had felt challenged, useful, and more creative. She occasionally felt this way at school with her friends or at home with her parents, but the feeling had been much more powerful on the street.

And even though Jill had run again, there were some differences the second time. First, she had called her parents from one of the youth programs to let them know that she was okay. And although Celeste and Dan were still terrified, they had handled it better. Of course, they knew how to file a missing person's report and could quickly access all the phone numbers for the youth shelters, but this time they also worked as a team, supporting each other. After Jill returned, when she told Celeste and Dan that it wasn't personal, they first listened carefully and then let her know that although they understood that she felt this way, her running away was both terrifying to them and dangerous to her. They were clear with her about limits and their future expectations. Still, Jill's parents were able to acknowledge why life on the streets, and with special, older friends, might be so attractive to her. Jill, in turn, really listened to them— perhaps because they had listened to her.

It was my job, of course, to listen to all three of the people in this family. I could hear the passion and excitement in Jill's voice at the same time I heard the panic in her parents'. Although Jill's and her parents' feelings were quite different, each had a sense of intense urgency. Jill talked about wanting to be with her friends of three days as though they were her long-lost family. Celeste and Dan were able

to talk about what Jill meant to them and to explain vividly how terrified they had been when she was gone. Speaking honestly and re-
specting what each other said was a very good start. But I knew that
Jill and her parents still had to understand each other's feelings
even better if we were going to help Jill decide to stop running
away.

Celeste and Dan had already taken important steps to help Jill.
They had recognized her first runaway episode as a serious problem
and obtained help for her by coming to see me. (Parents frequently
make the mistake of not recognizing a risk behavior if it occurs
alone and is not preceded by some warning of other risky behaviors.) Celeste and Dan had also determined consequences for Jill's
behavior, which included grounding and restricted telephone contact with her friends. They set clear rules for the house, including a
specific prohibition on running away and other risk behaviors.
Lastly, they let her know that they didn't want her to run away, not
only because it terrified them and caused her to miss school but,
more important, because it exposed her to a lot of genuinely dangerous risks. What more could be done?

One of the most important things to realize about adolescent
risk-taking is that it's complex and can take some time to figure out.
Teenagers are not all alike, and they can be engaging in many risk
behaviors for very different reasons. Parents can be doing all the
right things, and their child may still put himself or herself in high-
risk situations. Part of the solution lies in allowing time for a teen to
develop some experience with risk-taking. With time and gradually
increasing challenges, a teen learns to assess risks better and is then
able to modify risky behaviors. Frequently parents, teens, and clinicians can wait for that to happen, but Jill's situation was different.

As I've mentioned, Jill had not talked about a desire to run when
she was recovering from the coccidiomycosis. That period had been
challenging enough for her. After the second runaway episode, Jill
began to talk about what she thought was missing from her life. She
loved her parents, but she felt lonely and bored much of the time. At
fourteen, she was very young; waiting passively for her to develop
better risk assessment skills might take several years, and in the
meantime she was taking very dangerous risks. We didn't necessarily have time to let her "outgrow" it.

Different strategies have been used to help teens modify their risk-taking. Perhaps one of the most dramatic and well-publicized was the "Just Say No" antidrug, antisex campaign in the late 1980s; this effort made parents and teens aware of risk behavior but did little to stop it because it failed to acknowledge that teens are individuals, risk behaviors are diverse, and the reasons adolescents engage in them are varied. It is important to tailor the approach to the individual teen. A fairly basic consideration is how well-adjusted the teen taking dangerous risks is. Formerly well-adjusted kids like Jill seem to respond best to an approach that both educates them about risk behaviors and helps them explore and develop healthier ways to take risks and to set and meet their goals.

This is where Jill, her parents, and I began. We had a pretty good idea about Jill's goals—to create less loneliness and more excitement in her life. First, her parents educated themselves about teen risk behavior, focusing on running away but branching out into other areas such as the consequences of unprotected sex, including sexually transmitted diseases and pregnancy. They began by talking with me and each other about these risk behaviors and then gradually introduced the topics in conversation with Jill. As they did this, Celeste and Dan became aware of a number of things. In the beginning they weren't very comfortable talking with Jill about any risk behaviors, let alone the taboo subject of sexual risk-taking. They learned to talk, however, and it became progressively easier. It helped to role-play challenging parenting situations with each other.

Thinking honestly about their own teenage years also helped. Like many parents, they remembered themselves as risk-takers during adolescence. They did not want to tell each other the risks they had taken when they were younger, let alone share that incriminating and somewhat embarrassing information with their daughter, so they had omitted it from their conversation entirely. As a result, Jill had never heard about how her parents, when they were young, took new risks and learned to make choices, gradually modifying their behavior. Celeste and Dan had been very vocal about their current opinions and values, but they had failed to show their daughter how they came to make their own decisions. In fact, until we began talking about it, they hadn't seen that learning to make decisions is an evolutionary process. They had some pretty vivid memories of the risks they had taken as teens, and they knew where they stood now, but it was as if they had amnesia for the twenty-five years in between.

Like Celeste and Dan, our culture often fails to recognize that learning to make decisions that reflect good judgment is something people do over the course of many years. Risk-taking, especially during adolescence, is romanticized rather than identified as the first phase of a lifelong process that can at times be anything but glamorous. Even as adults many of us have taken some risks that were not successful (with jobs, relationships, etc.). But as parents we can realize that our adolescent children are learning "from scratch" how to make decisions and just beginning to learn how to assess risk. When you're young, danger can seem exciting, and because excitement feels grown-up, it's very seductive. Parents can, however, promote the excitement of positive risk-taking and draw their child away from more dangerous behaviors.

Gradually we were able to do that with Jill. It wasn't easy. We made it a group project, encouraging her to participate. Her choices—the tiny studded ruby in her right nostril, paired with a magenta-colored streak in her brunette head—were initially jarring. However, they were neither life-threatening nor even physically harmful. They gave us opportunities to talk about risk-taking and help Jill figure out what she had learned.

Celeste came up with some great ideas. She encouraged Jill to participate in a summer-school program making creative videos, and Jill loved it. Of course, she initially said that this, too, was boring, but she grew to revel in it and made a video filled with images of her adolescent life, including her friends and the Presidio. The film was dedicated to the four friends and offered her a way to combine different aspects of her life: her memories of her Rainbow Family and her ongoing life as a teenager in South San Francisco. Jill's video was recognized for artistic achievement and shown at the San Francisco Museum of Modern Art.

The video also represented an achievement of another sort for Jill. In it, she portrays herself as she was when she was living on the streets, and she uses the name she was given then by her friends. Her character is a runaway girl who describes what life on the streets is like. Watching the film, I couldn't help thinking about how difficult it had been for Jill to put the pieces of her life together.

Like creating a film, putting an identity together during adolescence involves both the courage to take risks and the courage to edit.

The Rainbow at Home

Besides helping their daughter with both ideas and opportunities for positive risk-taking, Jill's parents worked at reconstructing their family to include a teenager in search of herself. They acknowledged that their family was only a three-person unit, not a large blended family like the one in *Full House* or the large extended families that Dan and Celeste had grown up in. In many ways the smaller number of people in their family made their job harder. Jill, at fourteen, was searching for contact with others. She was actually looking for new family members, adopted brothers and sisters she could add to her life.

Although Celeste and Dan couldn't give siblings to Jill, they did expand their own roles in her life. They became more involved with their daughter. This change was most remarkable with Dan, who had been somewhat stand-offish with his daughter when she was twelve and thirteen, admittedly uncertain about his role as the father of a teenage girl. He now spent hours helping her on the computer, an area in which he had skill and Jill had interest, and switched his work hours so that he would be available to spend more time with his daughter after school. In important ways, when Celeste and Dan expanded their roles as parents, their family became not larger, but closer. This type of adjustment, which involves tracking teens more closely and spending more time with them than when they were ten, eleven, or twelve, is a helpful change that I've observed many parents make.

After all, risk behavior is a signal that the adolescent is having trouble taking on challenges. It offers parents an important opportunity to provide guidance, but they also have to modify their own behavior. If they guide the adolescent in the same way they did when the child was two or six or ten, the effort can backfire, resulting in being ignored or further defied in the heat of the power struggle such an approach invites. It takes time, and it is complex, but healthy risk-taking can be both learned and taught. The first crucial step is parents beginning to understand it.

Celeste and Dan made positive changes. They acknowledged the importance of the Rainbow Family to their daughter but recognized that their own influence over Jill was far stronger that that of this magical, far-off community or Jerry Garcia.

None of the stories in this book has a perfect ending; like most lives, the lives of teenagers don't proceed in particularly neat fashion. Jill is currently on a good course. Since she made the video, she has been able to channel her enthusiasm for challenge and her love of risk into nurturing her creative talents rather than participating in dangerous behaviors. At "forks in the road" Jill now has made some better choices, and her parents are better equipped with knowledge, experience, and the confidence that they, too, will make the right choices in continuing to guide their daughter through adolescence.

Jill has a different way of looking at risk today: "I think on both sides now. It wasn't like that before. I might think about what I wanted at the moment but never look at the complete picture."

And Jill is currently taking on a new risk. Although only sixteen, she is entering an arts college program to continue exploring her creative talents and building an identity she feels good about. Still, there are no guarantees. Opportunities to pursue risk behaviors will always appear, and Jill will have to continue to make choices, just as Celeste and Dan will have to continue to pay special attention to this area of their daughter's life.

Chapter Two

Ghosts from the Past

I seem to want to go down in a really big way.

— Ariel

When Ariel, a fourteen-year-old adopted girl who lived with her single mother, came to see me, she was confused about the unhealthy risks she was taking. What she and I both didn't understand for some time was that buried traumatic experiences from her early childhood were placing a burden on her everyday life, causing her great pain. She was repeating the abuse from her past by taking dangerous risks in the present. Ariel was also plagued by a serious depressive illness, a significant contributor to risk behavior in adolescents. Her mother, frightened, confused, and angry about her daughter's actions, suffered as well.

On the outside, the University of California Clinics Building, situated high on Parnassus Avenue in San Francisco, is an inscrutable glass and steel structure, often enshrouded in icy gray fog. Located in one of the coldest, windiest spots in San Francisco, it's not exactly inviting. In this way it's a lot like many adolescents—filled with life but wrapped in an exterior that somehow sends the message to parents to stay away. For the brightly lit second-floor clinic offers a sharp contrast to the building's facade. It is crowded with colorfully dressed teens talking in small groups and sitting sprawled in the hallways. This clinic sees the remarkable mix of San

Francisco teens and offers them care on a sliding financial scale. It was here that I began my work with Ariel and her mother.

I had been "prepped" about Ariel by both the clinic director and the doctor working with her. She had become a familiar visitor to the clinic, showing up each time in the aftermath of a different type of risk behavior. Most recently she had had a frightening experience after taking LSD.

Ariel walked into the small clinic weigh-in room, tripping over stacked boxes of baby formula. (Many of the young women seen in the clinic are mothers.) Petite, Hispanic, and beautiful, with green eyes and auburn hair, she entered the tiny space that is my office on Monday afternoons, looked around somewhat disgustedly at the infant scale covered with boxes of diapers, and huffed, "Nice office, huh?" Then, very slowly, she started to cry. She slumped down on the plastic chair and said, "This is not a very good beginning for me. I'm sorry. . . . I like you. You have a nice face. . . . I'm just so upset. Things aren't working out well for me. I mean, the acid, I took it, you know, it really messed me up. I don't know what to do about it. I don't seem to be very good at figuring things out. . . . They told me you were nice."

Taking to heart Ariel's comments about herself, I asked her what she thought the problem was. She said she really wasn't sure but she had noticed that she seemed to end up in trouble a lot; she didn't know how it happened, but she wanted it to stop. She was also worried about her mother's reactions to her "messing up"; taken from an abusive home and adopted at the age of five, she was now concerned that her adoptive mother would desert her if the problems continued. I asked Ariel what specific risks she had taken, and she answered, "I've never had sex. I don't want to have sex; I want to be older when I have it. I would really like to be a virgin when I get married."

I pointed out that I had asked her about risks she had taken and that she had told me about the ones she hadn't taken, but added that I was glad to hear about those, too. She laughed and said, "Yeah, I want you to have a really good impression of me. I mean, I have taken risks. You know about the acid, but I also smoke cigarettes, and I do stuff with guys at school, hang out with them, kiss them, let them touch me. Sometimes I smoke marijuana with them. . . . I seem to get in trouble all the time. My school counselor says that I dress in sexy clothes, too sexy for my own good. What do you think of these?" She stood up so I could assess her short, form-fitting, striped T-shirt and tight, patched jeans.

I smiled and said, "Well, Ariel, it seems really important to you what I think about your clothes. We will be spending some time talking about them, but today I need more time to think about it."

She laughed. "You're smart. You knew that if you said something, I would get real obsessed about it, but then if you acted like a shrink and didn't say anything at all, I'd also be obsessed about that."

During this first interview I began to tell her about what therapy could be and promised her that we would look together at all of the risky things she was doing. She smiled, looked relieved, and said, "I want to understand it all, too, but it's complicated."

Ariel's intelligence, unusual in any fourteen-year-old, was one of the first things that struck me about her. She had an incredible vocabulary, was extremely verbal, and showed a remarkable maturity in her capacity to work in the "talk therapy" I do with many of my young clients. Even during the first visit I found that I had to thread my way through her sophisticated language to find out what she really understood.

At the end of my first session with Ariel I also spoke with her adoptive mother, Elena, an almost fifty-year-old, careworn businesswoman. Like her daughter, Elena had questions: "How can you help her? I mean, I want to believe that you can, but it's really tough with her right now. . . . She was a wonderful little girl, but then the problems started right about the time she became a teenager. It's so difficult right now. I don't know if I can hang in there, but I'm trying. I love her so much."

Remarks from her pediatrician, Dr. Allen, a determined young resident specializing in adolescent medicine, weren't very different from Elena's. "Ariel can be rough, Lynn. She's hard for me now. I mean all the phone calls I've been getting about her, the acid, the emergency room visits, all that stuff. She also has these attacks where she gets incredibly angry and can't seem to hear anyone. I think she's really interesting, though, and I want to know what's going on with her. I hope that we can figure it out." I hoped that we could figure it out, too, but I agreed with Ariel, her doctor, and her mother—it was complicated, and it was going to be tough.

During Ariel's second visit I began searching for factors that might be contributing to her risky behavior. I explained my purpose to Ariel and stressed the importance of a partnership, and her role in this joint investigation, by describing the two of us as a team of detectives working together. I generally adopt this direct approach with the teens I see. I might refer to a partnership such as that between Sherlock Holmes and Dr. Watson, for example, being careful that the teen is familiar with the characters I use.[1] Ariel caught on immediately and did her part, telling me, "I've smoked dope several times, tried some alcohol on Haight Street, mostly with friends. I seem to keep getting into trouble at school for the clothes. They [the school counselors and administrators] say it's sexy. I don't have sex, only French kiss. I do end up in situations with guys alone a lot, though, on the street, bathrooms. Stuff could happen."

She was quite forthright, both during the initial meetings with me and throughout most of her treatment. Such honesty may surprise parents who expect teenagers to hide their risky behavior, but it's typical of what happens with adolescents when they're asked directly about their behavior by someone who is not their parent.

I thanked Ariel for being so open and then asked her what she thought might happen to her. "You mean like a fantasy-type thing?" she asked with a strange smile.

"Any ideas, really." I waited.

"How much do you want to know? I mean, I've got ideas. . . . I seem to want to go down in a really big way. I don't drink that often, but when I do, I don't stop until I'm totally out of it. I stop myself from having sex because of the virgin stuff, but I could see myself going with it, totally, with a lot of guys. I want to be totally out of it when they do it to me. It's the same thing with drugs. I'm trying to get really low, to that out-of-control point. I imagine myself really debased, like a street person on Haight Street. Afterwards I always feel really depressed and wonder, 'Who was that girl?' "

Ariel was telling me her thoughts about what she was doing, mixed in with fantasy and her predictions for the future. It was all interesting and important, but I had to obtain some specific information quickly about how depressed she was. I asked how she felt after these episodes. She waited a while before answering. "I'm not going to kill myself, if that's what you mean. I think I'm depressed about what I'm doing, but, you know, I don't even know that for sure."

Ariel's open style revealed the beginnings of a deep curiosity about her own actions. This was an advantage in developing our partnership in her therapy, as it is for anyone who seeks self-knowledge and who develops and grows as a result. But she was also right about the crux of my question. I had wanted to find out how depressed she was and whether she was suicidal.

During these early interviews I was trying to determine the role that psychological problems might be playing in Ariel's behavior. I probed, pried, read the recent treatment records (early records were not available), and talked to her doctors, her former therapist, her teacher, and her mother. Was she going to kill herself? I didn't think so. She denied it, she had no concrete plan, and she hadn't made any previous attempts. There were, however, big clues about other underlying problems—using drugs and alcohol until she passed out, for example—and I wondered exactly what she meant by the "stuff" with "a lot of guys." After several weeks Ariel's risky behavior remained a mystery to me. I wondered whether it was serving a more unconscious purpose, and whether she and I would be able to discover it. Sometimes there's no direct route to this information.

Psychological problems often show up at the same time as risk behaviors.[2] This seemed to be the case with Ariel. She was exhibiting both high-risk behavior (that is, taking risks beyond what would be considered normal for an adolescent) and, I was fairly certain, symptoms of a depressive illness. Depression can be a serious psychological problem for adolescents, and I judged Ariel's to be severe. At our second visit Ariel had volunteered a number of symptoms, including an ongoing depressed and irritable mood, problems sleeping, a decreased ability to concentrate on her schoolwork, a loss of energy, and persistent feelings of worthlessness. Obviously she was able to recognize and acknowledge that she was depressed now, but she didn't know if she had been before the risk behaviors started.

I spoke with her mother and the school in an effort to discover when Ariel's depression had begun. Not too surprisingly, no one was sure.

Ariel felt as though things had "snowballed." The more depressed she got, the more she drank, used drugs, and exposed herself vulnerably to groups of guys; the more she engaged in risky behaviors, the more depressed she got. I knew that I had to treat both her depression and her drug and alcohol abuse. Both problems were dangerous, and both were seriously affecting her ability to assess risks. I continued to wonder about the other factors that contributed to her risk behaviors, and about what I would find if I kept working with her.

Taking Risk Apart:
Investigating Dangerous Behaviors

When normal adolescent risk-taking crosses a line and becomes a pattern of more dangerous activities—in other words, risk behavior—it is an important signal to pay more attention to what is happening in the adolescent's life. Ariel was definitely at this point. Risk-taking and risk behaviors are complicated. A variety of negative factors can play a role when teens engage in unhealthy risk behaviors rather than healthy risk-taking. Adolescence is a developmental period during which many kinds of troubling psychological issues from childhood may be reactivated. The teen is almost never aware that this is going on; it typically remains unconscious. What is visible—to parents, teachers, family members, friends, and sometimes even to the teen himself or herself—is that he or she is taking unhealthy risks.

There are also positive factors that influence teens; these can help an adolescent to avoid risk behaviors altogether, or they can have enough of an influence that a teen engaging in dangerous behaviors can be helped to move toward the healthier end of the risk-taking spectrum.

Factors working in Ariel's favor included Elena, a very supportive adoptive mother who went "the extra mile" and beyond for her daughter. Elena organized and campaigned for quality schools, promoted involvement with other family members (aunts and cousins), and supported Ariel's therapy. Ariel's intelligence and articulateness were protective factors as well. Clearly they were advantageous in our endeavor to help her learn how to assess her own behavior and make safe choices. This combination of protective factors was strong, but the negative factors were also formidable. Ariel's depression was a big negative factor. There were also signs of something more going on, something that Ariel herself wasn't conscious of.

Like Elena, Ariel valued achievement and already saw aspects of her own behavior as dangerous and deviant. And yet unlike Jill in chapter 1, who knew why she longed to take dangerous risks, Ariel felt lost about the motives behind her behavior.

As mentioned, Ariel had been adopted by Elena at the age of five. When I began my work with her, her former therapist told me that Ariel's childhood had been difficult. Her biological mother had been a young, unmarried woman struggling to provide for three little children. The therapist believed that Ariel and her two siblings were removed from their mother's home because of "neglect," probably due to the mother's inability to provide for them adequately. The other two children, both younger than Ariel, had been adopted together by a family in the Southwest. There had been some question of parental drug or alcohol abuse, maybe depression, possibly involving both her biological parents. So it was even possible that Ariel was biologically susceptible to both depression and substance abuse.

My understanding of Ariel's early environment and her genetic background was obviously limited by missing information—specifically by a lack of information about her biological parents' mental health histories. As I worked with her, I began to develop serious questions about her home life during those first five years. In our initial interview Ariel had said that she didn't remember much about this early period. She had mentioned liking her mother and described a few fond memories. I didn't want to stop talking about her early life because I had a hunch there was more to it than her memories conveyed, but my approach to it was going to have to be very careful.

Other factors were easier to investigate. In her "perceived environment"—how Ariel experienced role models—her conservative adoptive mother, teachers, and family provided models of extremely conventional behavior, but the friends she had made hanging out on Haight Street had provided her with models for deviant behavior as well. One negative factor in Ariel's personality contributing to her risk behavior was low self-esteem, which also was a factor in her depression. (Influencing factors, whether positive or negative, can often overlap or work together.) Ariel's teachers had been especially concerned about this, believing that it helped to explain her choice of inappropriate clothing. (I, too, was seeing this particular manifestation in the very revealing outfits Ariel wore to the clinic each

Monday.) Most important, Ariel also showed a propensity for getting involved in risk behavior. This is a difficult factor to define. Ariel found herself getting involved in much more risk-taking than her peers, and her first reaction to an opportunity for risk-taking was usually to jump at it, regardless of the type of experience it might turn out to be for her.

Ariel's story illustrates the large number of factors that play a role in determining adolescent risk-taking style, and how important it is to take time to understand a teenager's behavior. The process of obtaining an understanding often resembles solving a mystery, so the metaphor of Dr. Watson and Sherlock Holmes does capture important parts of it. Ariel, her mother Elena, and I were all working together. Part of my job was to help us develop a team effort in what looked like a long process.

When I asked Ariel the details about a specific risky incident—coming to school after drinking, an episode that had left her teetering on the brink of expulsion—I asked her what she thought the long-term consequences would be. Not only did she think there would be no consequences, but she didn't think she would have a future. It is no secret that teenagers are not exactly tuned in to long-range thinking; getting them to think about what they'll be doing later the same day can be a feat in itself. But Ariel was different from most; she did not believe that she would have any future at all. When I asked why, she looked right at me with a cool stare and said that she would be dead.

Serious depression can affect anyone's ability to imagine his or her own future. Was Ariel's depression acting alone to influence her behavior negatively, or was there more? Children who have experienced serious trauma may be unable not only to talk about their futures but to perceive it at all; for them it just doesn't exist. I wondered with increasing interest about her early years of "neglect."

Doing the Work: Ariel's Treatment

Two weeks into the treatment I began the first of many conversations with Elena on the topic of Ariel's behavior. Risk behaviors are powerful adversaries; although Elena was physically and emotionally strong, she was also drained. She felt that previously she had coped well enough with Ariel's behavior, but that now things were no longer working. She was beginning to lose hope. "Dr. Ponton, I'll always love her, but I don't know how much longer I can take it. It's affecting my work. I get phone calls when I'm at the office, and then I have to go pick her up in some terrible situation. I don't even want to have friends over to the house anymore, her bad language is so disturbing." I asked Elena to be as specific as possible about what was happening. "It's like her personality changes. She gets so angry; she screams obscenities at me, won't listen to anything I say. It seems like she wants me to hate her."

Although Elena would not be more specific, blushing and stammering when I asked about Ariel's profanity, these conversations with her provided important clues about Ariel. I began to wonder about what happened to Ariel when she got angry. So far it hadn't happened with me. At the time, early in our work together, Ariel was going through a phase of idealizing me. In her eyes I could do no wrong. I was going to have to find out what Ariel's angry moods were like in some other way.

Elena's reticence about Ariel's profanity made me wonder how comfortable she was with her daughter's provocative, dramatic, and sometimes sexually overt behaviors. I asked her. Turning bright red, she drew herself up to her full height and asked me how comfortable I would be having a daughter run around town in the sexy little number Ariel had worn to the clinic that day.

I smiled at that thought, acknowledging that I probably wouldn't be comfortable with it, but then I mentioned to Elena that she seemed to be taking Ariel's behavior as a direct affront aimed at her personally.

"It does feel that way to me, but I see what you might be getting at, that she doesn't intend it as an attack on me."

"Exactly—in fact, she seems embarrassed by the idea that she's upsetting you. It appears to be more connected to something inside herself," I said.

"So if I don't take it personally, maybe I could deal with it better, help her figure it out," said Elena slowly, with new determination.

Well, easier said than done. Many people can grasp this idea in the abstract, but when it comes to putting it into practice with their

own child, it's just not always possible to slow down the almost unconscious processes by which we end up feeling hurt or angry.
Elena and I still had a lot of work to do.

Not long after this session I asked Elena what she knew about
Ariel's childhood and told her I suspected a hidden story. Elena had
adopted Ariel knowing about some of the problems with Ariel's
mother, and she commented to me that Ariel and her siblings "probably weren't watched carefully. There was a concerned social
worker involved. It was probably worse for Ariel's brother and sister, who were younger." Although matter-of-fact, Elena spoke very
empathically, and the story was moving—three little children living
with their young mother alone in a hotel room in San Francisco—
but the details were missing. Again, it left me wondering how I was
going to find out more. I could try getting access to the earlier
records and maybe try approaching the topic with Ariel again.

This time Ariel had a Buddha-like expression on her face when I
asked about her childhood. "I don't remember. I know I loved my
mom, but I don't really remember anything. . . . If you can get a picture of her, I'd like it. I think I might look like her." I talked with both
Elena and Ariel about getting the records. These are frequently
sealed in adoption cases, but I had managed to find them in my work
with other teens, sometimes with the help of private investigators.
Why did I want to know exactly what had happened to Ariel?

Recent debate in psychology and psychiatry has focused on outlining the dangers of therapists working to uncover traumatic memories in individuals who initially have no memories of trauma or
abuse, and this controversy has alerted the culture at large to the
danger of therapists promoting or developing "false memories" of
trauma. Some patients stimulated by such therapists will "remember" abuse where none actually occurred. The usual clinical scenario, however, is not one of provocative therapists carelessly
inducing memories. Many adolescent and adult patients are plagued
by painful memories and behaviors related to early childhoods that
are known to have been highly traumatic. Even with these patients
caution should be exercised; a therapist doesn't have to uncover
"buried" memories to be of help to the patient. In fact, the therapist
may decide after a comprehensive investigation of the behavior to
forgo exposing the memories; it is most important to have a good

understanding of the patient and to be able to provide a treatment that helps him or her feel and perform better.

Keeping all of this in mind, Ariel was revealing authentic, hard clues that she had been exposed to serious trauma. Her "live for today" philosophy, which partly explained the repetitive nature of some of her risk-taking behaviors, was evidence of her inability to envision her own future.[3] Clearly she was more impaired in her ability to see a future for herself than most teens.

Ariel's episodes of rage that came "out of the blue" demonstrated her compromised capacity to anticipate the consequences of her own actions. These dangerous episodes seemed to be of two types: rage directed toward others, and rage directed at herself in the form of provoking situations in which she was victimized by others. In the first type, Ariel would be talking to someone, disagree with them, and feel tremendous anger. She would then lash out furiously. As she described it to me, "I want to make them feel like I feel. They deserve it. They are the lowest of the low. I feel like I want to hit them; sometimes I do." The anger could be about something very small, such as not being given the right brand of potato chips by her mother. In the second type of episode, Ariel would "arrange" to have herself be beaten or attacked by others. These incidents also began with Ariel experiencing anger but continued with her goading others, generally boys her age, to hit her.

Needless to say, both types of behavior were beginning to get her in a lot of trouble and keeping her mother, her pediatrician, and me very busy. During this part of the treatment we felt like we were on a merry-go-round. Ariel was also starting to shift risk behaviors, a common danger sign when a teen is in serious trouble: one week a drug overdose in Golden Gate Park; the next week sexy language with the boys at school, resulting in expulsion; the week after that a violent fight with a girlfriend. At this point, nearly three months after treatment with me began, Ariel and I were working very hard together in therapy, but I didn't believe we were making the kind of progress needed to help her solve her problems. I was also worried that something dangerous was going to happen in the meantime and that I wouldn't be able to help her soon enough. Ariel and I talked about how she and I needed to work out ways for her to handle her feelings other than engaging in unhealthy risk behaviors. I reminded her of our central goal: figuring out how to assess risk and make reasonable choices.

Then some of the information that I had requested arrived. Through Elena's efforts, I received a copy of a court order that had been issued when Ariel was five years old, describing interactions among Ariel, her birth mother, and her two younger siblings. Perhaps most revealing was the information from the file compiled by Children's Protective Services. A social worker who had worked with the family for several years described years of parental neglect. She wrote a lengthy report on a home visit when Ariel was four years old; Ariel's mother had told the social worker that her little girl was "weird," that Ariel gave her strange looks, and that she was hitting the other children. During this visit the mother also had requested that another home be found for Ariel. All of this was said in front of Ariel.

This was terribly sad information, but I needed to be aware of it in order to help Ariel effectively. The five-page report described an extremely unhappy environment for a four-year-old girl. It appeared that Ariel was frequently placed in charge of her one- and two-year-old siblings in a small, dirty hotel room and often left alone with them. It was quite likely that she ended up hitting them, possibly to get them to mind her. I kept thinking about the incidents that were currently most problematic for Ariel. She got into situations in which she would become very angry and then would want to hit people, or she would set herself up, usually in front of a group of people, "to get dumped on" in order to get to the point where she felt most debased.

One of the most striking findings from case reports of children who have been chronically abused is the pattern of anger and rage that can show up years after the abuse. Lenore Terr stresses the rage of the repeatedly abused child, noting that it can show up directly (Ariel getting enraged about little things and finding herself screaming obscenities and hitting people) or as its opposite, extreme passivity (Ariel getting herself into trouble with two or more boys and literally having to wrestle her way out of danger).[4]

Ariel had recently told me about a situation she almost wasn't able to get out of. She had been trying to "turn on" a guy at school with sexy clothes, looks, and language, but when she tried to stop it, things became scary. He thought Ariel had said something "disrespecting" about him. Furious, he confronted her, pushed her into the boys' bathroom, and pinned her up against the wall with several of his buddies looking on and cheering him. He was stopped by school authorities before he hit her. In this situation Ariel took the passive role in a rage-filled, highly dangerous situation. It doesn't take a lot of imagination to picture Ariel as a little girl being beaten by her mother or her mother's "friends" in front of her siblings, watching her siblings get beaten, or even being the one to hit them.

Patterns of behavior termed "traumatic reenactments" are defined as the repetition of traumatic events in actions and behavior. When a child is exposed to trauma that is both serious and repeated, the trauma takes a major toll on the development of his or her personality. The situations Ariel was finding herself in appeared to be re-creations and re-experiencings of traumatic events during her childhood.[5] Reenactments, of both traumatic and nontraumatic events, can serve important purposes in an adolescent's or an adult's psychological life. They allow a person to reexperience events or even aspects of a particular relationship at a later point in time, opening up the possibility of handling things differently. Although the underlying (usually unconscious) goal is to "master" the traumatic or otherwise troubling situation or relationship, traumatic reenactments are often not healthy. For an adolescent, when old trauma is not reworked constructively, traumatic reenactments can cripple his or her development. This was the situation with Ariel. The hope for mastery and understanding was lost as she became trapped in a pattern she could neither understand nor stop.

Evidence is also accumulating that a child's initial response to trauma may affect cellular and molecular processes that inform brain structure, promoting the development of new, threat-sensitized pathways. A traumatized child's response to future trauma will always be altered; he or she may be under- or overreactive to later traumatic events. Understanding that biological and psychological responses to trauma are intimately connected is important in my work with children and adolescents who have been traumatized, contributes to my recognition of the symptoms I see, and encourages me to help these young people find better solutions for themselves.[6]

Repeated rageful episodes like Ariel's that are enacted without understanding can permanently distort a child's or teenager's personality and result in an angry, explosive adolescent who abuses others or sets herself up for victimization. Ariel was steadily moving in that direction. At this point in her treatment I thought we had very little time and worried that it was too late to help her change this pattern.

The problems that Ariel and I were struggling with were intimidating. Armed with the information I had obtained from her history, I was energized but still unsure about how to proceed. Years had elapsed since the abuse had occurred, allowing for much developmental change, but those early traumatic experiences had shaped Ariel's character and still appeared to be dramatically affecting her life and causing her a lot of pain. I believed that helping her see a connection between the traumatic experiences and the current repetitious behavior would be useful to her.

We began by talking about what had happened in the bathroom, taking the experience apart piece by piece. I asked questions and Ariel added details. As we talked, she began to remember an earlier incident, one that had taken place several years before, when she was in the sixth grade. First she remembered that the kids in the sixth-grade class had hated her; she then remembered that she had "made them" jeer and shout names at her. Recounting this incident was very painful to her. I empathized with her and said that I was sorry about what had happened, adding that even if she felt as if she'd put herself in this situation, it is horrible to have people yelling and shouting at you. I suggested to her that we would have to work hard to figure out why it had happened.

In the next session Ariel began to talk about feeling that she didn't amount to very much; she even used some of the same words that had been quoted in the report written by the Children's Protective Services worker, calling herself "a piece of shit." I acknowledged how sad it was to feel that way but added in a slightly frustrated tone of voice that it didn't seem to be helping her at this point and that we needed to understand and change it. I was immediately upset with my own irritation and sorry that I had so clearly shown it to Ariel. I told her so. "It's okay," she said softly. "I think my mother saw me like that, too. Not Elena. I think that my real mother thought I was weird." There was a long pause, and she cried quietly for several minutes. This moment was very difficult for Ariel, but important for us to share.

Acknowledging your own feelings with an adolescent is usually necessary, but often difficult. Until that moment in treatment I hadn't realized how upset I was myself. Some of the impatience I expressed was very much an authentic response to the current situation. But reenactments are like powerful undertows—parents, therapists, and teachers can all be pulled into situations where they are cued to play a certain role that re-creates a situation from the child's past. It's important to be alert to our own behavior; when it feels out of place or like an overreaction, this can be a crucial signal about what is happening. I had shown Ariel my irritation with our slow progress, some of which was genuine, and some of which was provoked by Ariel herself at an unconscious level, much as she had provoked her own attacks by peers. In response to my curtness, Ariel had started to remember a mother who had been more than just irritated with her, a mother who had criticized and humiliated her constantly.

After this beginning the story began to come out. We took the next months in therapy slowly. Ariel filled in pieces that she began to remember from her early childhood. Not all of it compared with what I had read in the social worker's report, but most important to our work together, they were *her* memories and perceptions of the earlier situations, and they gave us a starting point from which we could begin talking about the painful material. Many of Ariel's recollections and thoughts focused around watching her brother and sister, hungry, in dirty diapers, and crying at a sleeping mother with glazed eyes. Accessing the information from her history clearly helped me to be more attentive and curious about some of the details and allowed us to better understand how the early trauma contributed to the whole cycle. Talking about the situation with the boys in the bathroom and her current risky behavior had offered us a vehicle to begin to understand Ariel's patterns.

Also important during this part of the therapy was how valued Ariel felt herself to be in her adoptive family. The love, patience, and discipline shown by Elena made a significant difference. She believed that Ariel wasn't weird but, rather, that she was strong and had the capacity to work with others to solve her problems. Elena reminded Ariel of times when she had demonstrated strength and courage by helping a younger cousin out of a jam or by obtaining medical assistance for a friend who had tried drugs. Her mother's recognition of her strengths was key, as was the fact that she stood by her through the hard times.

Taking a Role: How a Parent Can Help

As I emphasize throughout this book, not only do teenagers enjoy taking risks, it is also a necessary and important part of their development. Taking on new challenges is thrilling, and their rapidly developing brains allow adolescents to see situations from new perspectives. Being able to see things from different perspectives is just a beginning, however, in learning the complex process of risk assessment. To take risks successfully, an adolescent should be able to weigh the dangers and benefits of a particular situation and know how his or her own strengths, weaknesses, and biases may affect the consequences, all of which help build self-confidence. Learning to assess risks in a thoughtful manner is one of the most important developmental tasks of adolescence.

Adolescents taking risks today confront some of society's most serious problems; these problems, in turn, are major contributors to the challenges that mark this period. Easy exposure to serious risks at an early age is a major societal problem. One would like to see adolescents gradually exposed to increasingly serious risks as they acquire more refined tools for risk assessment. But the ready availability of cars, sex, easily abused drugs (including alcohol), and lethal weapons short-circuits this important developmental process, frequently with fatal consequences. Increasing poverty and violence, as well as the advent of HIV as a fatal risk of unsafe sex or shared needle use, exacerbate the dangers for young people in our culture.[7] Parents need to take an active role in this area. Honestly educating children and adolescents about risks is an obligation of every parent. Educating ourselves first, of course, is mandatory.

Not all teens who engage in dangerous risk-taking carry the serious burden that Ariel did. Most children are not seriously abused early in life, locked in closets with younger children while their mother sleeps in a drugged stupor. Most people's histories are not locked away in file drawers. Learning how to take risks successfully is difficult enough for children who come to it unburdened; for Ariel it had become a chronic problem.

The period during which Ariel and I worked on her risk behaviors proved to be a very challenging time for her mother, too. Elena worked hard to understand what was going on with her daughter and slowly comprehended that improving Ariel's ability to make better choices was a process that would take a long time. Elena was very worried about the role that risky companions were playing in Ariel's risk behaviors. I acknowledged the role that friends have in adolescent decision-making, but also discussed with Elena the important difference that a parent can make.

Observations of adolescents over the past decade have shown that overall adolescents' lifestyles reflect the ethnic and social-class lifestyle of their parents significantly more than that of their peer group.[8] This finding underscores the importance of parents examining how they themselves assess and take risks. When Elena recognized this, she shared more with Ariel about how she herself made choices in risky areas. She was able to discuss candidly some of her own mistakes by addressing things she had missed out on, as well as healthy risks she might have taken, such as more travel, education, and relationships with men. She also began sharing with her daughter what she had learned.

In this process, Elena had become more receptive to hearing about Ariel's life and no longer seemed to blush at the first mention of sex or profanity. Elena and I also worked together to better understand the factors that were negatively influencing Ariel's ability to assess and then take healthy rather than unhealthy risks. Understanding Ariel's thinking and being aware of her past and how it was reverberating in the present enabled Elena to be more patient with her daughter as we all worked together to practice hypothetical risky situations and to better understand Ariel's choices and behaviors. Through this exercise, Elena was able to be less critical of Ariel, and more often than not, mother and daughter operated as a team and were able to talk about what happened between them when Ariel engaged in risky behavior.

This process was difficult but exciting for Elena, who had been an extremely cautious risk-taker during her own adolescence. Ariel's propensity to take risks frightened her, and it wasn't easy for her to understand which risks might be growth-promoting for her daughter. Yet parents can, and should, foster certain circumstances that support healthy risk-taking for adolescents. Many challenging sports and activities commonly engaged in during vacations, such as skiing, rock climbing, and rafting, offer opportunities for successful risk-taking. Challenge Zero is a work-oriented program in San Francisco that believes opportunities for risk-taking are instrumental to growing up. This program and others like it work with a spectrum of young people, including many former runaways and victims of serious abuse. Challenge Zero makes available to teens programs that teach computers or sophisticated silk printing techniques, a bicycle riding and repair program, and even a scaling wall where they can learn climbing techniques. Many young people are denied opportunities for healthy risk-taking in the United States because it is believed that such efforts require money. With only minimal financial support, programs such as Challenge Zero manage to present high-risk teenagers with healthy risk-taking opportunities.

Group sports, camping, running, and biking are also less expensive ways that adolescents can participate in risk-taking. Promoting and developing such opportunities is a crucial role for the parent of an adolescent. Traditionally this role has been relegated to fathers, but with the large number of single mothers raising teens it is particularly important that mothers learn about and promote healthy risk-taking.

Elena more than rose to the challenge. She took Ariel on several exciting vacations even when Ariel was actively engaging in high-risk behavior. Generally these vacations helped. Elena and Ariel returned home feeling closer, and Ariel often reported feeling challenged by the excitement of the travel and the new surroundings.

The vacations also served as restorative breaks for Elena. It is extremely important that parents protect their own strengths during the period when they are helping their teenager with risk-taking. I also encouraged Elena to have friends of her own over to the house and to maintain contact with her friends over the telephone when she didn't feel that she could leave Ariel alone in the evening. At all stages of a child's development, limit-setting and clear yet flexible communication of values constitute some of the toughest work that a parent will ever do. Many popular and professional books have been written on the topic of flexible limit-setting with adolescents. This is a worthy skill and an important part of helping an adolescent practice risk-taking and assessment.

Initially Elena was so upset by the enormity of Ariel's risky behavior and "wild streak" that she failed to see the use in clearly stating her own opinion and values when Ariel was in a difficult spot. It's hard to imagine a young girl's tantrum over something trivial, such as the wrong brand of potato chips, intimidating a physically powerful, mature woman, yet it can and does happen. By the same token, a tight T-shirt on Ariel could render Elena silent, but seething with frustration and anxiety. I encouraged her to speak to Ariel in a calm, direct manner about how she perceived her daughter's risky behaviors. If parents are to speak about risky behavior without obvious anger or disgust, it is often best to react slowly. Elena learned to do this and was gradually able to adopt the role of "consultant" to Ariel around the touchy topic of risk-taking. As children grow older, it is important that parents modify their parental style gradually, shifting their perspective from that of guide or benevolent dictator to that of consultant.[9] Elena became adept at offering Ariel sage advice; as a result, Ariel consulted with her more frequently.

My work with Ariel continues. We focus on helping her recognize situations that pull her into patterns from her childhood. She now knows that she has paid a pretty steep price for both her initial experiences and their return to haunt her adolescence. She has lost her idealized image of her birth mother, and some days her past seems all too close, but she has gained the courage to face it and go on with her life. Adolescents face many unbelievable obstacles. From my perspective, Ariel is a heroine, constantly fighting the ghosts from the past and, in so many ways, emerging victorious.

Chapter Three

Starving for Attention

*I imagine that they admire me
for being the best at being thin.*

—Hannah

Even a setting that appears to be protected and se-
cure for adolescents poses opportunities for unhealthy risk-taking. Hannah, an eleven-year-old girl
from an exclusive suburb, was slowly starving herself, demonstrating one of the most frequently seen
risk behaviors in girls. Poor body image and low self-
esteem are part of Hannah's story, but so are the limited opportunities for healthy risk-taking available to
girls. Parents can intervene not only by promoting
healthier body images for their daughters but by suggesting and demonstrating patterns of risk-taking
that foster, rather than diminish, self-esteem.

On a Wednesday morning in the middle of a northern California
fall, I was driving north across the Golden Gate Bridge. This
wasn't a pleasure trip, although the scenery was gorgeous. I was
planning to visit a private girls' school in Marin County, known for
its geographic beauty and wealthy residents, just twenty minutes
north of San Francisco. I was headed for a conference with a
teacher about an eleven-year-old girl named Hannah who had recently become one of my patients.

Hannah was one of three daughters, and a twin. Blonde and

blue-eyed, her major interests were horseback riding, clothes, and hiking. Her mother, Katrina, had described her daughter as "an all-American girl." I could see the characteristics her mother was referring to in Hannah's golden beauty, vitality, and good fortune in being a member of a stable, well-off family in peaceful Marin. In many ways, Hannah's family had captured the upper end of the American Dream—they owned a spacious home on a hillside with sweeping views of the ocean and a field where horses ran.

I had first met Hannah two months before. At that point she was seriously limiting her food intake, virtually starving herself. She was hiding food, pretending to eat, bargaining with her mother that she would eat "tomorrow," and had become so frail that her doctor was afraid to let her engage in any physical activities for fear that her heart might stop beating. For Hannah this prohibition was a great loss; she would have to stop horseback riding, which was very important to her. Hannah was showing the symptoms of an eating disorder, anorexia nervosa, and it was my concern about this that had prompted me to make the drive to her school.

Until this point Hannah hadn't been an easy child for me to work with. On the surface, there was nothing that pointed to difficulties in Hannah's life, most of which looked picture-perfect. But about six months earlier Hannah's weight had begun to decline steadily. Her parents had noticed that she was changing her eating habits. She stopped eating ice cream and started to ask for salads without dressing. She said she wanted to be a vegetarian and frequently avoided meat or chicken, but she wasn't substituting food from other food groups.

She had spoken very little during our first meeting, part of which was a joint interview with her mother and stepfather. I heard from Hannah's mother that she believed Hannah had also been depressed for a period of time before she started showing symptoms of the eating disorder. Katrina had taken Hannah to other therapists in Marin, but no one who was experienced with adolescents, and Katrina was worried that if she didn't get to the bottom of what was going on with Hannah, her daughter was actually going to disappear.

When I met Hannah, I had just completed a study of childhood-onset eating disorders and was very interested in eating problems in girls between the ages of eight and thirteen.[1] What drove these girls who were younger than the adolescents who typically suffer from serious eating disorders? Some of them were vomiting, a symptom commonly associated with bulimia nervosa; others were restricting their food intake, a behavior more frequently associated with anorexia nervosa. Many, however, were exhibiting odd behaviors such as spitting up, hiding food, strange dieting patterns, or unusual preferences for certain foods. Describing oneself as overweight is an important diagnostic criterion for eating problems in older adolescents. Many of these younger girls did *not* describe themselves as too fat. Often, in fact, they said that they saw themselves as too thin and expressed the hope that they would gain weight. Hannah fit this description. She did not see herself as too fat and said that she wanted to gain weight. Doing so, however, was proving extremely difficult.

Although these preteens say they feel too thin, suggesting a certain self-awareness around their bodies, the psychological work with them does not proceed any faster than it does with older teenagers. It's almost as if the younger girls can't cognitively grasp the dangerous situation they're placing themselves in by engaging in this risk behavior. With older teens, cognitive development is a factor in both risk behaviors and psychotherapeutic treatment approaches; it can be easier to work with the older group simply because they're that much more developmentally able to learn about and tackle their problems.

As I rounded the first wide curve on route 101, the road connecting San Francisco to Marin, I was again struck by the beauty of the scenery and moved away from thinking about Hannah to thinking about my own family, my husband and two daughters. Why did I still live in the city? Why didn't I move to this protected suburban world and obtain the "golden life" for my family? This fall morning wasn't the first time I had had such thoughts. They were recurring. Many of my friends had taken this drive across the Golden Gate Bridge, found a home on one of the Marin hills, and were now raising their children there—in a world that included public schools with comprehensive after-school programs, children and teachers unafraid of violence in the schools, and enriched curricula.

I was living the Marin dream in my head when the third almost identical curve on the sweeping highway made me pay better attention. I'd better not miss my turnoff, I thought. These beautiful, repetitive vistas were almost hypnotic. Even the name of the exit was reassuring: Paradise Drive. No street in urban San Francisco was called Paradise Drive.

Although not as majestically beautiful as route 101, Paradise Drive had its own appeal. I noticed bird-filled marshlands that I imagined to be ideal for Saturday hikes with children. I also noticed the shopping centers, attractive, tidy rows of shops with names like "The Village" and "Strawberry." So much of this world looked alike, from the echoing curves of the highway to the rows of tidy shops and the well-spaced clusters of golden homes.

When I arrived at the school, I was immediately struck by the cluster of blonde, blue-eyed girls outside on the playground. I'm hesitant to say that the girls all looked alike because I always resent such comments about people, but as I looked at the girls I realized that they didn't represent a lot of social variability. Entering Hannah's classroom, I wondered what it was like for her to live in an environment where all the girls her age looked so similar, from the hair barrettes and uniforms to the socks and shoes.

I was pulled away from my thoughts by a very pleasant, middle-aged, but youthful teacher who extended her hand to me. Ms. Wilson smiled, pointed outside to the beautiful fall colors, and suggested it was a wonderful day to get out of the city.

I agreed and followed her into her office. Unlike the teachers in the urban setting I was familiar with, Hannah's teacher had a large office filled with windows looking out over a large field. There was a certain peace here, but what was most impressive was her interest in Hannah. Ms. Wilson shook her head and said, "I don't understand Hannah. It's really puzzling to me. The girl has a wonderful family, and she's beautiful and talented. Lucky, too, with a great sister. And they really seem to care about each other. But this whole situation is a puzzle to me. The weight loss has been so dramatic, starting about six months ago. I remember her in her last class, when her teacher had mentioned that she seemed really focused on weight. And then she began my class this fall, and her weight has steadily dropped. It's scary. I keep thinking about it, wondering what could be causing it."

In the United States eating disorders are quite common in adolescent girls.[2] And I knew from my own research that younger girls could have them, too. The fact that Hannah had such a stable, even privileged, background didn't seem to have protected her.

As Ms. Wilson and I talked about Hannah's situation, she asked whether I'd like to see some of Hannah's drawings. I mentioned that Hannah drew cartoon figures during some of our sessions in my office, and I had been wondering about them. Ms. Wilson and I looked at the drawings together. The first thing I noticed was that none of the figures in Hannah's drawings was beautiful. Many were stunted, with large heads and dwarfed bodies. Others were bitingly sarcastic and in that sense quite funny, but there was an almost freakish quality to many of the figures. Ms. Wilson watched my face as I looked at the pictures. I mentioned that they were a surprise, although they resembled some of the drawings Hannah had made in my office. She said that they had been a surprise for her, too. I asked her what she thought about them, and she said that she didn't know, that Hannah really was a mystery. But she agreed with me that these drawings might provide a key for us to better understand what was going on. I said that Hannah had been drawing some political cartoons for me in the office and that this was an important part of our developing relationship. I asked Ms. Wilson whether Hannah had shown any political interest in the classroom.

"It's funny you'd mention that," she said. "We have a lot of elections because we encourage all of the kids to run for something here, to be political successes." She smiled at that and said, "You know, more of this 'perfect' world. But it's curious. Hannah seems to be interested, but then doesn't want to run."

As I've mentioned, my therapy sessions with Hannah had not been easy up to that point. Remarkably, in my first hour with her Hannah was totally silent. She had immediately curled up into a cocoon on the couch in my office and stared outside at the trees.

Like many adolescent psychiatrists, I am familiar with kids who cannot or refuse to talk in sessions. I am a very talkative doctor who has learned a number of skills under such pressure, and I pride myself on being able to engage almost any adolescent in conversation. But Hannah seriously tested my powers.

In my waiting room before our first session began, Hannah's mother had taken out an Oscar Meyer Lunchable meal and set it before her daughter. After introducing several topics that met with her silence, I asked Hannah about the Oscar Meyer Lunchable. I might have smiled at this point, and it appeared to me that Hannah hid a quick smile behind her hand. Seeing a sign of shared humor, I mentioned that she was the first patient who had come to my office bringing an Oscar Meyer Lunchable meal with her. She nearly laughed at this point but again lapsed into a long silence. I introduced other topics—her family, her school, her peers, her interests—trying to get her to talk about anything else, and was met with more silence.

After two more sessions marked by frequent silences, one afternoon I noticed that Hannah was moving her fingers on one corner of my couch and appeared to be imagining herself to be drawing. Remembering that girls this age are often still very much involved in play-related activities, I offered Hannah a pencil and paper to see whether we could do some art activities together in the office.[3] I encouraged her to draw, and when she refused, I began to draw a little picture and then pushed it over to her. She laughed at my drawing, which revealed my obvious lack of artistic skill.

This technique of sharing pictures back and forth is something I've found to be successful with young adolescents, though it's not something I felt naturally comfortable with when I first started my work with children and teenagers. My drawing skills are minimal, as my patients are usually able to see with the first drawing. But I've realized that I can use my very lack of skill to relate to adolescents, who often feel ill at ease in their first session and can more readily identify with a doctor who is willing to reveal her own imperfections.

As Hannah laughed at the picture, she stated that I could use some lessons drawing comics, adding that if I needed any help she was available. I told her that I certainly could use those lessons and would be glad to take them from her. She then began to draw a very extensive and sarcastic drawing of a political figure. She and I laughed about it. I was easily able to recognize this person and expressed surprise and delight at Hannah's skill. She continued to say nothing but did volunteer that she would bring her own pen to the next interview.

For the session that followed my school visit, Hannah brought with her some drawings she had worked on. One depicted the governor of California, and the others were of political figures I did not recognize but whom she was able to inform me about. All of them were well penned and demonstrated a sophisticated and sarcastic sense of humor as well as considerable skill. We looked at them together, but once again, Hannah was not very vocal. For me the drawings were clues that might explain part of the puzzle of Hannah's problem. I wanted to know more and asked her whether she had ever had any political interest. She smiled and asked what made me ask that. I said that the drawings were clearly the work of someone with a sharp, eager political eye. She was pleased with that and said that she was interested in running for representative of her class but felt that she was such a weakling, and that others in her class saw her that way so much so that there was no reason to think they would vote for her. Why not vote for the bigger, healthier twin, she said, the one who was so pretty, instead of the one who had to be carried around all of the time and had to have someone help her tie her shoes? (This was quite literally true—Hannah had become so weak and moved so little that she could no longer bend her legs and tie her own shoes.)

I listened and wasn't exactly sure how to respond. Hester, Hannah's twin, had accompanied her sister to several sessions. Hester was several inches taller than Hannah and attracted the attention of several adolescent boys in the waiting room who developed crushes on her. I, too, had seen Hester's obvious exuberance, high energy level, and physical beauty. I was sure Hannah had a keen political interest and was beginning to believe that a key to her treatment would be developing and promoting her self-esteem and ability to engage in her areas of interest. I said that, yes, I had seen Hester, and that, yes, being compared to her must be quite a problem. The fact that I acknowledged this difficulty seemed to allow Hannah to trust me a little more. She grew silent, but then grabbed a pen from the box on my desk and began to draw. This time the picture was of her sister and herself drawn in a cartoonish fashion. Hannah said, "She's so wonderful to me all the time, but she's always there, and she's always better." As we talked further, it became quite clear that Hannah saw herself as the weaker of the two sisters, and to some extent as the victim. Being a very frail young girl was consistent with her self-image.

Opening Up: The Beginnings of Change

During the next couple of weeks Hannah continued to give me lessons in cartoon drawing. She was an able and energetic teacher. I was an inept but curious student. Each of us probably had more than the immediately observable purpose for participating in these lessons. On my part, I continued to find out more about Hannah. My initial impression was correct — she did have a good sense of humor punctuated with sarcasm. At times she was very entertaining. On her part, Hannah was at least talking to me in the sessions now, but I still didn't have a very good idea about how I was going to help her get better.

Her symptoms continued to be quite serious. When she first came to see me, Hannah was a little over five feet tall and weighed seventy-three pounds. Although at this point in the treatment her weight appeared to be stable, having leveled off around seventy-five, she was not able to gain weight. Some young girls with eating disorders are not only unable to gain weight but fail to go through pubertal development at all, never developing breasts or beginning menstruation. I have worked with several older teenagers who never completed the steps of puberty, sometimes beginning to menstruate but then stopping and not starting up again. I knew how important it was for Hannah's psychological health to push forward and begin to turn around, to change the pattern she was locked into. It was also important to do this in time for her body to develop normally.

As a first step, she and I would have to find a way to communicate and talk about her eating problem. So far, we communicated best through drawing. It seemed that I would have to fit the two together. I waited and looked for an opportunity. This chance presented itself when Hannah let slip during a particular session that her boyfriend really liked her drawings. Pseudo-casually, I echoed the word "boyfriend," and said, "Hmm, first time you've talked about him." She smiled and retreated into her usual silence. I asked her which drawings he liked. She showed me the one he liked the most, and then said, "He's encouraging me to run for school representative. He says that even though I can't tie my shoelaces, he thinks I stand a good chance of winning. And he doesn't think that my sister's going to run against me. He says he doesn't think she really wants to be involved in politics. He wonders why I won't take a risk."

When Hannah mentioned the word *risk,* I jumped in right away. "Risk?" I said. "You're taking some risk in other areas." She asked me how. I said, "With the eating, you know? You risk stuff with your health to stay thin." She then repeated in an automaton-like voice that she had no desire to be thin, she just couldn't understand why she wasn't gaining weight. I said that I understood that she didn't want to be thin, but that her behavior was risky and that thinness was the inevitable result. She listened to that and then questioned me. "You mean I'm taking a risk even though I don't quite know about it?"

"That's the way it appears to me," I said. "Or maybe you do know about it. But either way, you are taking a risk, and it is having some serious implications for your health that you don't appear to be that aware of or concerned about."

She paused for only a second. "I've been doing this so long," she said. "I mean, you know, the way I eat and everything, that I don't even remember when it started. It's been going on for years. You're right. Now that you've said it, I do see it as risky. My older sister, Rachel, dieted a lot, too. I kind of remember when it happened. I don't know if I was imitating her at first, or maybe trying to be different from Hester."

"Hester's pretty hard to outshine," I said.

"Yeah," said Hannah, looking very sad. "I think Rachel got a lot of attention for screwing up her diet. I mean, you're right about outshining people in the house. My mom is so beautiful and so successful. And then there's Rachel—she's also beautiful, but she's got a lot of problems. I know that. And then there's Hester. She's perfect. And last, there's me."

"Doesn't leave a lot of choices," I said.

"Nope," she said, "not many choices at all."

Wanting her to see that there were options, however few they may have been at the time, I asked Hannah what she thought her choices were around the serious situation of her weight loss. She paused, a thoughtful kind of silence instead of her usual hiding.

"This is the first time that I've thought that I even do have choices. I mean, I've been doing the eating stuff without even thinking that I've got choices. I basically think I do it to get attention from my mother and to feel like I'm special in some way. I know it's a big thing at school, too. Lots of other girls want to be thin, and I imagine that they admire me for being the best at being thin," she said. "I still see myself as being successful when the other girls look at me, successful at being thin." She smiled at me and said, "I guess being the thinnest isn't exactly what you're suggesting. You asked about choices."

"Hannah," I said, "it is your choice, but I think you've got other options."

She looked straight at me and said slowly, "I feel like I have no options. I guess I could be successful at politics, you know, running for class representative. Would that mean that I wouldn't have to be successful with the weight?" she asked thoughtfully. "I don't know."

The process that I was trying to begin with Hannah was one that would first help her recognize the risk that she was engaged in and then teach her how to assess it and come up with some alternatives. Just as she did not see herself as having a lot of choices, quite frankly, neither did I.[4] One of the most frustrating things about working with girls of Hannah's age is that their opportunities do become narrower as they get older, and I have to work with them in an active way to search out some realistic, available options. In contrast to boys, who engage in a much larger variety of risk behaviors, young girls most commonly resort to just two—pregnancy or risky dieting.[5] This lack of choice is symbolic of the restricted opportunities we offer girls in our culture. Certainly it's life-saving that girls are not involved in more risk-taking behaviors, and no one would advocate that girls expand their repertoire of dangerous risk behaviors. Disordered eating does, however, on one level represent girls' limited choices, and asserting choice is at least partly a way of exerting control over one's life. Whether the hyper-control of restricting food or the lack of control around bingeing, both behaviors involve control; they are simply the unhealthy extremes of a continuum of behavior that results from feeling helpless or overwhelmed or otherwise out of control of one's external or internal world.

Hannah didn't even remember when she had begun to restrict her food, let alone the feelings associated with that time. This is fairly typical of young girls who suffer with this problem. The restrictive abnormal eating behavior begins very gradually and often develops in different ways so that the initial feelings and patterns are lost to the girls—and to those seeking to help them—forever. What we're left with is often a very serious disorder with no direct pathway that we can describe as "the cause." The behavior is often reinforced by the family, whose members may initially want the girl to be thin and attractive, some even making disparaging comments about her physical development. The behavior can also be reinforced at school.

Widening the Net: Working with Hannah's Mother

Eating disorders are tough adversaries, particularly in very young girls. At this point in Hannah's treatment I had made some headway. Her weight was low but stable, and perhaps most important, she was beginning to recognize the serious nature of the situation she was in. I believed that I was successfully establishing a treatment alliance with her but felt that it was going to take time before she would be able to change her behavior. I wondered whether I was utilizing all of my options and thought it was probably time to include Hannah's mother more actively.

I began with an educational approach. Katrina held some common misconceptions about adolescent development, but she also possessed a remarkable degree of common sense. In our first meeting Katrina volunteered opinions that followed G. Stanley Hall's and Anna Freud's views of adolescence as a developmental period in which stress and turmoil are normal.[6] Katrina had put forward the idea that Hannah's severe restriction of food was a variation on normal female development, particularly in a girl having difficulty facing puberty, and then stated hopefully that Hannah would "grow out of it."

I'm sure that my serious facial expression indicated that I didn't share this belief. Gently I explained to Katrina that although in the past doctors treating adolescents held the belief that adolescent turmoil was normal, this perspective is now changing. Adolescent growth is currently seen as following any of several patterns: one with few difficulties; a second wherein difficult periods and easier times alternate; and a third—no longer considered "typical"—characterized by difficulties and problems.[7] After saying this, I told Katrina that I was worried about her daughter's behavior.

Katrina actually looked relieved after I said this and admitted that she was seriously worried about Hannah, too. She was worried that Hannah's problems, if untreated, would accompany her into adulthood. She then acknowledged something Hannah had already alluded to, that her daughter Rachel had also experienced serious problems with her body image and had vomited to control her weight. Katrina believed that there was a lot of pressure on her three daughters in their sheltered, affluent community to be thin, and that there didn't seem to be anything that she as a mother could do to fight this. She described how she tried to communicate good feelings about her own body to her daughters, never discussing dieting or her own worries about being overweight with them. I told Katrina that I agreed with her; her eleven-year-old twins were under a lot of pressure, and I believed that she was trying both to understand it and to fight it. My comments were a clear overture to Katrina, intended both to credit her efforts to help her daughters and to enlist her to join with me in order to first acknowledge and then treat this very difficult situation with Hannah.

I sensed that I wasn't working effectively with Katrina, however. I wondered whether I was jealous of what I viewed as her "easy" lifestyle, or swayed by the fantasies I had about life in Marin County. I decided to meet with her regularly, something I try to do with the parents of seriously ill children but had failed to begin yet with Katrina.

Now I began to understand why I had been reluctant to do so earlier. Katrina talked a lot about the societal expectations frequently imposed on women in her immediate circles—makeup, designer clothes, entertaining. She offered lengthy descriptions of California cuisine meals that she had cooked and Hannah had only picked at. As Katrina spoke, I realized that she was experiencing many of the same societal pressures and the same lack of opportunity that her daughter was, but I also realized something else—that along with whatever part of me envied her relatively luxurious lifestyle, I could see the problems she was struggling with. As women, we shared the experience of facing constricted choices in our society or having to create choices ourselves, whether in our roles as professionals, as parents, or in other aspects of our lives. Once I identified with Katrina in this way, I was more able to be sympathetic. Just what were her options as a woman and as a mother?

Katrina shared many things with her daughter, one of which was a fear of taking risks. At the time we started meeting regularly, Katrina was struggling with her own patterns in trying to make changes. I spoke to her about how hard it is for girls and women in our culture to take risks, and how limited the opportunities for healthy risk-taking are for females of all ages. I then described specific ways in which this limited Hannah's life. Even finding risks to engage in was challenging. After my comments, Katrina smiled. "If I read between the lines, it's a message for me, too."

Pursuing that tack, I discovered that Katrina wanted to move away from affluent Marin County to Montana. She didn't think that life in Montana was about designer clothes and meals, and believed that living there would be healthier for her three daughters and herself. Hannah's illness was just one more thing that kept her locked in. Once I understood that she wasn't running away from her problems but actively searching for solutions, I encouraged her to visit Montana and investigate her dream, reassuring her that Hannah would be okay for a few days without her.

And Hannah was indeed okay while her mother was away. She didn't gain weight, but she did seem to acquire increased respect for Katrina for pursuing her goal. The role of a therapist working with girls or women with eating disorders is both to provide general education about the illness and to help girls, women, and families understand how societal expectations and their own choices—or lack thereof—fit together to limit their growth, physically and otherwise. Helping Hannah acknowledge her dream to be a political figure was important. A parallel process was occurring with her mother, and Hannah benefited from witnessing the changes her mother made. As she watched Katrina come closer to realizing her dream of a better life, Hannah commented on her mother's strength for the first time. Adolescent daughters' perceptions of their mothers are crucial elements in their own struggle for power and growth. Katrina's willingness to grow and change was invaluable to herself and to her daughters.

Again, an important step in this treatment process was my recognition of my own feelings about being part of a culture that propels younger and younger girls into a struggle to be thin. Each day I worked with girls and women who were scanning their bodies searching out the smallest imperfections. I am also the mother of two young daughters, one of whom is exactly Hannah's age. Like Katrina, I felt that I needed to know more about eating problems, including why they were striking younger and younger girls, in order to be able to protect and advise my own daughters.[8] I also knew that my thoughts about my own body played an important role in my understanding. Like Katrina, I felt pressure to maintain a slender appearance, but I had tried to be tolerant of the fluctuations in weight that are a normal part of every woman's life. I remained angry, however, about the pressures on women to meet unreasonable standards regarding their personal appearance. Working with Hannah and Katrina made me acutely aware of this pressure.

Going Further Still:
Working with Hannah's Stepfather

William, Hannah's stepfather, was a tall, relaxed man who clearly enjoyed his three stepdaughters but was mystified by Hannah's weight loss. "I just don't understand this thin business. I'm beginning to see that it's a serious problem for Hannah, even for Rachel. Maybe for all girls." William's response paralleled that of many fathers I've worked with whose daughters have had problems with eating. They don't understand the behavior and frequently express the opinion—often directly to their daughter—that everything would be okay if she would "just eat." William was ahead of the game in some respects because he knew that it wasn't that simple.

With fathers, I have struggled to find different ways to describe this problem of weight, body image, and the desire to be thin. Frequently I'll look for metaphors in their own lives that might aid in understanding. Looking at William's lanky frame, I asked him whether he had ever played basketball. He chuckled and said that he had played in college, not very successfully. I asked him why he felt it hadn't been successful. "Right body type, height, arm length," he said, "but not very coordinated, I guess." I asked him whether he had ever felt pressure to play. "I see where you're going with this," he said. "I think most boys and men feel a pressure to play and be good at sports—football, basketball, baseball, and now soccer. More than that, because I look like a basketball player, people assume that I am or have been. Are you saying that it's like that for the girls today? A lot of pressure to be a certain way, and a lot of assumptions based on appearance?"

"Yes," I said, "but it's more than that. There is a lot of pressure on girls to conform their bodies to an ideal image focused on being thin rather than building the body of an athlete. And unlike boys, the body type that girls aspire to is basically *un*healthy, affecting their ability to develop breasts, have a period, and participate in sports in a healthy way. Most adolescent girls feel this pressure, don't think that their bodies measure up, and are deeply dissatisfied with the way they look. Although some boys are dissatisfied with their physical appearance, overall body satisfaction among boys is much greater."[9]

After reading several articles I gave to him and Katrina, William thought that he understood it. "I'm beginning to get it. The message to girls is insidious, and it's everywhere. I don't know what I can do to help Hannah." I told William that his emotional support for Hannah and Katrina and his reading the articles were very important. I also told him that no one was sure of the role fathers play in the disorder. I emphasized that it was a complex illness caused by many factors occurring at the same time, including a girl's satisfaction with her body; social pressures from school, home, and television and magazines; and internal biological and psychological factors. I underscored that Hannah appeared to value success very highly but thought she could attain it only by becoming very thin. She didn't recognize her other talents and was very reluctant to take risks and test them. William thought about this and then suggested a role for himself. "What you're saying parallels what I've been thinking about. Each time I mention the weight or her body, she goes ballistic, but I can get her to try new things, with horses or sports. Of course, she's got to be healthy enough to do it. Sticking with your sports metaphors—you're the coach on eating, and I coach the other area, but it's a team effort."

William was different from many of the fathers and stepfathers I've worked with. Like many men, he understood and responded to sports metaphors and could even take them a step further, but most important, he was a team player within the family who could understand his role in that context; he didn't have to be constantly at the basket or in charge. Hannah's issues were already complex. Fortunately, her stepfather didn't add to them; in fact, he even worked to help lift the pressure. He was equally able to support Katrina in taking on the risks she was contemplating.

Growing Bodies, Growing Problems

Although dedicated researchers such as Daniel Offer, among others, have conducted several studies that dispel the myth that turmoil is a normal part of adolescent development, there has been some effort to resurrect the Sturm und Drang hypothesis of adolescent development and attach it to the pre- and early adolescent developmental period (ten to fourteen years of age), which Hannah and her twin sister were in. Even before menstruation, hormones can be active, and conventional wisdom held that adolescent hormones were responsible for much of the wildness seen in teens.[10] This theory of adolescent turmoil, prominent for over five decades, held that normative turmoil was part of early adolescence and that its importance in younger teens had been missed because most of the conflicting studies used older teens. In a final effort to lay the theory to rest, however, studies that used pre- and early adolescents convincingly demonstrated that although adolescence may be a challenging period of life, young people traverse it with varying degrees of difficulty, and some move through it with little or no trauma at all. Still, the idea of tumultuous teenage years as somehow inevitable lives on in the minds of parents.

This is not to say that adolescent development is not accompanied by certain risks that can have a major impact on the development of eating disorders. First, improved nutrition has allowed puberty to develop at progressively earlier ages for decades. The average age of pubertal onset in girls is eleven years, with a range of eight to thirteen years; for the vast majority of girls, therefore, puberty begins in latency (the developmental period from ages six to twelve).[11] It is important to understand that puberty is a lengthy process, averaging four years, but it also can be completed by girls by the age of twelve, before adolescence begins, meaning that these girls have fully developed women's bodies, with all of the associated social commentary, before they even enter adolescence.

This phenomenon of progressively earlier puberty has had some interesting effects. Recent studies have found that early pubertal development in boys is related to an initial drop in self-esteem, but then improved body image and finally higher self-esteem, whereas early physical maturation for girls is associated with dissatisfaction with their appearance and lowered self-esteem.[12] Why are girls dissatisfied with their changed appearance? One answer centers on how the physical changes associated with puberty for girls—weight gain, increased body fat, larger-proportioned breasts and hips—are viewed culturally. Cultural standards for attractiveness in women, most notably an emphasis on thinness, affect how girls feel about puberty. Studies show that many girls themselves know that they have something to lose when they undergo the normal and expected body changes associated with puberty.

The cultural value placed on thinness in girls is most disturbing in its insidious effects. Omnipresent in the media, this value is absorbed by girls at the very time when they discover that opportunities in their lives are being closed off. Society's rigid expectations about the physical appearance of adolescent girls limit more than their body size. Such standards also limit how girls see themselves and how freely they take risks. Many girls are aware of and expressive about this process. Andie, a young patient of mine who wanted to play professional baseball, put it most succinctly. "It's like there's a conspiracy to get me to look pretty and sit in the stands. I belong out there on the field." This thirteen-year-old athlete told me about the negative comments she had received regarding the size of her arms, muscular arms that pitched an amazing fastball. She was angry that others were critical of a body trait that she saw as an important asset. She was very angry about her missed opportunity to be a professional ballplayer, and had toilet-papered the homes of several boys on her team. The anger Andie felt was healthy, even if the toilet-papering was not the best expression of it. Her anger contrasts sharply with Hannah's feelings, which she internalized with grave consequences for her health.

Frail Hannah was a far cry from robust Andie, but they shared several important similarities. Each girl was between the ages of eleven and fifteen. Dedicated work by a child psychiatrist interested in epidemiology, Dr. Alexander Lucas at the Mayo Clinic, has shown that the only age group experiencing a demonstrable increase in eating disorders during the past forty years has been girls of this age.[13] Although Hannah was one of the first eleven-year-old girls to appear at our clinic, she was not the last, and she represented the beginning of a wave of nine-, ten-, and eleven-year-old girls who were on unhealthy diets or, in the extreme, vomiting or starving themselves. Eating disorders are old illnesses that have been recognized for centuries. They are no surprise to psychiatrists. The increase in eating problems in the younger age group, however, is new. Parents, teachers, and doctors can all fail to recognize the problem.

When girls enter puberty and start to experience physical changes, they also experience pressures to begin dating and sexual activity. Not surprisingly, these experiences are also occurring progressively earlier in girls' lives. Along with young athletes, the girls at highest risk for developing eating problems are early pubertal developers who also begin dating. For these girls, the biological and social pressures coming together at an early age give them less time to understand and feel comfortable with their bodies and to resolve psychological issues and conflicts related to this development.

Limiting Choices: The Culture's Role

Certainly Hannah's restrictive eating behavior and many of the odd behaviors attached to it offered her a small degree of autonomy in a setting that provided only minimal room to be different. This was most evident in our individual sessions, when Hannah talked about her odd eating behavior being a part of her, even if it was a sad way to define and separate herself from her friends, sisters, and mother.

Restrictive eating behavior is also often reinforced by the child's social network. Friends will support the behavior. Boyfriends will support the behavior. Another active agent in this regard is the media. Recently I read an editorial in one of the teenage glamour magazines disclaiming responsibility for eating disorders in its adolescent readers because the magazine chose models who were *naturally and safely very thin.* The editorial was framed by pictures of very anorectic-looking girls. It's true that some of them, though extremely thin, probably had no disordered eating behaviors, but the high rates of disturbed eating that we see in the girls who read such magazines are very discouraging. All of these factors work to make the eating disturbance grow once it has begun, so that a mildly disturbed eating behavior, such as hiding food, monitoring food intake, or going on unusual diets, can progress, moving toward a more entrenched disorder that has grave health consequences. *Often this behavior is not seen as dangerous risk-taking because it is socially and culturally reinforced.* Even when girls are at their sickest, with frail spines protruding and regular episodes of fainting, they are complimented on their appearance.

Disordered eating covers a whole spectrum of behaviors, from the very mild, such as periodic abnormal dieting, to the full-fledged illnesses of anorexia nervosa and bulimia nervosa. This specific risk-taking behavior tells us something very important about adolescent risk-taking in general—that gender and culturally sanctioned gender stereotypes play a role. As editors of the *Handbook of Adolescent Health Risk Behavior*, my colleagues Ralph DiClemente and Bill Hansen and I were all struck by how strictly risk-taking follows gender lines. As noted earlier, girls surpass boys in only two risk behaviors: disordered eating and the consequences of teenage pregnancy.

More Choices and a Happy Ending

Slowly things began to change in Hannah's life. Our therapy together went on for twelve months. I had to learn to wait for Hannah, forgetting my expectation that her changes would happen quickly. Yes, Hannah had a serious medical illness, one associated with mortality and delay of puberty. It was scary. The physician in me was eager to get her better fast, yet I was forced to come to terms with the psychological underpinnings of the illness. It had taken Hannah years to get to this serious point. She was deeply jealous of her sisters and her mother, and took pride in her role as the frail victim in the family. In the final leg of her treatment my training as an analyst encouraged me to be patient and recognize that she was, in fact, working with me and that together we would be able to help her get better.

Gradually Hannah was able to talk about her jealousy of her mother and sisters. The sarcastically drawn cartoon political figures were replaced with equally sarcastic drawings of the family. We also talked about the "ugliness" of several of her drawings, and Hannah freely admitted that she saw herself as painfully ugly—a frog in a family filled with princesses. Although Hannah was the "older" twin, she felt like the youngest, the littlest, and the ugliest in the family. She was also able to talk about feeling that her sisters had let her down, describing how she used to look up to her big sister but stopped when Rachel became a teenager ashamed of her body. Gradually Hannah acknowledged the considerable impact that Rachel's eating problems had had on her own feelings about her body. When Hannah said, "I wanted to be thin, but I wasn't going to be trapped like she was, depressed and vomiting," she was letting herself admit that she was, in fact, trapped.

Adopting the risk behavior of restricted eating had been Hannah's choice among what she perceived as a very limited number of options. In similar fashion to boys who take risks to prove their manhood, girls who can be the thinnest prove that they are attractive. Hannah took on the risk of dieting to achieve that goal of thinness and was unaware of what would come with it—frailty, lethargy, and depression. Even when she recognized the negative aspects of her disorder, she wasn't able to see herself as having other choices. Here the therapy was helpful in showing her that, however limited, she did have more choices than she realized.

Hannah ran for representative of her class and won. One year later her weight was not only restored to normal but stabilized. Two years later she and her family moved to Montana.

After that first meeting Hannah's teacher and I continued to share ideas. I dropped off some articles on both eating disorders and healthy food patterns for teens, and she shared these with parents. At the parents' request, I returned to lead a discussion about risk behaviors in teen girls that lead to serious eating problems. I was no longer seduced by the drive up to Marin. Meeting Katrina and other parents gave me a different view of that life—perhaps it was golden on the surface, but it certainly put a number of complex pressures on adolescent girls.

I also came to a better understanding of my relationship with Katrina. I was most afraid that she and I would lose ourselves or our daughters to a world that does not offer the full range of choices to women.

Things are going well for this family now, and occasionally I get phone calls from Katrina. In one of these calls she described the mountains she can see from her kitchen window. "All these amazing colors, always different," she laughed. "It's amazing how many choices there have turned out to be."

Not all Marin families have kids with eating disorders. Many are able to create an atmosphere of challenge for their teens in which they learn to recognize and combat the pressure to have just one kind of body or engage in one kind of behavior. Understanding that this pressure is real is the first important step; then girls and their families can fight back. Hannah's stepfather learned about pressures on his daughter that he had known nothing about. Coming to understand these pressures not only expanded how he saw Hannah, and life for girls her age, but also helped to create more emotional room within the family for Hannah's feelings.

Not everybody can, or should, go to Montana, but Katrina and Hannah both found places inside themselves that gave them more space to make their own choices. They each learned to take risks safely.

Chapter Four

Dangerous Bedfellows

*I guess I've always felt ashamed
about how I got pregnant.*

— Maya

*When it comes to sex, guys have to
know it all, be able to do it all.*

— Tom

Two harsh consequences of sexually related risk-taking behavior are teenage pregnancy and sexually transmitted disease. Taboo, gender stereotypes, and genuine fear continue to play their part in parents' reluctance to communicate clearly on this subject, but the importance of correcting misconceptions is especially crucial when two such poorly understood areas as adolescent risk-taking and sexuality intersect. Parents, kids, and other adults have to learn how to talk about both of these areas, and that's not easy in our society. If we don't, though, the consequences are life-altering — and sometimes life-threatening.

I was sitting outside the UCSF clinics building eating lunch the first time I met fifteen-year-old Maya. A tall African American girl with meticulous rows of braided hair, she was slowly pushing a stroller up steep Parnassus Avenue. As she and the stroller neared

the plaza where I was sitting at a table with a colleague, I could see
the child in the stroller, a smiling little girl wearing a bright purple
jacket and matching hat. My colleague, a social worker in pediatrics, noticed them, too. "There's your next patient, or should I say
patients—mother, daughter, and generations to come," she said. Before I could pursue her remark I was interrupted by a gentle tap on
my shoulder and a polite, soft-spoken voice. I looked up to see the
young woman in braids, her child now in her arms, looking at my
name tag and then at me. "I'm Maya, and this is Tanesha. We're set
up to see you this afternoon. We took the subway and two buses to
get here from Oakland, but we've spent the past hour wandering
around the medical center trying to find your clinic. Then how
about it, Tanesha and I just find you sitting right outside eating a
burrito. I thought I was going to miss this appointment." She extended her hand.

I moved toward her hand with my own, only to have it quickly
grabbed by Tanesha, who simultaneously knocked over my iced tea,
which landed on my lap, soaking my skirt. Although she was an
adorable baby, about fourteen months old, with one of the most engaging smiles I had ever seen, I found myself upset about suddenly
being so cold and wet. Maya apologized profusely for her daughter
and whipped out some Kleenex that she said she carried with her
for just such accidents. I told her that no harm was done and that I
looked forward to spending more time with her and Tanesha that
afternoon, and then I pointed her in the direction of the clinic.

I was already aware of feeling angrier than I would have expected to be from one wet, slightly sticky skirt and the brief interruption of my lunch hour. I sat back, trying to catch the last few
minutes of sunshine before I returned to the clinic, and wondered
about what could be making me so angry. I was always being interrupted during my free time—phone calls from parents, schools, teen
shelters, pharmacies—and I had a spare set of clothes with me in my
gym bag. So what was it? Had my lunch companion been on to
something when she disparagingly described Maya and Tanesha as
"your patients, mother, daughter, and generations to come"? I didn't
even know Maya yet; did I already have feelings about her being a
teenage mother? I professed to allowing teenagers the opportunity
to make their own choices and decisions in the very important area
of sex and sexuality, but what were my true feelings when their ac-

tivity resulted in a baby? Would I have felt differently if Maya had been twenty-one instead of fifteen? I was still wondering about all this when I returned to the clinic and began to look through Maya's chart.

That day would be a first-time visit with a psychiatrist for Maya. Although she had been seen in the adolescent clinic before (they had even diagnosed her pregnancy when she was thirteen), she had never been referred to a psychiatrist. That fact by itself was really no surprise. More teenagers get pregnant in the United States than in any other country in the Western world. More than one million girls become pregnant each year—in other words, 40 percent of America's adolescent girls.[1] One-half of that group decides to carry the pregnancy to term, and although almost all of them receive some counseling about their options around the pregnancy, very few see psychiatrists or other therapists.

I spent twenty minutes reading Maya's history and had to admit that I was moved by it. Her chart gave a picture of a courageous girl struggling to make a life for herself and her daughter. Maya and her baby lived with Maya's mother and two brothers in a three-room apartment in East Oakland. Her own father had disappeared when she was four years old. The family lived in subsidized public housing, and according to a social worker's report, Maya's mother, Angelina, struggled to support her family by holding down two jobs: she was a nurse's aide during the day, and in the evenings she sewed custom-designed hats, most from her own designs. Maya helped her mother with the millinery venture but had dropped out of school shortly after Tanesha's birth. The social worker also reported that Maya had not named Tanesha's father and had refused to say anything about how she became pregnant. The social worker had been impressed with Maya's skill as a mother and noted that Angelina was a good role model for her daughter.

I wondered why, if it was all so good, she was being sent to see a psychiatrist. I kept looking for a clue, and then I saw it, handwritten, at the end of the report. "Maya has talked about a fear that she will become pregnant again. She has asked to talk with someone who understands teenagers' problems. She won't say anything more but asks us to help her find someone."

This simple statement impressed me. Very few teenagers ask for help directly. Most do come willingly, in contrast to popular belief, but they are generally brought in by their parents, at least for that all-important first visit. Maya was a fifteen-year-old teen who had come by herself; in fact, she had traveled two hours with her baby daughter on crowded public transportation to see me. Now I was feeling impressed, but I still hadn't figured out why I had felt so pissed off initially.

The First Session

Maya and Tanesha were sitting on the floor of the crowded clinic consultation room, playing with a set of blocks, and both smiled at me when I opened the door. I pushed aside a packing crate of baby formula and sat down on the floor with them. I had been trained to work with mothers and infants using the model of Selma Fraiberg, one of my professors in residency.[2] Fraiberg underscored the importance of working therapeutically with parents of very young children to help them early in their child's life to achieve their potential as parents and especially to understand any "excess baggage" they might be bringing to their parenting from their own struggles in the past. The importance of this type of assistance, most commonly referred to as early intervention, has been recognized, and it is now used throughout the country. It focuses on promoting the mother-child interaction. As I sat on the floor with Maya and Tanesha, watching them build a tower of blocks, Maya interacting with Tanesha energetically and effectively, I wondered whether Maya wasn't already close to achieving her potential as a parent. I thought about the handwritten note at the bottom of her chart and asked her why she wanted to talk with someone.

"Well, I'm glad you get right at it, even though you didn't say exactly what you felt about the iced tea, getting it dumped on you."

I smiled then, acknowledging that she was right about my reaction, and she started to tell her story.

"My boyfriend's pressuring me to have another baby. I'm pretty sure now that he wanted me to get pregnant the first time, with Tanesha. He was around a lot then, pestering me to have sex with him, didn't want to use a condom, ever. I went along with it. It was like I didn't know my own feelings about it one way or the other, so I kind of let it happen. Then he disappeared at the end of the pregnancy, wasn't even there at the delivery. I was so angry." Maya's tears were spilling onto the block tower, and she reached out to touch her daughter's hand. Tanesha was still playing with the blocks and seemed unaware of her mother's pain, but I wondered.

"Then he starts showing up again about six months ago and acts like he wants to have another baby. He starts taking her out in the stroller, acting like a proud papa. I just don't know what's going on."

"It sounds like you've got a pretty good idea. You figured me out pretty well around the iced tea," I said.

Maya smiled at that. "I did, didn't I? You were trying to be so nice." She paused. "I guess I think he gets some kind of status from having kids."

"How do you feel about it?" I asked.

"I love my daughter, but I don't know. It's like before she was born, I didn't know how I'd feel then. In some ways I still don't know. I guess that's why I'm here, to figure out how I feel."

I saw Maya for a couple of sessions, both times with Tanesha, and although we talked, I wondered whether she might be avoiding talking more candidly, specifically about her questions about sex, because her daughter was present. Before our fourth session, and with Maya's agreement, I called the child care service developed for mothers using the UCSF clinics and arranged baby-sitting for Tanesha during Maya's next session. When Maya arrived after dropping Tanesha off, I noticed that she looked younger without her baby daughter. When I had first seen her pushing the stroller up Parnassus, she looked strong and responsible. Today she looked not weak, but vulnerable. She sat down and immediately began to talk. The session was different without Tanesha; Maya cried through half of it.

"Whenever I thought about what I was going to say today, I'd start feeling sad. You've been telling me that I'm real good at figuring out what everyone else wants and not so good at figuring out what I want, and I think that you're right. I kind of go with the flow. My mother's like that. She's a real strong lady, takes good care of my brothers and me, but I think that she caters to them too much."

"How does she do that?" I asked.

"Lots of ways. I don't know if she thinks they're so special just because they're boys; actually I think she just doesn't want to get into it with them, too much work to fight with them."

"Do you fight with them?"

"With them I do, it's with Justin that I don't. I really don't want another baby, but I haven't been able to tell him that, hadn't really figured it out myself until today. At that day-care center where I dropped Tanesha off there was a candy striper just my age working there. She smiled when she took Tanesha, said she was adorable, but I know what she was thinking—that I got stuck with this baby, only her age, just fifteen, and already stuck with a baby."

"What do you think about that, Maya?"

"I think she'd be partly right. It was kind of like that because I didn't know what I wanted. I'm starting to figure it out now. I don't think I want another baby for a long time, and I want to be back in high school."

"What's stopping you?"

"Lots of stuff. I hadn't wanted to leave Tanesha alone, put her in day care; she's only a year old. Then, because I haven't been able to say no to Justin, I'm just like my mama. I guess I think I'm going to end up with another baby anyway, so why bother."

"You will end up with another baby if you don't do something about it."

"Like say no and mean it."

"Like that. What's stopping you?"

"Less now, but you just don't start saying no when you haven't been saying anything."

"Why not?"

She smiled. "Why not?"

Meeting Mother's Mother

The next day I received a call from Angelina, Maya's mother. Although I had phoned her after the first time I saw her daughter, extending an invitation to come and meet with me, this was the first time I'd heard from her.

Like her daughter, she came right to the point. "You've helped my daughter. I want to come in and talk to you."

I suggested that she talk with her daughter and that they come together next time.

Angelina, Maya, and Tanesha all showed up for Maya's next session. I invited them into my office and readily caught the infectious mood of enjoyment that was obviously a major part of their family life. Sitting with three generations of a family is always informative. Working with adolescents, it's not uncommon to meet family members, but it is not usually the pleasure it was that afternoon with Maya and her mother. Angelina had brought in some designs of her hats because Maya had told her I was "hat-poor," and Tanesha was particularly enchanting toddling around the room modeling her grandmother's designs.

Although I was thoroughly enjoying the fashion show, I knew that Angelina had specific things she probably wanted to share with me, and I wanted to talk with her about my concerns about her daughter. I was looking for an opening when Maya said, "Tanesha wants to go visit that candy striper, so I'm sure you two have a lot to talk about."

"Is that okay with you?" I asked.

"Okay, yes, but I'll be back to join you. I have my own ideas, too."

"Don't we know that," said her mother as Tanesha and Maya walked down the hall to the child care office.

Angelina quickly thanked me for helping her daughter, then said, "She says that you and she have been able to talk about things. I've tried to talk with her about these matters, too, but she has a real hard time sticking with it."

"What do you mean by 'these matters'?" I asked.

She paused and then stammered out the word "sex." Then she repeated it with greater determination and ease. "You won't believe it. It's not like I can't talk about sex. With my girlfriends I can tell the dirtiest jokes, and it doesn't shock me, but start talking about the sex lives of my kids, and I develop a speech impediment."

"Oh, I would believe it. You're certainly not the only parent that it happens to. It's a lot harder with your own kids," I said.

Angelina looked considerably more relaxed and started to laugh. "So it happens around here, too. You're great with talking to other people's kids about sex, the Joyce Brothers of teens, but put you with your own kids and you're tongue-tied."

We were laughing hard at this point, partly because Angelina had a humorous and understanding way of putting the truth, but also because sex is not an easy thing to discuss even between parents, and laughing about it releases a lot of tension.

Angelina began again more seriously. "Knowing it's hard for you too does make it easier for me. I want to talk with her about sex. I know that she's struggling with that boy Justin. I guess I just don't know what to say. I feel like I should have done it years ago, and now she's already got one baby and I still can't do it."

"Some things don't get a whole lot easier. What do you want to say to her?" I asked.

"That her own life counts for a lot, and that I'd like her to go back to school. She had plans to go to college a couple years ago. Not any longer. That her baby is wonderful, but she doesn't have to keep having them to prove that she's a great mother or a great person. That sex is wonderful, but if Justin doesn't want to respect her wishes, she should tell him he'll be having it alone." Angelina stopped short, surprised that her speech disorder had disappeared so quickly.

"It looks like you're the Joyce Brothers of parents. What's stopped you from saying this to her before?"

"It's uncomfortable talking about this with my own kids, but I guess mostly embarrassment. I haven't been so great at telling off the Justins in my life. I've either sworn off sex completely or been sucked into it totally—either way it's not a good model for Maya. I guess I was thinking you'd be a better role model for her."

"Don't you think that you could tell Maya what you just told me without going into the details of your own sex life?"

"Hmmm. Maybe so. I guess I haven't seen it so clearly, how I've let my own mistakes, or even what I see to be my own mistakes, hold me back. That's not like me. I'm usually pretty direct."

"I can see that, but sex is a taboo area. Even though we see it plastered all over movies, television, talking frankly about sex with our own children is difficult."

Angelina, still anxious but definitely ready to try talking more directly with her daughter, said, "Let's start right away with you sitting right there."

"I'm not going anywhere."

When Maya returned after dropping Tanesha off, the three of us began to work on this sensitive topic. I began by asking Maya whether she thought her mother could be helpful with the struggles she was going through.

"Kind of. I really admire her opinion about most things, but this whole area is pretty embarrassing."

"Sexual matters are embarrassing for kids and parents, but that doesn't mean that you shouldn't try and talk about it together."

"I guess my biggest concern is this thing about having another baby."

I watched Angelina's face, and she was ready to move in quickly here, starting with, "What do you mean . . . "

I attempted to redirect her comment and asked her what it had been like for her when Maya had had Tanesha.

Tears came to her eyes immediately, and she looked at Maya as she spoke. "I love your baby girl, you know that, and she's been welcome in my home. I see that you are a wonderful mother and have amazing dreams for her. I am *your* mother, though, and I have my dreams for you, and now that you're older I want you to have dreams for yourself. When you get locked into making other people's dreams happen, you can lose your own. I don't want you to lose your own dreams."

Maya was moved by Angelina's comments. She spent several minutes visibly struggling with what to say. Her mother and I sat patiently and waited.

Looking her mother in the eye, she said, "I'm glad you said that Tanesha was welcome, Mom. I know that you love her, but I wasn't really sure that you welcomed her. I guess I've always felt ashamed about how I got pregnant. You and I never really talked about my decision to have her, even though we talk pretty easily about everything else. Part of that was my fault. I felt so badly about getting pregnant that maybe I would have taken anything you said as critical."

Slowly Maya and her mother worked their way through the potentially stormy topic of the first pregnancy and what had led up to it. Maya was able to tell Angelina that in hindsight she wished that her mother had talked with her bluntly about sexual activity before she became pregnant. Angelina agreed that it would have been a good idea but told her daughter that she felt like she'd had her "head stuck in the sand and didn't want to believe that my thirteen-year-old baby was having sex." Then, with a growing awareness of her daughter's struggles, she turned to her and said, "This problem hasn't exactly gone away, has it? You're still struggling with Justin about this, aren't you? I feel like I let you down big time back then, but maybe I can still help you."

Relieved that her mother finally knew, Maya nodded her head in agreement, presumably to both parts of what Angelina had said. This session was the first of several during which Angelina and Maya talked more directly about sex. These conversations weren't easy for either one of them. Maya confronted her mother about her relationships with men—describing what she saw as Angelina's endless search for the dream man and inability to say no to any of a long list of candidates—and what she believed was her mother's unfair treatment of her brothers. Angelina admitted that for years she had been looking for a man to take care of her and her children instead of relying on her own skills and abilities. But she pointed out to her daughter that things had been different for the past few years, that she had in fact been relying on herself to take care of herself and her children. Both mother and daughter agreed that she had been doing a pretty good job. Angelina also agreed with her daughter about how she had treated her sons and admitted that she had different "rules" for them. She disagreed with Maya about "being easier" on the boys but acknowledged that she had treated her sons and daughters differently in the important area of sex.

Angelina had expected her sons to have sexual intercourse at an early age and had even purchased a box of condoms for them. With Maya she had mentioned sex only minimally and, like many parents, mostly in a threatening or punitive way ("You'd better not get pregnant . . ."). The limited communication between Maya and Angelina in this area had contrasted sharply with their extensive discussions about almost everything else. Now, with new awareness, Angelina was willing to examine her behavior and make changes. Most important, she recognized the urgency of the situation. Maya could very easily end up with a second baby. Several of the important factors that had contributed to her first pregnancy were still at play. She still hadn't figured out how to say no to her boyfriend's wish for a second baby, or even what her own wishes were. Having a baby had limited her options and short-circuited the process of assessing and testing out new, healthy risks. Having a second baby would limit that process even further. Once Angelina understood that her earlier silence had contributed to Maya becoming a teen parent and that there was a possibility it could happen again, she was able to nurture and support her daughter's capacity to think before she acted, to use reason and judgment to consider the consequences of her actions beforehand, and to make her own choices accordingly. Angelina also was able to acknowledge—without going into any specific details about her own sex life—the mistakes she had made in her own choices and with her children. In this way she modeled for her daughter a capacity for self-analysis, for evaluation of new risks (after all, talking frankly with her daughter about sex was, for Angelina, a new risk), and for change.

Lastly, Angelina was able to help her daughter deal with the stigma surrounding both teenage pregnancy and illegitimacy. That stigma still exists in our culture, and it is felt by millions of teenage mothers who have babies outside of wedlock. Recovery from such a fall from grace is difficult, if not impossible. Angelina realized now that her own silence around her daughter's first pregnancy had been interpreted by Maya as shame for her daughter, and that this had reinforced Maya's painful fears about the reactions of others.

Angelina helped her daughter to see that just because she had made one choice to have a baby as a teen, she didn't have to make the same choice again. Her faith in her daughter's future helped Maya to identify and make her own choices.

Understanding Accurately: Adolescent Pregnancy

The mixed message about sexuality that American culture communicates to young people is believed by many to be responsible for our high rate of adolescent pregnancy.[3] Sexually explicit music videos, movies, and television send a message that sexual intercourse for teens is fun, carefree, and something they should try. Not only do the responsibilities of sexual activity go unmentioned, but an antiresponsibility attitude that discourages both male and female adolescents from considering the consequences of their actions may even be encouraged. At the same time that teenagers are exposed to this onslaught of sexual stimulation and pressure, they hear and see the opposite—adults blushing, avoiding sexual topics, and issuing prohibitions against sexual activity during adolescence. The double standard plays an important role here, too: girls who participate in sexual activity suffer more than boys, at least in terms of public opinion. Our culture's approach to sex education, or lack thereof, is not only confusing, it has been characterized as schizophrenic by knowledgeable sex educators.[4]

Teenage pregnancy is a result of risk-taking for all teens who are sexually active, and a risk behavior for most. It occurs in a context of social confusion about adolescent sexuality and sex education; even so, not all teens participate in intercourse resulting in pregnancy. How does the testing process break down, resulting in the serious consequence of pregnancy and teen parenthood? What factors play a role in a girl's decision to take risks that could result in pregnancy, and perhaps equally important, where can parents intervene? For most girls, both the decision and the behavior that results in teenage pregnancy are very complex. Like other types of adolescent risk-taking, sexual activity for girls may be a way to test out both her new physiological "equipment" and her developing identity.

Biology certainly plays a role. Both boys and girls have been developing earlier than in the past, but for girls puberty often begins as much as two years earlier than in boys. With puberty occurring earlier for girls, the vast majority of them now enter this developmental phase in late childhood, at an age we do not usually associate with developing sexuality.[5] Girls who mature earlier are more likely to engage in sexual activity. We don't fully understand why, but it is believed to be the result of a combination of physical and cultural pressures. Unfamiliar physical sensations are confusing enough; when the media sexualize children and focus on immediate gratification, the confusion is compounded by pressure to act.

Maya's physical development had actually lagged behind that of her peers, but she had become pregnant with her first sexual experience, which followed shortly after her first menstrual period. This is not uncommon. My discussions with Angelina revealed that she had postponed discussions about sexual activity and contraception with her daughter because Maya wasn't yet menstruating. She was as surprised as Maya when everything (first period and pregnancy) happened so quickly. To make a good decision, Maya should have been receiving guidance and thinking about the choices that she would soon be facing *before* she faced them. In Angelina's words, parents put their "heads in the sand" by not acknowledging first to themselves, and then to their children, that regardless of upbringing, morals, social class, or religious beliefs, all young people in our culture are going to face choices about sex. It is much better to be well prepared for them ahead of time.

Psychological factors also play a role. In chapter 3, I discussed how eleven-year-old Hannah felt that she had only limited choices. As Hannah and many of her female peers approach adolescence, they begin to think that they have no options for exercising power other than to adopt the waif-like appearance being foisted on them by the media and society. As their male counterparts are beginning to enjoy the preferred status our culture affords them in the classroom, on the sports field, in career guidance, and more, preteen girls, no longer adorable little girls, are slowly confronting the ways in which their own power in the world appears to be diminishing. Hannah, at age eleven, chose weight loss as a way of seizing control. Maya, at thirteen, reclaimed power by having a baby.

Maya had begun to see a world where she believed that boys were treated better, even in her own home. Having a baby was one thing that girls could do that boys could not. She knew other girls who had made the choice to have a baby, so pregnancy presented itself as a very real option. Then, perhaps most important, at a time in her life when she felt that she had few options, no adult talked with her about what her choices actually were. Her boyfriend, however, did talk to her about what he wanted.

Maya's interaction with Justin shows how cultural factors can affect adolescent risk-taking. A recent study conducted with African American girls indicates that they have difficulty initiating discussions about birth control, specifically condoms, with their partners, believing it is not their role to do so.[6] Part of Maya's inability to express her own opinion to Justin—not only about contraception but on the question of a second baby—was certainly related to her uncertainty about what she actually wanted, but openly disagreeing with a boyfriend or any man was also extremely difficult for her. Talking with me, Maya related this to what she viewed as her mother's inability to challenge her sons and male friends. This influence on Maya certainly played a role, and it was fortunate that Angelina came to understand this and was working on changing it, but it was also Maya's individual responsibility to look at her own behavior and take control of her own life.

Again, as a culture we are not addressing the simple fact that very young girls do face choices that can lead to pregnancy and parenthood when they are still children themselves. These girls need support from the adults in their lives in order to know their options and think about their decisions before they act. Discussions between parents and children about consequences are always important. In the area of sexual activity, they are crucial.

Finally, Maya's young age at the time of sexual initiation—thirteen years—was also important. It is much more difficult for girls to acknowledge to themselves their own needs and speak out about them during the early adolescent years. Postponing sexual activity for a few years can give them time to develop psychological skills to accompany their body's physical development.

How teens make decisions about contraception is very interesting. In contrast to the popular myth that most teen sexual activity happens impulsively, owing to their hormones being out of control, for a majority of teens the initiation of sexual activity and the use of contraception are largely conscious decisions that they do think about rationally. Many factors play a role, particularly their perceptions and understanding of specific birth control methods and their views on social expectations in their environment.[7] How a teen perceives the wishes of parents, physicians, and sexual partners is key. When one looks at Maya's situation before her first pregnancy, one can easily see the role that the wishes of others played. At thirteen, Maya's mother had not discussed specific birth control methods with her child, nor had she taken her to a physician who might have done so. Angelina had cautioned Maya once about pregnancy but provided no specifics. At the same time Justin, Maya's boyfriend, had mentioned several times that he did not want to use birth control and actively campaigned to have a baby. Weighing the opinions of these two important people in her life, it becomes clearer why Maya made the decision she did. More than two years later her mother's clear articulation of her wishes for her daughter played an important role in Maya's final decision.

Having said that, it is important for parents to recognize that although most factors in this process are conscious, not all elements of adolescents' decisions about contraception and pregnancy are. For example, a teenager from a small, single-parent family may have an unconscious wish for a more socially structured family, with mother, father, and child, and may decide to have a baby to create that. This type of wish indicates how important it is for parents to be talking with their adolescents, both listening and communicating their wishes and values.

A couple of years later Maya was able to speak clearly and with insight about the choices she had made at thirteen: first, to have unprotected intercourse with Justin, and second, to give birth and to keep her baby once she discovered that she was pregnant. She related to me that she wished her mother had spoken out about the importance of her choices in life, about the potential rewards of postponement, particularly before Maya had decided to have intercourse. Lacking her mother's clearly voiced wishes and pursued by Justin, who was strongly pressing her first to have unprotected sex and then to keep the baby, she felt adrift; thirteen-year-old Maya chose what she saw as the easiest path. It was clear that she had spent time thinking about her decisions; however, the wisdom and guidance of experienced adults would have been invaluable.

Maya's story illustrates how important it is for kids of all ages to have the opportunity to talk about making choices. They also need guidance as they learn—first, that not all choices are of equal importance (what one wears to school one day is a less important decision than whether to have unprotected sex), and then that the important decisions should be made carefully, slowly, and with some sense of the personal consequences of the various choices they could make. This complicated process requires that adults have serious conversations with teens about responsibility; it may, I think, have had something to do with my anger after Maya's daughter spilled my iced tea when we first met. Like many adults, I recognize how difficult it is to parent. It requires a tremendous amount of skill and effort as well as resources. The decision to take on this job, to become a parent, should be made very carefully and only after a great deal of thought. Also like many adults, I believe that in general teens cannot make this commitment. Maya and other mothers like her help to prove me wrong, but the decision to parent is not one that adolescents are really prepared—psychologically, emotionally, or economically—to make. Maya rose to the challenge after the fact, and it was her good fortune to have an extremely helpful mother, but the process by which she made the choice to get pregnant and have a baby is not one that should be advocated; even Maya herself was not willing to repeat it.

Sexual activity, sexuality, and sex education and values continue to have very different messages for adolescent boys and girls in our culture. The contrast is clear in comparing Maya's situation with the questions that came up for Tom around sex.

"I Saw It in the Video"

With his straight, sandy blond hair, permanent tan, and sparkling clear blue eyes, Tom looked like the television version of a California boy. This healthy-looking, articulate, educated sixteen-year-old boy had been referred to me by a local clinic because the therapist there was worried that Tom was participating in high-risk sexual intercourse with seemingly little regard for his own welfare or that of others.

It wasn't clear to me what Tom's high-risk sexual activity had been. The therapist reported that Tom had told him that he had been having sex with several girls without condoms, but when questioned, Tom clammed up completely, refusing to talk about it. Curiously, Tom was willing to come see me, an adolescent psychiatrist, partly I think to escape from a therapist whom he found too intrusive, and partly because in my work at the adolescent medicine clinic I function as a doctor who bridges both medical and psychological areas with teens. This middle ground of part-medicine part-psychiatry is easier for some adolescents to deal with.

So Tom arrived at the UCSF clinic willing to see a medical doctor, somewhat curious about his own psychology, but definitely not ready to talk about sex or sexual risk-taking. A comfortable physical atmosphere with brochures on sex that matter-of-factly describe sexual development as well as risk behaviors can both soothe an adolescent and pique an already overwhelming curiosity. When Tom commented on a particular poster, a drawing of a pregnant teen father, I picked up on his interest and encouraged him to tell me what he thought about it.

He laughed sheepishly. "It's kind of stupid—a boy pregnant like that."

"Only happens in the movies, never in real life?"

He laughed again but seemed to relax a bit. I went on. "So if boys don't usually get pregnant, what do you think the risks about sex are?"

"Are you going to bug me about not using condoms like that other guy?"

"'Bug' isn't exactly the way I'd put it, but I am curious about why you don't want to use them. I bet you've got a reason."

Suddenly Tom changed his angry expression and asked me whether the clinic had any sex videos. "You know what I mean. Not educational stuff, but real sex, so you can see how to do it."

Intrigued but still not quite understanding Tom's meaning, I asked him exactly what kind of videos he was talking about. "The university probably hasn't purchased them, but I would like to know what you're interested in."

"Well, my dad lets me rent these videos. That's how a guy really finds out about sex."

"Is that how you found out about not using condoms?"

"Sort of, yeah. . . . All these guys on the videos have sex with women, sometimes with a condom, and then pull out and take the condom off, for the pleasure, you see. I guess that's where I got the idea." He stopped suddenly, surprised, I think, that he had told me so much.

"So let's see if I follow you. You remove the condom for pleasure—your pleasure, the girl's—and then you ejaculate?"

"Yeah, that's what the videos show."

"You've tried this out?"

"Yeah, but that's where I've gotten into trouble. The first two girls, no problem, but this last girl screamed about getting her pregnant, giving her AIDS, didn't I know this was San Francisco. . . . She kept mentioning infections."

"Is that why you went to the clinic?"

"Yeah, I started to believe I'd gotten an infection, maybe even AIDS."

"Your dad knows that you watch these videos?"

"Yeah, he gave me his card, told me they'd help me, be educational. When it comes to sex, guys have to know it all, be able to do it all. It's not easy to figure out."

"No, it's not."

That night Tom went home and spoke to his father about his visit to the clinic. They came back together a couple of weeks later.

David, Tom's father, possessed some of the same California charm that his son had, but he also exhibited considerably more sophistication. He let me know that he had been a single father for several years. His ex-wife, Tom's mother, lived in an eastern state and had sent Tom to live with David when he was ten years old so that he could spend time with his father. The relationship had worked well; father and son shared a lot and could communicate well about most things, but like Angelina and Maya, sex was not one of them.

David admitted that he hadn't talked to Tom much about sex. He had purchased a box of condoms for Tom, and, yes, he had encouraged his son to watch the sex videos. "I felt like he had to find out about sex." Echoing his son, he said, "A man has to know a lot."

"Did you talk with him about it?"

"I guess I could have. He told me about how he got the idea about taking off the condoms and all. I guess I could have helped him figure that out."

"You can now—you're here."

Like Angelina, David was a single parent struggling to raise his child and confused about how to handle the topic of sex. But poor communication about sex can occur in *any* family; two-parent families are in no way exempt. Parents who are raising a teenager alone just have a bigger job to do, usually with fewer resources.

Maya's and Tom's stories both illustrate the pressure that strict gender roles can place on parents and teens in the area of sexuality. My later conversations with Angelina revealed her belief that she was supposed to encourage her sons to have sex so that they could "become men." Making condoms available to them was part of that, but talking explicitly with them about their responsibility regarding relationships and the possibility of pregnancy was not. With her daughter, Angelina discussed relationships but could not focus on specific issues about pregnancy and choices—and certainly not when Maya was twelve, when the information was needed, the year before she became pregnant.

David, too, was hamstrung by what he saw as gender roles, both his own as a father and what he hoped would be his son's as "a man." Providing a credit card for instructional sex videos fit in with his sense of what a father should do for his son. Having conversations about the nature of intimate relationships did not. David's attitude that men "have to know" illustrates some of the pressures that strict gender roles place on boys. As Tom was discovering, having to know it all or pretend to know it all before he'd even had a lot of experience complicated the already difficult process of sexual experimentation and risk-taking.

It is still remarkable to me, even after fifteen years of practice working with teens and their parents discussing sex, how different the sexual standards for girls and boys continue to be. The idea that "boys will be boys" and that they need sexual experience, sometimes characterized as "good clean fun," is pervasive. If parents are not able to teach sons about responsible sexual behavior, then who is? Many parents feel a certain amount of resignation about the issues of responsibility, sexuality, and boys; moreover, some parents have said to me directly that they view sexual activity as a son's birthright.

But sex is not all about fun. Watching Maya push that heavy stroller uphill illustrated that very clearly. It is also about relationships, risks, and responsibility. Teenagers have to be taught about all of these things in order to make good choices for themselves in the area of sexual activity.

David and I met alone on two separate occasions, and then I saw him several times together with his son. The individual visits were particularly illuminating. In those sessions David admitted that he was just beginning to find out about relationships himself. He felt that he was finally building a relationship with Tom's mother, even though she lived on the other side of the country, and that they were beginning to coparent together. He also described a developing relationship with his sister, who lived in San Francisco. He mentioned that she gave him lots of good ideas about raising Tom and celebrated holidays with them. As David and I spoke, it emerged that he didn't think he was very good at either developing or maintaining relationships, so what did he have to teach his son? We talked about the fact that he was still learning about relationships and agreed that it was important for Tom to know this—that relationships are difficult and can take a long time to understand, and that even his father was still learning. I asked David what he thought about his son's sexual practices. He admitted how scared he was, first discussing the risk of HIV and then talking about how sad he felt about his son repeating what had been his own life pattern of many sexual liaisons without real relationships and, ultimately, feeling lonely at the age of forty-eight. In fact, it was having his son live with him and becoming a more active parent that had started David's examination of these issues.

After these meetings David and I met together with Tom, and David was able to tell his son about some of the problems he'd experienced with relationships. These conversations were not easy for David, and he needed support from me to initiate them. We started with the topic of the sex videos but then were able to expand the discussions to address how to develop a relationship, and then intimacy. David stressed the importance of taking time to know people before the sexual element started.

Talking with Teenagers About Sex

Sexual risk-taking often presents the most daunting challenges to parents of adolescents. I receive more questions from parents about this area than any other, frequently from parents who have very successfully negotiated other areas of parenting their adolescent children. What would make it easier for parents and their teenagers to communicate well about sex and sexual activity?

One of the most important things I've learned about sexual issues is that they bring up our own biases. It is important for parents to speak directly with their teenagers about sex and to use simple language to describe both feelings and activities. Many parents believe that they can exert control over their child's sexual activity through loosely framed, highly prohibitive, barely articulated restrictions. Angelina had attempted that unsuccessfully with Maya. This approach only builds more barriers between teens and parents.

The most effective tool parents have in assisting their adolescent with developing a capacity to assess and negotiate any risk is their relationship with their child. Parents absolutely must learn to listen without being judgmental and to develop this ability as early as possible. If parents wait to address sex until their child is already a teenager, and then frame their discussions of sex only in terms of fears and prohibitions about pregnancy, risk of disease, HIV infection, and so forth, it will be nearly impossible to develop reasonable communication. But if a parent begins early, and in a relaxed setting—for example, beginning by discussing the meanings and uses of "dirty" words when the child is seven or eight years old, then spending one dinner hour's conversation each month on sexual matters—all family members are prepared to expand the discussion into more complex areas as the child grows.

Parents must also remember that sex, sexuality, and sexual activity are all confusing for young people. Despite the explicit music videos, movies, and television programming to which young people are exposed, the important adults in their lives, such as parents and teachers, stammer and stall when asked to discuss sexual matters. By doing so, they make an already mysterious subject only more difficult to understand. In addition to developing a capacity to speak with their children honestly and directly about sex, parents should acknowledge to their children that they are likely to encounter extremes in our culture's attitudes toward sex—from Victorian embarrassment to sexual provocation and exploitation.

Parents of teens also need to recognize the role that other risk behaviors may play in sexual risk-taking, and vice versa. As mentioned throughout this book, risk behaviors often appear in clusters; parents who detect their child engaging in one risk behavior should be alert to the possibility that there may be others. For example, many teens are using either drugs or alcohol at the time of their first experience with sexual intercourse. And the younger a teen is when he or she engages in sexual activity, the greater the statistical risk that a pregnancy will result.

A whole range of sexual, cultural, and psychological factors affect adolescent sexuality, both positively and negatively. Parents need to be alert to the complex ways in which these factors come into play. For example, early sexual abuse can play an important role in the development of a child's adolescent sexuality and can also contribute to destructive patterns—though not always, by any means. It is the parents' job to remember that this may be a factor and to assist their child, getting professional help if necessary.

Talking with teenagers about sex doesn't mean that parents should discuss their own sexual experiences. They can talk about their feelings and what they have learned without describing specifics. Choosing to leave issues of relationship and responsibility out of conversations about sex is not acceptable, however. Teens are starved for discussion about relationships. In fact, many teens have sex because it is one of the few experiences of intimacy available to them.

Lastly, it is important for parents to communicate their own values clearly. These values may include not having sexual intercourse before marriage. The wise parent recognizes that adolescence is about taking risks, however, and will want his or her teen to have safe, healthy options, even if he or she is engaging in a behavior that runs counter to parental values.

Part II

All in the Family: Risk-taking and Parents

Chapter Five

Mothers and Daughters:
The Slippery Slope

*But I'm not sure who I am, Mom. All I know is that I
seem to discover it best when I'm fighting with you.*

— Zoe

Mother-daughter conflict, a common phenomenon
during a daughter's adolescence, is a natural part of
the developmental process. Nonetheless, it can interfere with a mother's ability to do her part — validating
and encouraging her daughter's healthy risk-taking.
Zoe and her mother Jessica were affected by such
conflict; by the fact that Jessica's own mother was
never able to validate her daughter's developing identity when she was an adolescent; and by the close
identification that can confound the roles between
many mothers and daughters, obscuring who is taking what sorts of risks.

Jessica and Zoe were fifteen minutes late for their first session
with me. It was hard for me to forget this because each mentioned it repeatedly, blaming the other. During their first five
months of treatment this pair personified the long-standing stereo-
type of conflict between mothers and adolescent daughters. They
fought bitterly, beginning the minute they arrived. Sixteen-year-old
Zoe, whose beautiful, waist-length black hair curved over the edge

of her chair, just barely touching her mother's arm, opened the attack. "I don't understand it. We used to get along so well, now all we seem to do is fight. She doesn't see anything good that I do, and if she does say anything about it, it is always critical, goddamn critical. I really don't understand why she's the parent and I'm the kid."

After Zoe's jab, Jessica's eyes glared as she looked straight at her daughter and spoke in a caustic tone. "You, sweetling, you're the critical one around here; it's you, you're always attacking me. I feel like I'm constantly on the defensive in this family."

Zoe swerved rapidly around in her chair so that she was no longer facing her mother and spoke in a choking voice. "You've turned away from me. You still call me sweetling, but you don't mean it, that's just to make me feel guilty."

Nearly in tears, Jessica replied, "You're the one who's gone all the time. You never have time to do anything with me."

Jessica and Zoe sounded and looked like many married couples who come to treatment for help with their relationships. And like each partner in many couples, both actually saw their relationship in a remarkably similar fashion, although, of course, each viewed the other as the primary culprit, the one who had changed and thus upset the wonderful relationship they'd shared until about two years earlier. How they perceived their relationship wasn't the only similarity. Both Jessica and Zoe had very busy lives. David, Jessica's husband and Zoe's father, had died when Zoe was about five years old. Mother and daughter had left the suburbs south of San Francisco to move into a small condominium in the Marina District, an area filled with busy, single professionals who enjoyed the city life. For years Jessica and Zoe had functioned primarily as a duo and enjoyed their life together. A graphic artist, Jessica had opened a small studio in their condominium and did freelance projects. Zoe would come home after school and spend time in her mother's studio doing her homework as her mother worked at her drafting table. They enjoyed going out for coffee and a movie. Their shared activities had seemed grown-up—again, almost like those of a couple instead of a parent and child. Both Zoe and Jessica had liked their time together, however, and there didn't seem to be any problems.

Then life started to change, not only for Zoe, who was going through puberty, but also for Jessica, who was offered and accepted a position as a vice president of a small graphic design firm. Almost simultaneously, she began dating, the new job having brought her into contact with more people. In addition to all of this, her aging mother became seriously ill, and Jessica not only wanted to spend time with her but felt that she had to. She justified spending so much time away from home by noting that her daughter, too, was busier than ever.

Zoe had a part-time job in a record store. She was attending an excellent and challenging large public high school that focused on the arts, and, applying what she had learned from years spent near her mother's design table and computer, she was working to develop better computer graphics within the school. But when Zoe began to date Paul, a boy she had met while working on the graphics project for school, things between mother and daughter grew as difficult as they had once been easy. Zoe began to stay out with Paul progressively later in the evenings and then one night did not come home at all. When she returned the next morning, Jessica demanded to know whether she had been having sex with Paul. Zoe screamed at her mother that it was none of her business, and Jessica grounded her for two months. They had a brief respite from their now almost constant arguing when they refused to speak to each other for two days. It was several days later that they appeared in my office for the first time.

After directing their stinging opening remarks at each other, they sat without speaking. Still, in the silence they were communicating with each other. Jessica's eyebrows were extended, arching above her angry, piercing eyes, but at the same time her right hand was close to reaching out to touch a dark wave of her daughter's hair, which barely eluded her hand. Zoe's back bent both away from and toward her mother, an S-curve of ambivalence. Her body visibly trembled every few minutes, sending shock waves throughout the room. Locked in this tableau of anger and frustration, they appeared more vulnerable than aggressive or frightening. Rather than begin by commenting on this shared vulnerability, which I thought might make them feel weak and want to retaliate against me to demonstrate their strength, I chose to address their fighting head-on.

I began by complimenting them on the highly evolved techniques they had developed in their constant conflict. I really had been awestruck watching them, and now I noted particularly the rapid-fire pace of their exchange. Their fighting had a polish to it that could only come from lots of practice; other mothers and daughters striving to be gladiators would do well to imitate. As I had hoped, the unexpected praise took them off guard, and both Jessica and Zoe began to smile.

Then, feeling like a lone soldier riding into a battlefield, hoping my white flag would be visible to both sides, I said, "Not only are you two really good at the fighting, but it appears to be serving some purpose."

Zoe flashed a smile at this, and then the smile evolved into a sly grin. "Yeah, the purpose is she wants to dominate and control me, and I'm just not going to let her do that."

Raising my hand to halt Jessica's comeback, I intervened and said, "Honestly, Zoe, do you think your mom wants to subjugate you, the daughter she has put so much time and energy into building up?"

I've already mentioned that Zoe was both quick on her feet and had excellent comeback skills. "Good point, Doc. She has put a lot of energy into this relationship with me. Why is she destroying it?"

"Well, that's one of the things I would like to find out," I said.

I couldn't stop Jessica at this point. She began colorfully. "I have spawned a snake. She is eating me alive. I have no desire to 'destroy' our relationship. I'm doing this in self-defense."

"Jessica, you're right. You have given birth to Zoe. You are truly the mother. No one doubts this. And from what I can see, this does appear to be a mutual attack. So let me ask you: Why do you think your daughter would be attacking you at this point in time?"

"I don't know and I don't care. I just want you to stop her."

"I know the fighting is painful for you, but I'm not the one who can stop it. And I can tell you from experience that it's not going to stop until we understand it better. I think we will. We're getting a good start here, but I can't just tell Zoe to shut up and make it happen any more than you've been able to."

"You mean you're helpless with her, too. She wears everyone down." Jessica appeared disheartened but at the same time relieved that I hadn't been able to show her up.

"I'm helpless if I use the technique of telling her to shut up, but

I'm actually feeling very hopeful, not worn down, about you and your daughter. You've got a lot going for you, not the least of which is all the energy you've both been putting into fighting. This energy could be used in other ways."

The white flag of truce held for the next few minutes in my office while mother and daughter scheduled their next session, but not for long. I could hear them arguing about who would be driving the car home as they left the building.

Taking Our Daughters to Work

On 27 April 1995, the university medical school where I teach sponsored its first full-fledged "Take Our Daughters to Work Day," a national event initiated and supported by the Ms. Foundation. The campus hosted almost three hundred daughters, ages eleven to fourteen years, in a daylong program that offered the girls several exciting choices, including opportunities to see surgeries, listen to the heartbeat of a fetus, visit research laboratories, and talk to researchers and scientists, many of whom were women.

Recognizing that our daughters would get hungry, the university planned a brown-bag lunch during which I was asked to speak on the topic of adolescent girls and self-esteem. More than two hundred girls signed up. Then the phone calls began coming from their mothers; they wanted to attend, too. Most of the phone calls began with the same polite, tentative requests to participate. "I'm worried about my twelve- (or thirteen- or fourteen-) year-old daughter. She seems to be having a very hard time right now. I want to help her, but she doesn't seem to listen to anything that I have to say. I've read a lot and know that girls this age are supposed to be losing their self-esteem. I wonder if that's going on with her. I want to know what I can do about it."

So the mothers, and even a few fathers, came to the lunch talk with their daughters. First I spoke about the development of adolescent girls, outlined what I saw as the major reasons teenage girls were having trouble holding on to their self-esteem, and highlighted what kids and parents could do to promote it.

Shyly at first, the girls raised their hands, and then many in the group began to talk about how they saw it, including what they thought brought them self-esteem. Several things stood out from this somewhat surprising but captivating discussion in which the girls shared their ideas. Almost all agreed that they had experienced or were experiencing periods during their teen years when they didn't feel very good about themselves. Much of this part of the discussion focused on how badly the girls felt about their bodies. Many believed that there was a specific body type that was more desirable than all others, and none of the girls believed that she had it. It was more than a little depressing to hear this room of youthful, bright-faced young women talk about how their bodies failed to meet the standards they and others were setting. Parts of this discussion focused on the comments they were receiving about their bodies from strangers and those familiar to them. The girls described these comments as both provocative, in a pleasurable way, and harassing; many expressed the idea that they had "lost" their own bodies when they started puberty and began developing what now felt like "public property."

When the overall discussion shifted to building self-esteem, the mood brightened. The girls talked about things they had tried in their lives that had made them feel good about themselves. Many of these endeavors involved taking a risk; whether or not the girls had succeeded at the risks they undertook, they felt good about themselves for having tried.

I was surprised that all these girls would talk so openly in such a large group, but my surprise wasn't equal to that of their mothers, who sat silently through most of the discussion. Many appeared stunned and stayed to talk afterward when their daughters had gone on to the next activity. They hadn't realized that their teenage daughters were so aware of problems with both self-esteem and body image, and they also hadn't understood how the girls were actually working to combat it. Obviously their daughters had spent a lot of time thinking about this topic, and these mothers were touched by both the efforts their daughters had described and the courage they had demonstrated. It was also clear from many of the mothers' comments that they hadn't understood the relationship between their daughters' current and future self-esteem and the process of taking on challenges and risks. The types of risk the girls described were diverse. Many talked about sports, bringing up occasions when they had challenged themselves far past what they thought they could accomplish by skiing a scary slope, or trying for a hard goal in soccer, or running or swimming faster than they ever had before. For some girls even trying a sport at all was a challenge. The girls had also talked about the interpersonal risks they had taken with friends or family; they described being worried that they might jeopardize a relationship by speaking out about a painful issue but feeling that they had to go ahead and do it. They spoke about risks they had taken in school, pushing themselves in subjects where they experienced difficulty, and risks they took in their after-school activities, such as trying out for a part in a play they thought they hadn't stood a chance for. They also talked about other types of risks that could have serious negative consequences—drugs, alcohol, sex, shoplifting, and more. They described these as risks their peers had suggested they try but which they hadn't. (Or perhaps they were unwilling to admit they had in such a large group.)

Both mothers and fathers in our culture are encouraged to promote risk-taking in sons. And although there is a downside to all of this socially encouraged risk-taking for boys, resulting in higher rates for many risk behaviors, they are usually encouraged to participate in many positive challenges from which girls are discouraged. It is particularly difficult for mothers who have functioned as the primary protector when their daughters were younger to shift the focus and encourage the girls to take risks when there is any potential at all for danger, or even embarrassment. Several of the mothers who stayed to talk admitted frankly that they hadn't seen the two-edged nature of risk-taking. They had been focusing on the negative consequences, failing to see the advantages that this process could bring their daughters.

One of the important role transitions that mothers have to make as their daughters become older is to encourage and promote positive risk-taking. Not only are mothers faced with cultural barriers as they attempt to do this, but many remain conflicted about their own risk-taking. Mother-daughter conflict also plays a role. It can take up a lot of space, obscuring and interfering with a mother's desire to promote her daughter's development. Jessica and Zoe's story illustrates this situation.

Mother to Mother

Jessica and Zoe were not alone in their struggle. Within the frame of parental challenges, mother-daughter conflict has had a unique spot; the adolescent period is particularly well known for conflict and strife between mothers and daughters. In retrospect, my first conversation with Jessica alone began naively with a somewhat academic discussion about adolescent development. I underscored that a central task in Zoe's development of her own identity, as for many adolescent girls, was testing both her new ideas about the world and herself and newly achieved skills with her mother. Most teenage girls do so by challenging their mothers. They then carefully monitor their mothers' reactions to their challenges and internalize or digest this information both consciously and unconsciously. An observant mother can validate new ideas and developmental changes in her daughter, thereby encouraging and promoting her daughter's identity as separate from her own and from others'. This testing process sounds great in theory; in reality it is accomplished only with a certain amount of conflict and risk-taking. Many of the challenges that daughters present to their mothers appear to be personal attacks or criticisms on almost every topic, from clothing to behavior. The risk-taking they engage in can cross the same spectrum. The important idea here is that teenage girls are vigilant about watching their mothers' reactions and listening for their implicit messages.

I emphasized to Jessica that the testing manner that Zoe used with her might be brusque or even hostile, and that I understood how she could be so surprised by the argumentative nature of Zoe's testing that she became angry or refused to talk to her daughter. I then pointed out that while her silence helped them to avoid open conflict sometimes, it also made her forgo the opportunity to be a part of this valuable testing process by giving her daughter positive reinforcement for developing her autonomous identity.

I was right that this developmental process was playing a role with Jessica and Zoe, but it was the wrong place to start. They were locked in a struggle. Jessica brought me right back to it.

She listened impatiently while I described the process, and then said, "You've got a good theory. Now I'm going to share my theory with you. Zoe is just like her father and my mother. She looks like them, and now that she is a teenager she is acting and talking like them. All of their lives my husband and my mother tortured me, fighting with me constantly—Zoe's dad until he died, and with my mother it's still constant. I don't want this same thing to happen with Zoe."

"So you see Zoe's fighting with you as inevitable because she's similar to your husband and mother?" I asked, trying to understand.

"Exactly, but it sounds kind of silly when you say it that way," she said sheepishly.

"Why do you think your husband and mother fought with you constantly?"

"I've never been sure about my husband. Now that he's dead I'll never find out. The ongoing struggle with my mother still amazes me. She fights with me about everything. When I mention anything I've done or a great idea that I've had, she's always critical."

When she said this, I thought back to what Zoe had said about Jessica, using almost the same words. Jessica thought of it, too. She smiled and said, "Just like Zoe says I'm critical of her. Okay, maybe it's not all biology or genetics. Maybe it's interactive, too. What about this developmental process—testing, you say?"

I smiled, beginning to believe that Jessica and I could work together.

"You're right, too, though, Jessica, about character playing a part of it. And character isn't just biology or genetics; even this testing process could be considered part of character."

"So maybe I'm still going through this with my own mother. I've never felt like she's listened to me or was able to see me as a separate person when we're together. It always seems to be about her ideas. She's got a better idea always. Well, maybe she has got a better idea," she said, sounding an awful lot like her own daughter, "but I just want her to listen to mine."

Jessica and I talked about how important her mother's validation of her ideas would have been to her, both as an adolescent and as an adult. This led to a larger discussion about how Jessica saw her mother's life when she was a child growing up in New York City. Jessica said her mother had wanted to be a writer. Proudly, she mentioned several articles her mother had published in a socialist magazine in her early twenties. Her mother's writing had stopped slowly when she married and had four children in rapid succession.

Jessica was the second child and the oldest daughter. She had felt that she and her mother had a very close relationship, and that she was her mother's special friend and confidante, until her teen years. Jessica described how her mother took her to art openings and let her sit in on a writing group she held in the living room, and her eyes shone with tears as she remembered her mother passionately leading the discussions.

When I commented on her tears, she told me that she was remembering when all of this ended. Yes, it had happened at about the time she became a teenager, but there was more to it. Jessica's father had lost his job, and the only work opportunities in his field were in California. They had moved across the country, from New York to San Francisco, leaving the members of the writing group and those exciting living room discussions far behind. Sadly, Jessica told me that her mother had tried to start another writing group. It had never worked, though—she couldn't find the same East Coast intellectuals or political climate. As she recounted her mother's · story, Jessica realized that her mother had actually changed very slowly, over years. She had gone from being talkative and filled with ideas to being filled with bitterness and criticism—most of that criticism directed at her beloved daughter. The pain Jessica felt about this, something that had taken place more than thirty years earlier, was still shattering. Sitting in my office, she talked about how good the relationship with her mother had been before these events, and how she still felt robbed and angry.

After some time I asked her whether she had ideas about the impact of her relationship with her own mother on her relationship with Zoe.

Without even thinking about it she said, "I don't hold a lot of hope for mother-daughter relationships during the teen years. The magical spell of childhood is broken. The mother, now filled with bitterness, tells her formerly cherished daughter what the world is really like, and then the daughter grows to hate her." Tears were streaming down her cheeks, and she stared out the window.

"I feel like I'm caught in this place, doomed into repeating all of this with Zoe and, until this moment, not even knowing that I might be doing it."

"Although you say you lack hope, Jessica, it doesn't sound like that to me. You don't want to stay frozen in this spot, locked into re-peating this tragedy with your daughter," I said quietly.

Her eyes now focused on me, and she said, "I don't want to stay here, and I won't."

A Break in the Battle

I didn't want to lose the momentum that had developed during the individual session with Jessica. Previously, despite the early opti-mism I'd articulated to them directly, I hadn't found this mother or daughter easy to work with. In fact, I would steel myself for their sessions, anticipating nonstop conflict and animosity. Like Jessica and Zoe, I, too, felt hamstrung by their relationship. I was still searching for a way to help them break their cycle.

As usual, they opened the next joint hour with another fight, this one about upcoming Thanksgiving holiday plans. Zoe didn't want to visit her grandmother with Jessica. She argued that they should have dinner at their own house, and each invite over some of their friends. I noticed that in contrast to other arguments that Zoe had with her mother in which she appeared much more self-centered, here she seemed to be considering both her own interests and her mother's. I asked Zoe to describe how she saw the two Thanksgiv-ing possibilities, one at her grandmother's and the other at their house.

She liked my idea and jumped up, asking whether she could act it out. Figuring that this had to be more constructive than their con-stant arguing, but remembering that Jessica felt very vulnerable about her own mother, I agreed, and then watched Jessica carefully, ready to intervene if needed as Zoe began the holiday play.

Act 1 was at Grandma's house. For this drama, Zoe whipped her long black hair into a French twist and borrowed her mother's emerald green sweater. She began as her mother.

"Hi, Mom, here's the pie. Happy Thanksgiving!"

Instantly she became her grandmother. "Only one pie? That's not enough with Uncle Mortie and Aunt Sadie coming. They eat a pie apiece, dear. You'll have to go out to Lindenmeyer's Bakery." Squinting her eyes, "Grandma" asked, "Did you get a new hairpiece or just get up out of bed? Of course you got out of bed, you're still wearing your robe! With all the money you make you should be able to buy something pretty to wear to your mother's, dear."

"Mother, this is a Valentino suit." And then, as an aside, Zoe added, "What difference does that make when she can't see anything that's going on anyway?"

Watching her daughter carefully, Jessica was now close to tears.

"Where are you in this holiday drama, Zoe?" I asked gently.

My question obviously startled her. She thought about it and then said, "I don't know where I am with the two of them. I don't like being there, though. It makes me really sad to watch them. I guess I feel left out, and at the same time I feel sorry for them."

"Sorry for them?" I asked.

"Sorry for them, but also for me. They're trapped," she said.

Now Jessica spoke. "I feel sorry for my relationship with Grandma, too, Zoe, but it doesn't mean that you and I have to be trapped in the same place." With support, Jessica then shared with Zoe some parts of her life with her own mother.

Zoe listened carefully. When she performed the Thanksgiving drama, act 2, she decided to show how she would like it to be. There was a sugary sweetness to this little drama, contrasting sharply with the character of their relationship, but Zoe's sense of humor was also evident.

This act began with an aside from Jessica, who has just sampled a pumpkin pie that Zoe made. It is genuinely terrible.

"This is a wonderful pie, dear, so distinctive—it reflects your unique talent."

"I am so glad you like it, Mom. I made up the recipe and made it from scratch, trying to be different, show up your pies, and, at the same time, please you."

"You know, you please me the most when you are yourself, darling, especially when it is just like me."

Jessica was laughing now, clearly enjoying her daughter's play.

"But I'm not sure who I am, Mom. All I know is that I seem to discover it best when I'm fighting with you."

At this point Jessica, Zoe, and I were all laughing. Morality plays carry a message, however, and this one was no exception.

Zoe wanted her mother to support and compliment her on her new "recipes," even if the taste was bitter. She knew that when she said she was trying to show up her mother's pies and, at the same time, please her, that she had put her mother in a tough spot. This was the first time she'd been able to acknowledge this to Jessica. Zoe also knew, as did Jessica, that their constant fighting was not all some inherited repetition of Jessica and *her* mother. An important element of this fighting was Zoe's own rightful need—again, typical for all adolescent girls—to find out exactly who she was by pushing up against her mother.

Although there was a break in the battle before the Thanksgiving holiday, the truce didn't last for long, and Jessica and Zoe were pulled back into embittered struggles that lasted for months. The respite, though, gave me a chance to see where they could be: Jessica sharing the knowledge acquired from her painful struggle with her own mother, and Zoe and Jessica both becoming more aware that Zoe needed to test herself with Jessica first before she could try out new skills with the rest of the world. It was an important step forward.

I was also beginning to see the role that conflict played in relation to risk-taking with Jessica and Zoe. When Jessica felt less attacked by Zoe, she was able to look at her daughter's risk-taking—which largely took the form of challenges to her—more objectively and to recognize the benefits that the process brought her daughter.

The Dynamic Duo

The strong relationships that develop between mothers and daughters are characterized by more closeness and discord than the other three dyads that can exist in a family—mother-son, father-son, and father-daughter.[1] The potential for close identification between mothers and daughters is a crucial part of many relationships. Traditional views of mother-daughter relationships have been revised by some in recent years, but even so, all perspectives underscore both the importance and the intensity of those relationships. The study of this dynamic duo has a long history. In 1945 the psychoanalyst Helene Deutsch focused her work on relationships between mothers and adolescent daughters and reported a large amount of conflict. Her perspective largely developed from psychoanalytic sessions with adolescent girls who described considerable conflict with their mothers; Deutsch and others who followed her related such conflict to issues of separation between mother and daughter.[2]

This relationship has also been explored from a feminist perspective. In her important volume *In a Different Voice*, Carol Gilligan, a professor at Harvard University, reports that girls under the age of twelve speak with great surety and self-confidence; she notes that they have both a sense of outspokenness and an awareness of their authority in the world.[3] Her studies have gone on to show that girls in early adolescence appear to lose their ability to speak out and are less sure of themselves and less able to discuss honestly their feelings and observations than when they were younger. In numerous writings Gilligan describes a crisis that adolescent girls undergo, one she believes is a response to the demands of our culture, which both implicitly and explicitly tells young women to keep quiet. This crisis appears to be a slow, ongoing process that is initiated during the early years of adolescence when girls attempt to speak out, discover that it is no longer as acceptable as it once was, and alter their behavior accordingly.[4]

The role of the mother in this process is an interesting one. Although Gilligan does not specifically address the mother-daughter dyad in her work, it is covered by some of her followers in *The Mother-Daughter Revolution: From Betrayal to Power*. This book underscores the difficulties mothers and adolescent daughters face in what the authors view as a largely patriarchal culture. Elizabeth Debold and her colleagues connect the "silence" that girls develop at ages twelve or thirteen with an internal realization that they are facing a largely male-dominated and not particularly female-friendly culture. The authors believe that mothers communicate their lack of power in the world to their adolescent daughters and act as instruments to socialize their daughters to the limited role expected of them in a male-dominated culture. Debold and her coauthors support this argument by pointing out that adolescent girls express considerable scorn for their mothers and report that their greatest desire is to *not be like them*. The authors urge mothers to make a transition from teaching their daughters how to get by in a man's world (the role of betrayer) to one of politically awakening their daughters (the role of political activist).[5]

There is an important message in *The Mother-Daughter Revolution*, reflected repeatedly in my own clinical observations and, I'm sure, in those of many others: relationships between mothers and daughters do not occur in a vacuum; they are very much affected by the culture. Still, I question the perspective that minimizes what mothers have been able and continue to be able to accomplish with their daughters. The implication is that girls at age twelve can understand and appreciate what their mothers, with an additional twenty, thirty, or sometimes even forty years' life experience, have been unable to recognize—the personal damage and constraints of living in a patriarchal culture. This view implies that mothers of adolescent girls fail their daughters because they were unable to negotiate their own adolescence with their voices intact.

Clinically I see a wide spectrum of mothers and adolescent daughters, and universal truths are hard to find in this diverse population. In general, mothers show that they want the best for their daughters in both what they say and what they do. Despite significant amounts of conflict, both mothers and daughters are able to acknowledge that they love and care about each other. And whereas many daughters sense that something about their mothers' less than ideal roles in the world scares them about their own futures, most mothers are much clearer than their daughters about what it really means to try to construct their lives within a patriarchal culture. Perhaps the only universal truth among the mother-daughter pairs I work with is that the daughter's adolescence is a very intense period for them both.

Most of the mothers I see echo the concerns voiced by those mothers who brought their daughters to work with them in April 1995 and thoughtfully questioned both the developmental concerns their daughters were struggling with and the values of the adult world the girls were moving into. Obviously I see a limited population of mothers in the sense that they are mothers seeking assistance with their children, but nonetheless, I take issue with any perspective that assumes that mothers have let their daughters down. Each day I meet with mothers who are struggling mightily to help their daughters achieve what they could not. Imagining that teen daughters provide the leadership and direction for the pair is disrespectful of all that mothers do to provide guidance and leadership for their daughters. During adolescence this can be an especially difficult task.

The question then becomes, How can mothers improve on what

they are already doing? It is especially important that the mother of an adolescent daughter acknowledge the intensity of the relationship, understand that conflict is part of it, and see the conflict not as a sign of failure but rather as part of a developmental progression. When a mother dissolves into tears after her daughter attacks, it does give the daughter a message of weakness. On the other hand, it is also a mistake for mothers to be too reluctant to tell their daughters that their attacks are genuinely painful. Instead, mothers need to demonstrate their leadership role in the relationship by providing guidance about what is expected and appropriate in mutual relationships.

Adolescent girls also have a lot to contribute. Zoe gave a vibrant example of this when she acted out the holiday play. Her energy, perspective, and ideas were crucial components of her relationship with her mother. She let Jessica know that she needed not only her guidance but her validation of the important changes that she was undergoing to become an adult. Like a younger child moving away from her mother when learning to walk, an adolescent also looks back constantly, both to reassure herself that her mother is still there for her while she explores the world and to gain affirmation from her mother that this exploration—which is such an integral part of developing a self—is a good thing. Both the toddler and the adolescent want to see and be seen by their mothers as they come into their own. The way teenage daughters appear to feel and the general conflict between them and their mothers can make it difficult for mothers to provide this attention for their daughters.[6] After all, when the girls were little and cute, it was easy to affirm them. Grown taller and more sarcastic, argumentative, and private, teenage daughters present their mothers with quite a challenge. But if mothers can see that while the process looks different it is actually much the same, they may be better able to tolerate the challenges their daughters pose. This is not intended to suggest that mothers should tolerate rudeness or bad behavior—what's acceptable is different in every family—or condone dangerous risks. But mothers can remember that their daughters still very much need their guidance, even when they act as if they couldn't care less.

Even though they may deny it, adolescent girls want their mothers to notice the risks they are taking, both positive and negative. Walking across the room was a risk for the three-year-old; driving to a friend's house without an adult in the car may be the comparable risk for the sixteen-year-old. Healthy risks do need to be encouraged and validated, but as I mentioned earlier, it is not always easy for a mother to encourage her daughter to take risks, particularly if she has largely defined her maternal role as one of protecting her young. One danger for such mothers is in not knowing the difference between risks that are genuinely dangerous and risks that seem to be dangerous but aren't necessarily.

Obstacles to Encouragement

Mothers who experienced difficulty taking their own risks are described in this book. Jenny's mother Sarah was an impulsive risk-taker and could not provide guidance for her daughter in this area (see chapter 9). Eva, Cecilia's mother, was locked into an enmeshed twinship with her daughter and feared any risks her daughter took because they could lead to separation (see chapter 11). And in this chapter, although Jessica was a successful risk-taker—she had coped with a husband's death, trail-blazed her own successful career, and single-handedly raised her daughter—it was still not easy for her to encourage her daughter to take risks. It took us a while to figure out why.

The first and most obvious reason Jessica found it difficult to encourage Zoe to take risks, even positive risks, was that she felt attacked by her daughter. Feeling attacked, she reacted by limiting most of her daughter's activities. These limits were backfiring, though; they failed to provide the firm guidance that Jessica really intended and instead encouraged Zoe to sneak behind her mother's back and disobey her. This dynamic occurred repeatedly in their conflicts over dating. Zoe would want a later curfew hour for a particular evening, but in her attempt to ask Jessica about this, she would say something particularly sarcastic. Zoe's tone often made Jessica retaliate, thus escalating the tension; Jessica was not able to say calmly, "I can't talk to you about this when you're screaming or saying biting things. Let's take a break for a half-hour while we each think about it." Taking a quiet interlude can give mother and daughter time to regroup and think clearly about what they want to accomplish, and it interrupts a cycle of sarcasm and conflict.

A second reason Jessica was having trouble setting limits with her daughter was that Zoe was pushing specifically to take risks in the area of sexuality. As mentioned earlier, she was spending later and later hours with her boyfriend and one night had not come home at all. Jessica's demands to know whether Zoe and Paul were having sex predictably led to an eruption and the two-month grounding followed by silence.

As discussed in detail in chapter 4, the area of sex and sexuality is a particularly complex one for parents and teenagers because the key to guiding and promoting healthy risk-taking is good communication; sexuality in our culture, however, is simultaneously over-exposed and still taboo—thrust at us everywhere and talked about very little. This does not lead to good communication. As we subsequently discovered together, during her own adolescence Jessica had felt shamed by her mother, who had been both critical and intrusive about Jessica's sexual development. In an attempt to avoid that stance with Zoe, Jessica had veered to the other extreme, avoiding even normal conversations about general sexual matters and Zoe's sexual development. So Jessica's questions about Zoe's sexual activity with Paul were jarring in light of the fact that they did not regularly discuss anything sexual at all. Helping mother and daughter to backtrack and develop a vocabulary for discussing sexual matters was an important part of our work together.

An additional complication was that Jessica herself was just beginning to date again. The fact that mother and daughter were engaging in similar activities at the same time was confusing to both of them. Helping Jessica understand that she could provide guidance for Zoe in an area of life that had been long-dormant for her was also important. It was crucial to help both of them see that although they were participating in similar activities, it was not the same experience. Zoe, at sixteen, was dating for the first time and needed basic guidance about her developing body, the risk of pregnancy and sexually transmitted diseases, and dating etiquette. Jessica, on the other hand, had a backlog of experience but was dating after a moratorium of many years. She feared that relationships would reawaken grief about her dead husband. Jessica came to see that she could either directly provide or help Zoe find guidance in this all-important area, but that it was crucial to do one or the other if she didn't want to send her daughter the same negative messages about sexuality that her own mother had sent her.

One of the most memorable sessions with Jessica and Zoe occurred several days after they had each gone out on a Saturday night date. Not surprisingly, Zoe, who was now both closely identified and hotly competitive with her mother, was underscoring the similarities between herself and Jessica. "We each wore black dresses and went out to restaurants. Wouldn't it have been funny if we had ended up at the same restaurant? We're so alike, Mom."

Jessica, while able to acknowledge the similarities between them, was now clearer about the differences, and said gently but firmly, "Maybe the same dress, even the same restaurant, but we're different people, and I'm the mother and you're the daughter."

The Impact of the Outside World

The initial period of a daughter's developing sexuality generally occurs during the early and middle adolescent years and is affected by the cultural emphasis on and interest in young female bodies. The cultural reaction often consists of overwhelming and inappropriate attention for a developing young girl. Remember the reactions of the girls who came to "Take Our Daughters to Work Day" at the medical school? They felt that the comments of others simultaneously harassed and stimulated them. Many concurred with one girl's feeling that her body had suddenly become "public property." At the same time that daughters are receiving increased attention from the outside world, their mothers are usually receiving less. And for females of any age in many cultures, the body and general physical appearance is one of the primary means by which the outside world measures value and worth. Our own culture is one that admires the pubescent or even prepubescent bodies of young girls and often discounts the bodies of mature women in their thirties, forties, or fifties—the usual age range of mothers of adolescents.

So the adolescents who are suddenly receiving new attention aren't the only ones who have feelings about it. Jessica described her own reactions with unique candor. "It used to be that when Zoe and I went to a party, eyes were on me, and I'd hear people talk—

'Who's the beautiful young widow with the lovely child?' I can't say I didn't like it. Now when we walk into a room together, all the eyes are on her, and I'm fairly sure no one notices me. This hasn't been easy to deal with. . . . I want to protect her from attention that I don't think she's ready for, and at the same time I miss the attention for myself. Like everything about this time in our lives, it leaves me feeling angry and confused."

Jessica's comments articulated what many mothers have had trouble saying. It is hard, and painful, to be a forty-five-year-old woman and know that men your age receive as much attention and admiration as ever while your share of such attention has largely diminished. When your young daughter is showered with the attention you once received, it's bad twice over—the attention they're getting may not be coming to them in a quantity or quality they are ready to handle, and paradoxically, you're jealous of their gain, which seems somehow connected to your own loss!

How can a mother approach this tricky situation in the most positive manner? First, acknowledging her complicated feelings about it is important. Second, finding support from others—husband, mother, friends, siblings—can be a valuable help. These people can remind you that you can't change a cultural perspective overnight, but that you can make your own feelings heard. At the same time it is important for a mother who is struggling with an adolescent daughter to remember that she is the parent, and that if she feels confused about society's reactions, her daughter probably does, too. Mothers can intervene. They can limit inappropriate comments both directly and by working with their daughters to build their skills in taking care of themselves. This is an important area where mothers and daughters can work together to make an important difference in their own lives and in society as well.

Risk-taking is finally beginning to be recognized as an important task for both adolescent girls and women. Mothers, however, are not encouraged to be risk-takers if doing so removes them from their children for any length of time. There is an unspoken, threatening challenge: "What would happen to your children if something happened to you?" Yet mothers have the potential to be great risk-takers; after all, taking on the responsibilities of having a child is one of the biggest risks of all. Mothers need to acknowledge the risks they have already taken and teach their children what they have learned. If mothers ignore or are scared of risk-taking, however, they communicate these attitudes to their daughters as well. The mother who doesn't stand up for herself or challenge herself to experience new things may, at the very least, end up not respected by her daughter, who may, at worst, engage in dangerous behaviors in an effort to avoid ending up like her. Mothers who model self-reliance, self-respect, healthy relationships, and a willingness to take risks in order to grow offer their daughters a tremendous gift.

Chapter Six

Fathers and Sons: Taking Risks Together

*My father and brothers are so busy pulling out
their swords that they can't see what's going on.
Yet if I know it's so destructive, why do I want
so much to be a part of it?*

— David

The Greek myth of Oedipus tells of a deeply embedded competition between a father and his son, but it also depicts distance between father and son, a much more common problem that may or may not have to do with rivalry. In our culture today many fathers intentionally back away from their adolescent sons for various reasons, including the belief that boys become men by facing challenges on their own, without the "interference" of others, parents included. Like most adolescent boys, David still craved his father's attention. But his father Joseph was in his sixties, had already raised three children, and had some pretty fixed ideas about what he should and shouldn't provide for his children.

When David first came to my office, he was only thirteen years old and I was young in my field. I had just finished my psychiatric fellowship specializing in child and adolescent work and was beginning my psychoanalytic training, a process that would

122

take almost ten years to complete. Youthful enthusiasm can have its rewards, one being a wealth of curiosity, a trait that David and I shared. Through our work together we were also able to develop a successful partnership. During three separate periods over an eight-year time span that covered David's adolescence, he found answers to the questions about his life that he had brought to therapy, and I found answers to some of my questions about the role fathers play with sons and risk-taking. The partnership was valuable to both of us.

David was the youngest of four children in an Italian Catholic family. His brothers were eighteen and sixteen years older than he; his sister was six years older. David's father, a man in his late sixties, ran a successful grocery business and was identified by other family members as particularly close to his oldest son. David's mother, a woman in her midfifties, had recently been diagnosed and treated for breast cancer. She was in remission, and her doctors were very optimistic.

David's parents had called me because they were concerned about a drop in David's grades, from As to Cs, during the period of his mother's illness. His parents were also concerned that David had been discovered several times hanging out with a group of boys that included some who had been arrested for shoplifting. After my first meeting with David, I received phone calls from his two older brothers. They each wanted to set me straight and let me know what was "really" going on with David, although their initial approach was one of wanting to be helpful to David. After checking with David and his parents and getting their okay, I had a phone conversation with each brother, both of whom lived at some geographical distance but were still very connected to their parents and younger brother. Although each reported a somewhat similar version, Mike, the older brother, a professional hunter and wilderness guide in Canada, was more forceful in his tone. "I don't know exactly how to say this, but my brother and I think he's too attached to Mom, a real mama's boy. That's a dangerous thing for a guy, makes him less of a man . . . might even make him gay."

As I've already mentioned, this conversation occurred early in my career as a practicing psychiatrist, and I was more than somewhat taken aback. I remember that I stammered something into the phone and asked the older brother if he could be more specific about his concerns. "Lady, don't you get it? My brother could become a fag. My mother treats him like a real sissy. They were always spending all this time together at the hospital when she was getting her treatments, and my mother was always mooning over him."

"So you don't think their close relationship is a good thing?" I asked, still reeling from what Mike had just said. Mike responded by throwing in several expletives to underscore his point, letting me know unmistakably that he and his brother believed that David's close relationship with their mother was making him less manly and contributing to a confused sexual identity.

Conversations with David's father revealed similar concerns, but on the surface anyway, the issue seemed nonexistent for David. He was worried about his relationship with his father.

David was quite interested in therapy and early on expressed a rudimentary knowledge of the way his mind worked. "I don't know what's going on with me, Dr. Ponton. My behavior changed after my mother got sick. She was the only person in my family I could talk to. I've tried to talk to my brothers and my father, but it's hopeless. I know that I play a role in this, too, and if we could explore my ideas about it, I think it would help."

At this very young age, David was not only curious about his own thoughts and behavior but had an awareness of the unconscious, of the idea that he had buried thoughts and feelings that affected his day-to-day actions but were not readily accessible. With all the zeal of a new candidate in psychoanalysis, I mentioned that exploration of his dreams would be one way to explore his unconscious. He jumped at the suggestion and began recording his dreams in a journal. More important, he began to think about them and make connections to his life.

David began his description of one dream by saying that he thought it was "weird," but at the same time he "kind of liked it." The dream was set at an Italian wedding party. In it, a band is playing and guests are dancing. David would like to ask a girl to dance, but he is too shy. Then a girl with a clubfoot asks him to dance, and he accepts. While they are dancing, a stick falls out of his pocket, and both he and the girl trip and fall on the floor. His father and two brothers are watching all of this with stony-faced expressions. Their frozen faces are what David remembers as he wakes up.

On the day he first told me about this dream, David had very little to say about it. Then during his next session he asked me what I thought about masturbation. He said that he had been thinking a lot about masturbation since he had gone to confession the day before he attended the actual wedding that had appeared as part of his dream. I asked him what he imagined I would think about mastur- bation, and he presented me with two "theories." His first theory was that I was an "older married person" who would understand this type of thing but maybe wouldn't remember much about it (as- suming that masturbation occurs in adolescence and then disap- pears). His second theory was that I would be "hurt" by his mere expression of this idea. When I asked him about this, he stated that I might be so offended that I would faint and then injure myself falling on the floor. We were both reminded of the part of his dream when he and the girl with the clubfoot fall on the floor together. At thirteen, David was thinking about his sexual anatomy and develop- ment both indirectly, as revealed in his dreams (the stick "falling out" of his pocket representing his frequent erections and/or mas- turbation and fears of powerlessness and humiliation), and directly, as in the questions that arose in subsequent sessions. He asked me questions about masturbation and puzzling aspects of his sexual de- velopment. He told me that he had been masturbating and thinking about sexual matters a great deal at the time his mother became sick. Several months later David told me that he had felt responsible for his mother's illness: perhaps if he had not been so preoccupied with thoughts about sex, he would have observed the signs of her impending cancer.[1]

Our continued discussions gave us an opportunity to talk about some of David's risk-taking behavior. Because David saw his mas- turbation as risky behavior, he connected it with other risky things he was doing and ended up admitting to me that not only had he hung out with a group of guys who shoplifted, but he, too, had stolen. "Nothing big, a couple of tapes, candy bars," he said, "but I don't un- derstand why I did it, and it worries me. I could get caught." I asked him what worried him about getting caught. David smiled. "You al- ways want the specifics, I can't get away with being vague in here, not about jacking off, or stealing." I commented on his smile and sense of humor, mentioning that he seemed to appreciate my persis- tence. After all, he, too, was curious about his behavior. He laughed. "Some of the time. I hide a lot, of course, not only from you."

"From yourself, too," I replied.

In the context of this gentle bantering, I was trying to encourage David's curiosity about his behavior. It was through this process of joint examination and exploration that we would both understand it better. This early dream offered us an opportunity to discuss many things — David's recent pubertal development, his excitement and guilt about his "hidden stick," and his discovery of masturbation.

Peter Blos, a student and follower of Sigmund Freud, has written extensively on the topic of adolescent masturbation. Blos believes that the absence of masturbation in adolescence is abnormal, constituting an arrest in psychosexual development; the implication is that without masturbation, sexuality won't proceed along a normal developmental course.[2] Although I don't believe that the absence of masturbation in adolescence is necessarily pathological, masturbation does provide an important outlet for adolescent sexual drives and serves as an area of positive risk-taking for adolescents. The process allows adolescents to experiment with their developing bodies and changing sexuality, to develop sexual fantasies, and to engage in sexual experimentation. One serious consequence of the continuing stigma regarding masturbation in the era of HIV/AIDS is that many teens actually feel that masturbation is riskier than sexual intercourse. This is not to say that there are no problems with adolescent masturbation. Excessive, compulsive masturbation, engaged in to the exclusion of social activities, and masturbation associated with violent sadomasochistic fantasies are both problematic. Therapy offers adolescents one of the few opportunities to explore this often difficult area directly and to help them develop a healthy attitude toward it if they are troubled.

My discussion with David of this delicate subject helped him open up about other areas where he felt vulnerable. From his perspective, the fact that I was neither prudish nor hurt by such discussion meant that I could be trusted with other difficult topics, such as his shoplifting.

At this point David's understanding of his risky behavior was limited. He would admit that he engaged in it and that it troubled him. But therapy and his own development would expand his understanding about his risk-taking, as would our work around his relationship with his father.

In the first dream David described for me, his older brothers and father are watching his adolescent sexual antics stony-faced. David thought that they didn't approve of his developing, and perhaps still clumsy or awkward, sexuality. Remembering my conversations with these men, I knew that on some level he was right. But the dream also introduced the idea of David being shut out by his father and brothers. Mike, his oldest brother, had had more time to develop a relationship with their father, being eighteen years older than David. But David really believed that by virtue of his age and their collective disapproval, he had been excluded. Acknowledging the situation allowed him to talk about his anger. "What other kid has to deal with three fathers? One's bad enough—no wonder I have to fight so hard to prove that I'm a man!"

David and I had talked a great deal about his "gang" participation, and he had, for the most part, stopped spending so much time with that group. But we really hadn't understood why it had been so important to him. After talking about the dream, David also remembered that a couple of the boys in the gang had reminded him of his brothers. He had felt as though they were laughing at him and thought he was a sissy. David's eyes flashed anger as he said, "And I, stupid guy, fell right into it because I wanted to prove that I was a man."

Often when teenagers first acknowledge their risky behavior they see themselves as "stupid." I tried to help David see that, at age thirteen, he hadn't understood that he felt shut out by his father and brothers, let alone been able to recognize that some of these feelings were being replayed with his friends. I pointed out that this was a tough business to figure out, even with months of therapy. David then relaxed some and admitted, "I've changed a lot. I couldn't see it then. At least coming to see you got me out of the shoplifting gang, but it didn't change the way that I felt about myself—like a sissy who had to prove himself."

"You still feel that way inside," I said gently.

"Yes," he acknowledged, sounding sad.

Now David and I not only understood his risky behavior better but had begun to understand his negative self-concept as the sissy who had to prove himself, a view that easily guided him in a risky direction.

Life with Father, Work with Father

When Joseph first appeared in the office with his wife and son, he was elderly, quiet, and somewhat self-effacing. Even with her recent illness, his wife had a confident and understanding attitude about her son's problems. Joseph appeared genuinely perplexed. He said, "I really don't understand what's going on with David. You know, he is having a lot of trouble. We've been good parents to him, even through all the stuff with my wife. She's better now. She's just fine. What's going on with him?"

When I met with Joseph alone for the first time, the self-effacing demeanor seemed to drop away, and I began to get a sense of this man's power. Quiet, yes, but he was also extremely successful and self-confident. He had immigrated to this country at a young age and built a very successful grocery business. I had heard from everyone in the family that he was "a rock" to members of the extended family, to members of their ethnic community, to everyone who knew him. He was vital, supportive, and understanding, but he was nearly seventy years old. Parenting a teenager is difficult regardless of one's age, but Joseph was raising a son who was the same age as several of his grandchildren. Part of the difficulty with the fifty-seven-year age difference was obvious during this first visit. Joseph tended to see David as younger than he really was, as revealed in comments such as, "David's still a kid, problems like this shouldn't be happening with him." Joseph's lack of awareness about the role of David's two older brothers as second and third fathers was also evident during this visit. "Of course he should follow what his brothers say. They're great, they're like fathers to him."

I asked him whether he thought it might be difficult for David to grow up with three fathers. He paused, and then said, "Well, when you put it that way, maybe, but I didn't even have one. Three's got to be better than zero."

I laughed and said, "Yeah, three is better than zero, but it can still be difficult."

He smiled at that and said, "Well, what kind of problems do you think he's got related to all of this?"

I mentioned to him that my experience with some adolescent boys who had successful fathers and older brothers was that they felt they had to compete with them, measure up next to them. In our individual work, David was expressing difficulties in this area. He felt like he just didn't measure up. I asked Joseph whether he had any thoughts about this. He admitted that he was quite worried about David and felt that the boy was too close to his mother.

Remembering all too well the phone call with the brother who was the professional hunter, I asked Joseph whether he thought that was a problem. Joseph then confessed to his worry that David, being the youngest son, was mollycoddled by his mother and would turn out gay.

I asked him how he'd feel about his son being gay. He said, "Not good. I know you doctors have different ideas about that kind of stuff, but for me, a man has got to be straight to be a man."

"Do you feel like David's sexuality affects your manhood?"

He thought about it for a minute or two. "Yes. You're right about that. My manhood, as you call it, is affected by my sons—how they act, how they feel, what kind of men they are. If they are so-called gay, then I am not the man I should be." Joseph added that as an older father, he thought that he already wasn't enough of a man for David. He then expressed an idea I've heard from many men: that if the father isn't manly enough, then even "normal" contact with a caring mother, let alone contact that might be perceived as excessive, can "make" a son gay. Joseph was also letting me know something else very important—that for him masculinity was connected to age. Whether because of declining physical strength or diminished sexual potency, he didn't feel that he was as masculine as he was when he was younger.

"Well, Joseph, you're right," I said. "I do have different ideas than you do about this. For me, being straight or gay doesn't define what makes a man, but I can understand how and why you have these ideas." I also told him that the current psychological thinking was that the parents do not "make" a child gay, neither mothers nor fathers. We agreed that our job was to work together to help David, who was having a hard time. I told Joseph that David didn't feel that he could compete with his father and two brothers, that he felt as though he were defective in many ways, and that I believed that anything Joseph could do to help David feel like he was more of a man in a real sense would be very helpful both to David personally and to our work together.

He thought for a moment, and then he said, "Well, he can work with me. I like that, having a son work right alongside you. David's really good at that."

I asked him what David was especially good at. He said, "With figures, you know? He's got all of that. He's better at it than his brothers and me."

I asked him whether he'd ever told David that. He shrugged and said, "My sons just know it."

"Well, maybe the others do," I said. "But not this one. He doesn't just know it. He feels like he's fourth in line."

"Well, he *is* fourth in line," said Joseph. We both laughed again, but he was also hearing what I had said and beginning to think about what it might be like to be the fourth man in this household.

Part of the work with Joseph paralleled the process I try to engage all parents in—looking at their child's behavior with at least some sense of humor and trying to problem-solve together.

Several sessions later Joseph and I talked more about the concept of being fourth in line and what it felt like to David. David's feeling of being left out might explain why he felt so aligned with his mother. In her eyes, he wasn't fourth in line. What could make it different? "Well, I did tell him about the being good at figures stuff," said Joseph. "I think it might help. But then I thought about your idea that I should get to know him better and thought maybe we could start doing something together. I mean, I'm old." Again he smiled. "I guess you've noticed that. But I do play golf. I like it. David and I could play together. He's got a mean swing. He slices a little bit, but he's a lot of fun to be with. That kind of thing—is that what you're talking about?"

It was exactly what I was talking about. I told him to try it and let me know what happened.

After a rocky start, Joseph was a very willing parent. Advantages were immediately obvious in my work with him. First, he was direct. He didn't lie about his feelings but made an effort to put them right out there. I've found that many fathers share some of Joseph's feelings about masculinity, but few are able to be so candid. Second, he was goal-oriented and willing to try solutions, to test them out. This fit with his thinking as a successful businessman. Together we were able to establish an effective partnership, more limited but working in tandem with the partnership I had established with David. As Joseph developed a closer relationship with his son, he also became less critical of David's close relationship with his mother. Slowly, too, Joseph saw that the two older sons shouldn't be David's "fathers," and that maybe he was more than enough for David to battle against.

Challenging Our Fathers

Many fathers would like to be better parents to their sons. Like Joseph, who had lost his own father before he became a teenager, many fathers have not had role models. Their ideas about how a father should parent are much more likely to be rigid and strongly influenced by common stereotypes—for example, that fathers need to be rough and tough in order to make their sons rough and tough. Lacking a father in adolescence, Joseph believed that he had become a man by facing and taking on challenges on his own. As we talked about his adolescence after the death of his father, it became clear that he had not been alone, and that several members of his large extended family had played important roles. An uncle had paid for his passage to America. An aunt had found his bride and fostered his marriage. His grandmother had given him money to start his first business, a small fruit market.

Although Joseph had been a fatherless teen, family members had stepped in to assist him with some of the functions that fathers are expected to provide in a young man's life. As we spoke about this, Joseph confided that he was not happy about his relationships with his two oldest sons. He was proud of them, no question. They were responsible men with families of their own, and their masculinity was certainly not in question. But he did not feel emotionally close to either of them, and he was able to acknowledge that a bond like that would be valuable to him and to them at this point in their lives—better late than never. Joseph described having used a largely authoritarian style of parenting with his two older boys. He had spanked them several times, even into their adolescence, and although he had set up clear rules and guidelines during their adolescent years, he admitted that he was often inflexible, focusing on order for order's sake alone and forgetting that it was a tool he was using to raise his boys well. Even so, he remarked with surprise, it hadn't stopped the risky behavior. His second son, like David, had shoplifted and also smoked marijuana. And although Joseph felt that this son had "understood the rules," he also believed his son had been very angry with him, distant and rebellious. He admitted thinking that both of his older sons were angry with him, and he even wondered whether they were still afraid of him, acknowledging that fear had been one of the "tools" he had used to keep order in the house during their adolescence.

Joseph also told me that he was upset by the way his two older sons handled their children, spanking them and verbally humiliating them. He could see that his sons paid a price for the order they demanded in their houses and were not close to their own children. His oldest grandson was now already sequestering himself in his room and had told his grandmother that he hated his father. This was particularly painful for Joseph to see because at this point he and David were becoming closer. David was teaching his father about a new computer accounting program for retail businesses, and Joseph was steadily improving David's golf swing. Yes, they still argued constantly on the golf course, but their competitive banter during the now-routine Tuesday afternoons together gave them an opportunity to work things out. Joseph saw that David not only understood the "house rules," he was rewriting them with references and footnotes.

Of course, David was not the only one rewriting the rules. His father was shifting from an *authoritarian* parenting style to one that was much more *authoritative*. Authoritarian parents are able to set rules and provide structure for teens, but generally they are short on flexibility. Authoritative parents still exert control over their adolescents' behavior but tailor the rules and structure to the individual needs of the child and the parents—a frame of golf and accounting for Joseph and David. An authoritative parenting style still encourages verbal give-and-take, in contrast to the authoritarian parent who allows no leeway and is always right. An authoritative parenting style also leaves room for the important work of developing a relationship with the adolescent. In short, an authoritative style makes a supportive relationship the cornerstone around which discipline and structure can be provided. It emphasizes a flexible sense of order tailored to the family's needs rather than order rigidly imposed for its own sake.[3]

Changing Dreams

A year later David's dreams continued to provide interesting material for our discussions. Several focused on his continuing struggle to understand and be understood by his father. His brothers, too, frequently played a role in his dreams. Although David still wondered where he stood with his father and brothers, the message was slowly changing.

A year and a half after the first Italian wedding dream, David had another dream set in the same place. In this dream, David is marrying a girl, but, no surprise, his father and brothers are ignoring it; they are busily engaged in a sword fight with each other. David was upset when he first brought up this dream. In this dream, he has chosen the woman, unlike the woman in the first dream, who chooses him. He feels proud of his choice and would like his father and brothers to notice and acknowledge it as an accomplishment. Instead, they continue to be involved in their own activities and to ignore him. David is increasingly aware, however, of his own feelings—his anger and sadness—and his wish that his father and brothers would pay attention to him.[4]

At this time David was able to tell me that he had mixed desires about his father and brothers. Although he felt their constant "sword play" was ridiculous, he wanted to be a part of it; in fact, he wanted to be the winner, triumphing over father and brothers in a bloody, hard-fought battle.

"This is stupid," he said to me. "I can see how their competitive behavior has ruined my family. My mother is constantly being put down. I haven't been given a fair chance by them. Their own children are suffering. My father and brothers are so busy pulling out their swords that they can't see what's going on. Yet if I know it's so destructive, why do I want so much to be a part of it?"

There was no easy answer to David's question, and I told him that. He was a remarkable young man, increasingly willing to examine his thoughts, and I was gaining confidence in his ability to find an answer for himself. During the next months we spent a great deal of time looking at his feelings and his choices. Yes, he wanted to be a man recognized by the men in his family and to join in their aggressively destructive fights. That pull was strong. He believed that he would triumph over them as the youngest and most physically fit, but more important, he wanted to be recognized as part of their world. On the other hand, where would it get him? Where had it gotten them? They were constantly engaged in struggles, most concerned about who was on top, and alienated from their own children.

But things were changing with David's father. On their Tuesday afternoons together they were talking more and more. David discussed problems he was coming up against in high school and found that his father was starting to express his opinion in a different way. Joseph would still voice his ideas, whether or not they had been solicited (it was doubtful that anything would ever stop that process!), but he wasn't as upset if David disagreed. And he seemed to be listening to David differently, too. It wasn't a perfect match, by any means. Many times one or the other would storm off the golf course, shouting some obscenity and leaving the other wondering what he had done wrong, but the afternoons continued. Over time they even became calmer, more pleasurable.

I realized just how much David and Joseph's relationship had changed when David contacted me four years later when he was eighteen. We met briefly because he wanted to talk again about some issues with his brothers. David's oldest brother had criticized David's girlfriend at a family party. It was uncanny how this real episode resembled David's adolescent wedding dreams with his father, brothers, and "fiancée." A second episode, disturbing to the entire family, was the disappearance of the oldest brother's teenage son—the same boy who three years earlier had told his grandmother he hated his father. After a fight with his father, this teen had left a bitter note addressed to his mother stating that he loved her but couldn't live this way any longer, humiliated by his father, filled with bitterness and hatred for him.

Joseph told David that he thought his brother was wrong to be so critical of David's girlfriend in front of the whole family, and that he was proud of David's choices and the positive changes he had seen his youngest son make. David, still very angry with his oldest brother, asked Joseph whether he was going to intervene in the matter with his runaway grandson. Slowly Joseph said, "Yes, David, but not in the way that I used to. Mike is making the same mistakes that I made with my boys, and I led him down this road. Guidance and rules provide structure for young people, but the way

I handled it has left a bitter taste and an angry edge. I would like for you to learn from our mistakes and be a different type of father to your children. You and I, we talk. You listen, I listen. It was not that way with Mike and me, and it has not been that way with Mike and his son."

Joseph had changed. He had learned from his relationship with David and now saw that his desire to make his sons "manly" men, to teach them how to compete in the world, was not enough. Each of his sons was a strong competitor, and each could stand alone in the world, but the time that he and David spent together had helped both of them channel their energy in different ways. They competed, but more often than not they found that they were working together. There was room in their relationship for nurturance, caring, and close collaboration.

Dr. Kyle Pruett, a professor at Harvard University, has been curious about the role of fathers for several decades and has pursued this curiosity by studying families in which fathers are playing an increasingly larger role in caretaking. I was drawn to his work when he and I both participated in a mentorship program for young psychiatrists at the annual meetings of the Academy of Child and Adolescent Psychiatry. I had prepared what I thought was a series of dazzling slides on adolescent risk-taking, but it was Kyle Pruett's video of a father and son playing the piano together that captured the audience.

On the surface, this video clip appeared pretty simple—a father and child hanging out together, nothing unusual about it. What became apparent as we watched was how important the father's role was in the child's development, and also how much of a hands-on experience it was for both father and son. When the father moved in one direction, the son moved. When the father sang, the son sang. Their bond was visible. The discussion period following the talks was filled with questions about fathering. Young psychiatrists wanted to know how they could help their patients become the kind of father they had seen on that tape. As the discussion expanded, many of the men in the room admitted that they wanted to know how they could be that kind of father themselves. Stimulated by their questions, Pruett spoke about the potential nurturing abilities of fathers, outlining a perspective that he refines in his book *The Nurturing Father: Journey Toward the Complete Man*. Both men and women are born with a vigorous predisposition to procreate and nurture, and we can only hope that a time will come when fathers can love and nurture without embarrassment or fear, when they can be open and vulnerable without being perceived as less than masculine.[5]

The fathers in Pruett's studies indicated that this type of relationship could happen between fathers and children. It isn't mysterious: it takes time spent with the child, hard work, practice, and some ability to look at failures and learn from those experiences. Fathers learning to be proud rather than embarrassed about showing how much they care for their children is crucial.

Joseph had reexamined his method of fathering with his last son, and was able to see his role as a father in a more complicated, and hence, richer light. He no longer believed that he had to shut his tender feelings out of his relationship with his son in order to do his job as a father. He began to see that three fathers were too many to compete with and began to develop a relationship with David that was outside the competitive hierarchy he had built with his older sons. As their bond developed, their competitiveness decreased and father and son began to listen to each other. It was this step, the listening, that helped to change David's pattern of risk behaviors. David began to feel accepted in his father's eyes and no longer had to take on high-risk challenges to prove himself.

David told me about a new computerized billing system for the grocery business that he had discussed with his dad. He had described this plan to Joseph on a very hot day when they were playing their usual golf game but going more slowly. The way David explained it, he described the plan at the third hole, fought with his father until the fifteenth hole, and by the eighteenth hole his father could see some merit to it. David felt triumphant. His father was listening to him and acknowledging that he had some pretty good ideas.

Joseph also allowed David an opportunity to listen to him in a new way by sharing new parts of himself. Instead of being only critical, Joseph discussed David's ideas for a better billing system; furthermore, he began to talk about his own failures, acknowledging his belief that his earlier parenting style might have contributed to his grandson running away. So Joseph, a man who had been unable to confide in his older sons—who in fact had believed it to be detrimental to them—saw that he and David each benefited from such a relationship.

The last time I spoke with Joseph was when he called looking for a recommendation for a therapist to work with his grandson. I smiled as he again demonstrated what he had learned about the men in his family and competition when he said, "It wouldn't work for you to be his therapist. You're David's doctor. Wouldn't want to set up something that wouldn't work between my son and grandson."

Several months later David called to tell me that Joseph had died suddenly from a heart attack. David had been asked by his two brothers and mother to write and give the eulogy for his father because the others felt that he knew Joseph the best. David wrote, "It was most important that my father learned to listen to me. It showed me how to listen to him. We were able to learn from each other."

Chapter Seven

Mothers and Sons: Untangling Family Business

Dad hits you for years and then I hit you one time and you act like it's the end of the world.

— Mark

The staff in the Adolescent Medicine Clinic had told me about the family I would be meeting—Opal and her thirteen-year-old son Mark from up north in Humboldt County, an emergency referral from social services there following an episode of domestic violence: the boy had assaulted his mother. When a child overpowers a parent physically and violently, they are both in a dangerous situation.

Even with preparation, when I opened the door to the room where we were meeting, I was taken aback by the purple marks on Opal's face. As I got closer, I saw that it was not one bruise, but several, reflecting the pattern of the fist that had struck her. Mark was watching me stare at his mother's brutalized face, looking at me with an expression that was both surly and scared. It was visible even as they sat that Opal was petite and Mark was not only big for his age but on his way to becoming a large man. His long legs were stretched out nearly to the center of the room. He kept his hands in the pockets of his windbreaker until I offered my own to shake; his grasp was lazy and not at all menacing, but with the evidence sitting before us in the very next chair, it was hard to forget that this boy's man-sized fist had recently been used as a weapon. It may have been obvious where the physical danger between this parent and child lay, but there were surely other dangers that had allowed such violence to happen.

Fortunately, my work sometimes offers me a formal structure when I am at a loss for words. This was one of those rare moments. I introduced myself, shook hands with Opal and Mark, and then began by mentioning some of the history that the pediatrician had given me and describing the type of services we offered at the clinic. Halfway through my spiel I realized that I was avoiding talking about what had happened between this mother and son.

I looked at Opal and Mark. Both wore freshly pressed shirts tucked into their Levis, topped off by cowboy boots. Around Opal's neck was a small peace symbol hanging from a black leather cord. They came from Ukiah, a small town in Humboldt County, a beautiful area along the northernmost coast of California known for its rocky ocean vistas and massive redwood forests. It was also an area desperately in need of child and adolescent psychiatrists. For several years the county had paid for me to fly up from San Francisco to evaluate some of the most difficult adolescents. I hadn't forgotten those teenagers. Their cases were always complicated—ritualistic abuse, families "under the spell" of witchcraft, generations affected by incest, violent family arguments, and problems interconnected with the supply and demand of this farming area's main crop—marijuana. Not exactly a pastoral scene. Typically I address a risk behavior directly, especially one as dangerous as violence. Why was I holding back now?

Opal had been watching me wade through their chart, which they had brought with them from Humboldt County, and was fidgeting with her peace medallion as she heaved long and increasingly louder sighs of impatience. Finally she looked at me and said, "Don't just sit there, do something!"

Sharing her belief that I should be doing something, but still unsure about how to proceed, I asked her what she thought I should be doing.

"They sent us down here to get evaluated because you're supposed to be some sort of expert on teenagers." She eyed me suspiciously now, indicating that she thought Humboldt County had made a serious mistake and that she had made a four-hour drive for nothing.

Rephrasing my question, I asked what she would like to see happen if things were to go well here.

This sparked a comeback that I've heard from many parents of teenagers: "Make him ten again!" She started to smile then, looking at her six-foot-tall son and recognizing the impossibility of her wish.

Mark grunted at this. Sensing an opening for some communication with him, I quickly asked him what his wish would be. "I wanna be outta here," he said.

"Out of where?" I asked.

"Her life, I guess. She treats me like I *am* ten."

"So your mom wants you younger so you'll be easier to parent, and you want to be older so that you can leave home?"

He shrugged, but I sensed that this thirteen-year-old did not want to leave home. Then I looked straight at Opal and repeated her wish that her thirteen-year-old son could be younger, adding that if I could just change Mark's age in one direction or the other, things would, no doubt, be fine. Although I hadn't entirely redeemed myself at this point, Opal and Mark were both listening to me, so I decided to ask about the bruise on Opal's face. In keeping with my philosophy that adolescents should be held responsible for their behavior, I asked Mark first to tell me how it had happened.

"She was screaming at me."

"So you felt like it was okay to hit her?"

"Yes. No. She made me so angry."

"So it was okay to hit her?"

There was a long pause, and then Mark slowly said, "It's not okay, but I'm pretty sure it's gonna happen again."

"But at this point you're also agreeing with me that it wasn't okay for you to hit your mom?"

There was a long pause, and then Mark finally said that he agreed with me.

I then turned to Opal and asked her how she had seen what happened between herself and her son. She minimized it. "It's not a big bruise. I've had worse. I just want him to start treating me better now."

Worse? As far as I knew, this was the first time Mark had struck
his mother. But violence is often learned, and there may have been
someone else in their house who was setting the example. I chose
my words carefully. "Opal, your thirteen-year-old son hit you. This
could become a dangerous pattern. But I think that in order to help
you change things, I need to understand this episode. So how did it
happen?"

She began slowly. "I was trying to get him to clean up a mess that
he had left in the kitchen. The dishes had been there for hours. I had
asked him several times in a calm voice, but he kept ignoring me. I
started yelling at him, and still he did nothing. Then he just got up
and hit me across the face!" Opal was holding her face in her hands
and began moaning, "I can't handle it." Although she was still in the
room physically with her son and me, her mind appeared to have
drifted to some faraway place. Meanwhile, as soon as she had said,
"Then he got up and hit me across the face," Mark had started shaking. Several seconds later he stood up, still shaking, and stammered,
"That's not all, Mom. Tell her what you said to me. Tell her!"

Drawn back into the room but looking very frightened and still
somewhat removed, Opal appeared surprised by her son's comment. "What do you mean?"

"You're sure you don't remember, Mom? You said I was just like
him. You said, 'You're just like your father, that bastard.'" Mark
turned his body away from his mother and pushed his fist up and
down against the wall. His shoulders were heaving. I was struck by
not only the anger but also the tremendous amount of pain each of
them was feeling, and by their inability to reach out to each other.

After hearing what Opal had said to Mark, I was beginning to
realize that my impulse to hold back with them was probably related to how highly sensitive everything in this family was. Both
Mark and Opal were extremely volatile and reactive with each
other. It appeared that even small things could trigger their fighting,
and clearly most of the things we had to talk about were not small.

Taking something of a chance, I decided to bring up the topic of
Mark's father. First I asked Mark if he could join us again and sit
down with his mother and me. He agreed reluctantly, keeping his
face turned away from us. Then I asked Opal about her husband.

She began slowly, still fidgeting with the peace symbol on her
necklace. "Michael's in the merchant marines. He's still part of our

life, though, at least when he comes back to our house every few months—he has a room with a padlocked door where he keeps his things when he's not on ship—but the visits are horrible. I think Mark and I would both agree about that. He fights with me. Mark's seen a lot of that." Pausing, she added, "I guess he hits me a lot."

Immediately I asked the next question. "Has he ever hit Mark?"

"No," said Opal, sounding sure.

"How would you know?" said Mark accusingly. At that, Opal and I both turned to face him.

"She's right. I've seen a lot of it. I've seen him hit her a lot. She should call the police on the bastard."

"Has he ever hit you, Mark?" He didn't answer. "What happened between you and your dad when he was home last time?" I asked.

"Why do you want to know?"

"I need to know because I think it affects where you're at, and what happened between you and your mom. I also need to make sure you're safe."

"You think he hit me, don't you."

"Mark, I don't know."

"But that's what you think."

"I think what's most important here is that you be safe. We also have to deal with what went on between you and your mom, and with what you're thinking and feeling about all of this. If you don't want to tell me about it, you don't have to. It looks like it was a hard thing for you to handle alone, though."

Calmer now, Mark looked at me with his mouth twisted into a strange smile, both mocking and hopeless. "Yeah, he hit me. Once. The last time he was home. He hits her all the time. So what can you do about it? He's coming back again in three weeks." It sounded like a dare, but I knew he felt hopeless.

Suddenly I, too, felt caught in this family's hopeless cycle of family pain and violence. As I felt myself being sucked into their despondency, I tried to remember the energy of this family—Mark being courageous enough to admit the truth, and Opal caring enough about the son who had assaulted her to drive four hours to get some help.

Whether Mark acknowledged that his father had hit him or not, I had enough reason to suspect it was a possibility, and therefore enough reason to report my suspicions to either Children's Protective Services or the police, as mandated by law. As I thought about it, I wondered whether Mark had hit his mother because his father was scheduled to come home soon and he knew on some level that if he hit her, too, she would be pushed to act. Maybe he wanted to tell someone—his mother, me, the police—that his father was hitting him. Maybe he wanted people to know his father was hitting his mother. Maybe he was tired of watching her take it.

My assessment that day ended with brief meetings alone with Opal and Mark. I told them that based on what I had heard, I was going to speak with Children's Protective Services in Humboldt County. I alerted them to the possibility that the agency might call and perhaps even investigate the violence in their family. I explained what usually happened when they did investigate, briefly describing several situations with other families. I gave each of them a card for a shelter that provided assistance to victims of violence, and I encouraged Opal to join a women's support group for abused spouses. She was grateful and said that she would try to go even though it was an hour's drive from their home. I gave them a phone number where they could contact me at any hour and told them that I thought it was important that they come back to see me the next week. We found a time to meet that would work better with their long drive to the city, and I let them know that I thought they had taken a key step by starting to talk about the complicated problems in their family. Meanwhile, I told myself that we still had a lot of work to do, and not a lot of time, before Michael returned home.

A Week Later: Round Two

Violence is specifically addressed in this chapter, but it runs through many of the adolescent lives described in this book. Their stories illustrate that violence isn't bound to gender, class, or race, and that it is important to address and treat violence early in a child's life.

At the time of our next meeting I had collected a considerable number of articles and handouts on family violence to give to Mark and Opal. The American Medical Association recently reported that family violence is being more effectively handled in our country than are other categories of violence, including public violence, sexual assault, and what is now called "virtual violence," a term used to refer to violence in entertainment—song lyrics, films, television, video games, and the Internet.[1] Although this report indicates that the nation is doing a better job of working with family violence, largely because it is now easier to report and treatment is sometimes available, I believe that this assessment tells only half the story.

Family violence plays an important role in promoting other types of violence, often beginning a cycle of violence for children and adolescents from which they are later unable to break free. And violence, in all of its forms, is a risk behavior. Often unrecognized in its early manifestations, it can begin as a transition from risk-taking to risk behavior—for example, when a child moves from being assertive to being aggressive. This kind of warning sign had occurred with Mark when he was eleven years old. He beat up three children on the playground and was expelled from school. Like many risk behaviors, violence can make a child more vulnerable to other risk behaviors. After Mark was expelled from school, he ran away from home; though he was gone only for a few days, he stole a neighbor's car, which he took joy-riding, and started smoking, a habit he never broke as long as I knew him. Perhaps most important, violent behavior is often impulsive; it is the opposite of the carefulness and the thinking skills that adolescents need to acquire so that they can better assess risks.

Mark appeared exhausted, hungry, and angry for his second appointment with me. He and his mother had argued during the entire trip down in the car, unable to agree on which fast-food restaurant to eat at or who would meet with me first once they got here. Opal finally decided that Mark could start first with me but refused to feed him, at least by his report, and had dropped him off and gone off to her own choice of a drive-through food stop.

A hungry teenager is not a good candidate for psychotherapy, so I pulled several granola bars and a can of fruit juice from my emergency stash and sat down to meet with Mark. After he inhaled two chocolate chip bars, he began to talk, beginning with how things were going at school—not well. He hadn't gotten in any major fights since he was expelled from school five years earlier, but he still had a reputation as a fighter. Other kids shied away. I asked him what that was like for him.

"I don't know. I try not to think about it."

"What do you think about when you're in school?"

He smiled for the first time. "Not school, if that's what you were wondering about. I space out a lot." After a long pause, he said, "Nothing, I don't think about anything."

Mark's own comment about spending a lot of time thinking about nothing—which I understood as a way of trying to avoid thinking or feeling—seemed to surprise him. It was as if in telling me about it, he realized for the first time all of the minutes he wasted this way. He saw himself as an active, action-oriented type of guy, so all that wasted time bothered him.

I asked him whether he had any idea what kind of thoughts he might be trying to avoid having. It took him a while, but two things really bothered him: the possibility that, as his mother had said, he really was a bastard like his father; and the possibility that other kids saw him that way, too. He was a lot like his dad, after all. He knocked holes in walls. And now he had hit his mother.

Mark also said that his mother seemed out of it most of the time. His dad was out to sea, he said, but his mother might as well have been. He recognized that she was scared of his father, but it scared Mark when she did nothing or seemed to fall apart around this man.

I agreed with Mark about part of what he said, letting him know that I saw him as an angry guy, but I also told him that he didn't have to end up being like his father. I also said that it had to be hard for him to watch his mother get hit. He nodded. "It's the worst," he said. When we stood up, Mark looked relieved, a feeling that was heightened by his mother waiting outside with two Whoppers and two sides of fries for him. He had devoured half of it before she and I began our part of the meeting.

Although recently fed, Opal was less communicative with me than her son had been. When I asked her how things had gone for her during the past week, she began to cry softly. When she finally was able to speak, I could barely hear her, and the words were punctuated by small, choking sobs.

"Why does everything bad happen to me?" she whispered.

"What's 'everything'?"

"Everything—my marriage with a horrible husband, our farm under attack by the sheriff, my son mouthing off all the time and now turning violent."

The comment about the sheriff took me by surprise, and I asked

Opal about it. Apparently, far from attacking their farm, the sheriff who brought Mark home after he had run away and stolen the neighbor's car, had warned Opal about a relatively small crop of well-tended marijuana growing peacefully in the greenhouse behind their garage. She had told Michael the next time he came home, but he had instructed her pretty clearly to ignore the sheriff's threats. Opal told me that although she disapproved of drugs, she was afraid to stop tending the crop, fearful that Michael would beat her when he came home if she let the plants die in his absence. She was very clear with me that neither she nor Michael smoked—it was a cash crop. She said she had even imagined that she might find a way to take the whole crop, unharvested, and sell it to someone, using the money to help her and Mark move away from Michael. It wasn't working out the way she had planned, however.

"It does sound like there's a lot for you to handle," I said.

"There is."

"Where do you get your support?"

"I don't," she said, her overwhelming sadness beginning again. I knew that it was important for me to help Opal not fall prey to her usual pattern of helplessness, but I was beginning to feel frustrated by how lacking in power she felt herself to be.

"Opal, you did make this drive to San Francisco today. What did you think was going to happen here with me?" I asked this largely to provide us with a focus; it can be difficult to work with "everything is hopeless" and much simpler to deal with one specific person or problem.

"I guess I think that nothing will happen here either. My son and I fought the whole way down in the car."

"So why did you come?" I asked.

She was clearly taken aback by my question. "They recommended you."

"So that's why you made the four-hour drive a second time?" I asked.

"I guess that I think it helped some the last time, but not a lot."

"Not a lot, but some. Enough to come again. And yet we've barely begun to talk and you already have serious questions about whether this trip will do any good."

"Yeah."

"Opal, your life does seem to be very difficult right now—problems with your husband, your son, and the sheriff. Is there anything you think you can do about it?" I was thinking about what Mark had said about how she fell apart so much of the time, or did nothing. Getting her to focus might help get her to act.

"I don't know." Opal answered slowly, but as we talked, her own sad story emerged and the shadow of a plan began slowly to unfold.

Violence had been an early presence in Opal's life. Her father had started beating her when she was seven years old and hadn't stopped until she was seventeen, when she left home with her nineteen-year-old sister after one particularly painful beating. Opal told me that when she was young she had loved her mother deeply and always sought her soothing comfort and calm voice after her father's beatings. But over time, seeing how her mother couldn't, or wouldn't, stop her father, Opal began to see her mother as cowardly and weak, standing by silently while her children were beaten. Opal had vowed that she wouldn't be the same kind of mother—she would protect her children. And Michael never did beat Mark, or so Opal had thought. Hearing Mark tell me that Michael had struck him the last time he was home had jolted her.

Opal's mother had died many years earlier, but now the problems that Opal was having with Mark and the ongoing problems with Michael gave her a better understanding of what her mother's situation had been. And she knew that despite vowing not to, she had fallen into the very same pattern. She also wanted better for herself, and for Mark. She said that she had chosen to drive to San Francisco the first time when she heard that our clinic specialized in teens and families; the one in Humboldt County did not. Maybe with our special experience we would be able to help her and Mark.

When I asked Opal why she had stayed with Michael until now, she said she wasn't sure. She knew that, probably like her own mother had been, she was afraid of her husband. She also knew that she was afraid to be left alone, and now especially frightened to be left alone with her thirteen-year-old son, who was big enough to hit her, and apparently willing.

Michael had been a younger drinking buddy of her father's. Why that fact hadn't immediately put her off was hard for Opal herself to understand. Instead, she had married Michael hoping that he would change. He had changed—he drank even more. Verbal abuse followed, then escalated, and then he started hitting her. Now she knew he had hit Mark. Now she knew that she couldn't wait for him to change. She talked about the possibility of Mark staying with her sister while she tried to work things out with Michael. Maybe he would go to counseling with her. She had asked him to do this before, and he had refused. Maybe if he knew she knew he had hit Mark, he would be willing to try.

Even talking with me, Opal was not able to hold on to her hopeful feelings for long, however. She would start to cry and then shake, repeating to herself over and over again how hopeless things were for her. Although it was true that Opal had a number of very real and serious problems, her tendency to become overwhelmed was a major block. Knowing that our work was just beginning, I made a referral for her to work with a therapist who specialized in spousal abuse in Humboldt County, and then I suggested that she and I focus on her problems with her son.

Mothers and Sons

In chapter 6, Joseph and David illustrate one of our society's concerns about families, specifically, that sons will not be masculine enough. David's father and brothers were extremely worried that David would turn out to be gay if he was too close with his mother, and they struggled to separate him from her. It was during the course of that struggle that David began to participate in risk behaviors, in part so that he could prove to his male relatives that he truly was "a man." David's mother was a quiet partner in all of this; she knew that her strong relationship with her youngest son was beneficial to him, but being ill and cowed by her husband and older sons, she was reluctant to stand up to them.

Her actions are mirrored around the world. Many mothers feel pressured into "cutting the cord" with their sons during adolescence so that they can grow up into "men." Such attempts to separate may actually do real damage to the good relationships that mothers have developed with their sons, adversely affecting both the boys and their mothers.[2] Mothers may specifically back away from giving their sons advice about risk-taking, believing that not having an "overinvolved" mother will make them more masculine.

Although Opal was not backing away from Mark in the same

way that David's mother backed away from him, these two mothers did have several things in common. Opal was unable to recognize the important role model she was for her son. In fact, in light of Michael's absence and poor role-modeling when he was around, her behavior was even more important for her son's development. She began to see this in the family session that immediately followed my individual meetings with them, during which I focused on Mark and Opal's relationship.

When I asked Mark how he thought things with his mom had gone during the past week, he spoke up angrily. "My dad's coming home in two more weeks. Nothing is going to change. I'm sick of her being such a doormat. I wish she would do something about it or the same old thing is going to happen, fighting, screaming . . . "

"So you're angry and worried about what your mother's doing and not doing. How do you fit into it?"

"Because I hit her, too? Is that what you mean?"

"Well, aren't you responsible for your actions?" I asked.

Most likely remembering some of our conversation from the week before, Mark changed his tone. "Look, I'm responsible for what I do. I know that. But how come you're not getting on her case about what she does?"

"What is it you think she does, Mark?"

"She takes it. She lets him treat her that way."

At this moment Opal started to cry. Mark and I both looked at her. These weren't her usual tears of helplessness. She was really listening to what her son was saying and, it seemed, feeling genuinely bad about the way he saw her. Mark kept talking to me as though she weren't in the room.

"I'm worried about her, about us. That guy could kill us one of these times, maybe next time. And anyway, even if he doesn't kill us, what right does he have to beat up on us? She gets so helpless, it's disgusting. And she doesn't do anything about it."

"So it's very important that she face this situation, be strong."

Mark was now starting to kick one of my chairs with his work boot. "One of us has to be."

After I asked him to please stop kicking the chair, I turned to Opal.

"What do you think about what Mark is saying?"

"Even after seeing my mother when I was growing up, it didn't occur to me that what I did was so important. I mean, I was her daughter, you know? Mark's a boy."

"So you didn't see yourself as a role model for his behavior?"

"I guess not. I mean, I know his father's no role model, but it never occurred to me that I could be one for him."

"Well, it seems as though his father *is* a role model, but not a very good one," I said.

"No kidding," said Opal. Then, after a long pause, she added, "I guess I haven't been a very good one either, then. I mean, Michael and I both showed Mark that I could be hit."

I asked Opal whether she could talk about situations in which she felt that she had acted as a good role model for her son. It took her several minutes, but she was smiling as she said, "I don't know how Mark's going to like this, but I thought I did a pretty fair job of handling things after he hit me. I followed up with Social Services; I drove us here."

Mark was quick to come back after she said this. "That's your example, Mom. Come on, Dad hits you for years and then I hit you one time and you act like it's the end of the world."

"The doctor asked when I thought I set a good example for you. I don't think that I did all of the years with your dad. But when you hit me, I had to do something or you were going to repeat your father's and my life."

At this moment Mark started to look at his mother differently, the first sign of respect for her that I had seen on his face. Maybe he was angry about it, but he respected her standing up to him. During the rest of the session we continued to talk about how Mark and Opal could each recognize and take responsibility for their own actions. Opal was beginning to see the impact that her actions had on her son's life. During this meeting she shared her belief that she would be less important in her son's life after he became a teenager. Opal and I talked about the possibility that Mark might believe that violence and drugs were wrong but that, at thirteen, the picture he was receiving from his parents was a powerful negative influence.

Although Opal and Mark's situation, characterized by an atmosphere of fear and violence, is different from that of many mothers and their adolescent sons, much about their relationship is more typical. Unlike David's mother, Opal was not trying to cut ties with her son. As an essentially single mother, she knew she couldn't do that, but she failed to recognize that she was still an important role model for her son. All of her actions—including her helplessness when her husband beat her, her concessions around growing marijuana for him, however reluctantly—had tremendous impact.

Like Opal, many mothers of adolescent sons fail to recognize that they are still one of their son's primary role models and that, in some cases, they may be the most important one. And just like fathers, mothers role-model risk-taking, both positive and negative, for their sons. Mothers who take positive risks frequently and encourage their sons to do the same are powerful role models. Mothers who can't take risks, or who get locked into patterns of negative risk behavior, as Opal did, also transmit a powerful message.

Leaving that session, I could see that it wasn't only Mark who was looking at his mother differently; Opal was starting to look at herself differently, with slowly growing self-confidence and self-respect. She would need all of it in the upcoming weeks.

Finding a Way Out

The consequences of adolescent violence are staggering.[3] The lifetime costs for all persons aged twelve years and older who are injured owing to rape, robbery, assault, arson, or murder in a single year in America are estimated to be $178 billion.[4] Almost half of these crimes are committed by young men, who constitute only 8 percent of the total population[5]; that statistic indicates the importance of identifying and then working with adolescents at risk of participating in activities that are harmful to themselves, their families, and society.

Mark definitely fell into the category of young men at risk. He had been physically abused by his father. He had hit his own mother, almost causing permanent damage to her face. He had run away and stolen a car. He had also told me that some of his "friends" at school were encouraging him to steal and sell his mother's marijuana crop. These same "friends" were stealing cars, although they had not yet been caught. Without a well-developed treatment plan, I had little doubt that Mark would join that 8 percent of the population. How could we all keep working together to keep that from happening?

Mark and Opal had driven a considerable distance and "lasted" past the second visit. They were both talking to me, but I knew that this alone was not going to be enough. I would need to assess whether Mark had any underlying psychiatric problems that might be part of the picture of his risk behaviors. I could also work with Opal and Mark together to help Opal become a more effective parent and to help them both practice better ways to express and resolve their conflicts. But I was not in school with Mark, and clearly that was also a problem area: he spent much of his time there spacing out and teaming up with friends involved in dangerous activities. I also wasn't sitting on the youth probation board for the county, to which Mark had to answer after stealing the neighbor's car.

Violent behavior is extremely difficult to change. Mark was already thirteen years old. That's young for an adolescent, but old in terms of altering a pattern of violence. This is not to say that such patterns can't be altered—they can—but an active team effort, including individual and family therapy, collaboration with school and the probation and social service departments, and the assistance of other caring adults, is often required.[6] Stable adults who already knew Mark and took an interest in him might be hard to come by.

As we talked, Opal could understand the concept of building a team to help her raise her adolescent son. She came up with other people to add—a teacher at school and a neighbor. Where Opal ran into difficulty was around the question of what to do about Michael. She believed that when he came home, all her plans would be upset and she and Mark would again be sucked into the cycle of violence. We reviewed her options. She could do nothing now, wait for Michael to come home, and then confront him. That would most likely lead to a repeat of the cycle of violence: she would get beaten and might lose her newfound resolve. She could move out, taking Mark with her. That would be financially arduous, but it was at least a workable option. She could also get legal help to assist her with a separation from Michael, then call him while he was still on ship to outline the plan when he returned. She believed that he would threaten violence and maybe act on it when he returned to Ukiah, but she could be ready, alert the police, and have friends and family staying with her for added support.

Once we talked about these options, it became clear that Opal had a larger support system than many abused spouses. She had friends and family with whom she spent a considerable amount of time when Michael was at sea. Clearly this was a valuable asset. As this plan started to percolate for Opal, she and I also discussed whether Michael had ever used a weapon, in any context, and whether he currently owned one. He had been arrested several times for physical fights, but she didn't think he had any weapons. Although there were no weapons in the house that she knew of, we still didn't know what was in Michael's locked room, and there was nothing to prevent him from getting hold of one before he came home if he got angry enough when she talked to him by phone. We discussed what her best options were and decided that she and Mark shouldn't be at home when Michael got there. I recommended that she talk with the sheriff who had been lenient with them about the marijuana, and with the women's shelter in Humboldt County.

Mentioning the sheriff returned us to the question about what Opal should do about the marijuana growing in the greenhouse. Suddenly it didn't seem like such a big problem. Encouraged by our discussion, which showed that she could change the situation with Michael, she knew that she could figure this problem out. There were other ways to find the money she needed to leave the marriage.

Homecoming

Much has been written about the extremely complex subject of domestic violence. All too common in the United States, where it's reported to occur in two million households each year, it permanently alters the atmosphere of the families that experience it.[7] It scars the children and adolescents who witness it, emotionally and physically. One-third of children in homes with domestic violence are beaten by the parent who is doing the spousal battering. Another third are beaten by the parent who is being battered.[8] Even those children who are not being physically abused themselves but are watching a cycle of abuse between the adults in their homes suffer emotionally and are at risk to act out patterns of violence.

Stopping these cycles in a family takes not only one act of courage but many. Opal and Mark had begun that process during their family sessions. They came for one more meeting with me before Michael came home, after which Opal called Michael on his

ship and let him know that she knew he had hit Mark, that Mark
had hit her, and that she and Mark had been getting treatment. She
told him she had decided to work to eliminate the violence in her
life, and she once more asked Michael whether he would be willing
to get help for his behavior when he returned to Ukiah. Disappointed but not surprised when he again refused, she let him know
that she had made plans to live separately. She told him that by the
time he returned she would have filed for a restraining order that
would legally prevent him from seeing or meeting with her, and she
gave him a phone number where messages could be left for them. To
her surprise, Michael was not angry but instead pleaded with her
not to leave. Opal stayed firm and said good-bye to him, ending the
ship-to-shore phone call feeling both relief and growing confidence.

Once she had taken this step and followed through with it, Mark
stood by his mother. They stayed with her sister at first and then got
a small apartment in town. Things weren't perfect. Mark still
mouthed off sometimes, left his dishes in the sink longer than his
mother liked, and hadn't extricated himself entirely from the guys at
school who were, in Opal's words, a "bad influence," but he began
to prove he had his own values and could act responsibly, too. He
did chores, and he got a job at a garage after school to help Opal
with their budget. Even after the restraining order preventing
Michael from seeing Mark was lifted, he told his father that for the
time being he only wanted to talk to him by telephone.

Opal learned that she was a role model for her son and made an
effort to make decisions that she thought sent him the right message
around taking responsibility for your own actions. And Opal
learned something about herself, too: the more she managed to do,
the less overwhelmed and paralyzed she got. She and Mark even
started spending some of their free time with each other, Mark
agreeing to attend a folk music concert with his mother if she took
him to motorbike races down in Sonoma.

Obviously a lot went into improving the lives of Mark and Opal,
and none of it happened overnight. Again, violence is a risk behavior that requires a team effort to treat. Although our sessions together provided a starting point, many other people became part of
the team that worked to help them for years. Opal's therapist at
home, who specialized in working with victims of spousal abuse,
gave years of energy and ideas to help this mother change over time.

A year later a teacher of Mark's helped him get a different part-time job working with younger boys in the after-school program. And the sheriff continued to play a role in this family's life: it turned out that he shared Mark's passion for motorbikes, and he took Mark to some of the races. In fact, it was the sheriff who drove Mark and Opal back to their farm one year later, after Michael had finally left for good. Now, for both mother and son, coming home felt the way it should — safe.

Chapter Eight

Fathers and Daughters: The Cutting Edge

I pick up the razor blade and watch myself in the mirror, cutting my arm very carefully until I see the blood. It makes me feel alive.

—Maura

The first time I met Maura, she was getting her arm bandaged at the university hospital emergency room. On that particular spring afternoon, only an hour after school and soccer practice had ended, Maura had taken a brand-new razor blade, made four cuts on her left arm, and then headed over to the Adolescent Medicine Clinic at the university, not to have the cuts examined but because she was scheduled for her yearly sports physical. When the cuts were discovered during the exam, Maura first acted surprised, even curious about where they'd come from, but then she admitted that she had made them herself. Justifiably worried about this harmful behavior, as well as Maura's inability to talk about it, the clinic nurse called Maura's father; the emergency room; and me, the adolescent psychiatrist who consults to pediatric doctors at the hospital when they have a psychological question or problem.

By the time I arrived at the emergency room where the nurse had sent seventeen-year-old Maura for evaluation of the wounds on her arm, Maura's father, an orthopedic surgeon, was already there. Standing unobserved in the open doorway of the exam room where Maura was being seen, I saw her father arguing with the surgical resident who was on call that day, demanding that he page the plastic surgeon to examine the four narrow cuts that his daughter had made on her arm. His voice was raised, and he appeared to be struggling to control himself to keep from getting even louder and angrier. He didn't seem to be listening to the surgical resident, who was rapidly losing patience with this doctor dad, or to his daughter's pleas to not get so upset about it.

Still wearing her soccer uniform, Maura was sitting on a gurney, holding her backpack so that it covered her newly marred arm. Apart from the tears in her eyes and the scared expression on her face, Maura looked like a model young athlete. Her long blonde hair was pulled back with a scrunchie, and her freshly scrubbed face was dotted with freckles. Her shoes still had muddy cleats. I decided not to interrupt her father's encounter with the other doctor; even under the best circumstances it is not easy for parents to meet a psychiatrist about their child, and these weren't even close to the best circumstances. I decided to collect more information in the meantime.

First I spoke with the adolescent medicine social worker, David, who was writing a note in the chart. He told me that he had tried to assist the father and surgical resident in their discussion about what to do about the wounds, but he had finally left, believing that this was a struggle that could not be stopped, at least not at this moment. I asked him whether he knew anything more about the family, and he mentioned that he'd heard that a stepmother was also at the hospital, but he hadn't met her yet. Though frequently maligned, stepparents are often keen observers of how a family works. Scanning the emergency room, I sighted a gray-haired middle-aged woman carrying a cardboard tray with three cups of tea on it and pushing open the main door. She visibly winced each time Maura's father shouted another order to the resident and paused outside the door to Maura's room. Sensing an opportunity, I walked over to her and introduced myself.

"I'm glad you're here," she said apprehensively, still reacting to the voices inside the room. "We all need some assistance."

"Perhaps you can help me first. If you would introduce me to your husband and daughter, maybe we could move this process along," I said, nodding toward the door.

Not quite convinced but willing to try, she smiled and said, "I hope so." We entered the room together and distributed tea to Maura, her father, and the surgical resident. With the assistance of the stepmother, Sarah, I was introduced to her husband Edward; I immediately apologized for having to speak to the surgical resident right away and pulled him outside the room, saying I would be right back.

The resident looked at me, obviously relieved, and then looked around the ER sheepishly, wondering whether others had heard the raised voices. "I don't know how that happened," he said. "I could not stop fighting with him."

I smiled and said, "Something for you to think about. What about the cuts?"

"They're superficial, they don't need to be sutured. I think she's done it before, though. There are a number of light scars on her arms and a few behind her knees. They really need you," he said.

"Thanks for the vote of confidence. I can see already this isn't going to be easy. Do you think a visit from the attending on plastic surgery would calm the dad down? Surgeon to surgeon?"

"You know, I was thinking that myself, but then I got into such a hole with that dad," he said, shaking his head. "The plastics man is in-house this afternoon—I'll call him ASAP. Thanks." He went off, sipping the tea, glad to have his assignment made clear, glad to leave this family behind.

I took a deep breath and went back into the exam room after giving a quick knock. This time I introduced myself first to Maura, who was quietly crying and holding her backpack, slowly rocking back and forth. I told her that I needed to talk to her alone. I spoke to her father, saying that the attending plastic surgeon had been called and would be here shortly, and then asked whether he and his wife would mind waiting outside while I spoke with his daughter for a few minutes. He agreed and patted his daughter's shoulder as he left, seeming too overcome with emotion for words. I sat down close to Maura, wishing that I, too, had a cup of tea.

Emergency rooms make an exciting setting for a television series, but they can be frightening places for teenagers. Still, they offer one of the best opportunities for a psychiatrist to connect with a teen, partly because the adolescent sent there is obviously in some kind of serious trouble and so can often be made to recognize the severity of the situation.

At this point, though, I was doubting that any communication would be possible with Maura. As soon as her father and step-mother left the room she lay down, still clutching her backpack, and openly sobbed. I sat down next to her and said that I would stay there for a while until she felt more comfortable with talking, and I asked whether she would mind if I talked to her until she did feel more comfortable. She shook her head no, so I began to speak, first describing the emergency room where we were, explaining how it was different from similar places that she might have seen on televi-sion. Slowly, she began to nod at some of my comments and finally uncovered her eyes and looked at me. Searching for a neutral entry point for the more serious part of our conversation, I asked Maura how her soccer game had gone that afternoon.

"Not well. It's my dad's game anyway," she said shrugging.

I realized immediately that this wasn't going to be the neutral topic I'd hoped for, but I decided to pursue it anyway since she was alert and still looking at me, although the rocking had started again.

"It may be his game, but you're definitely wearing the uniform. Are you part of Viking League or Inter-School?" I asked.

Pleased that I recognized the leagues, she squirmed around to face me and pushed her backpack onto the floor. "Viking League to-day, although I play for Inter-School on Tuesdays and Thursdays."

"And for Viking League on Mondays and Wednesdays?"

She nodded.

"You play a lot," I said. "So how is it your dad's game and not yours?"

"He played in school. He wants me to play, too, just like him. Go to medical school just like him, too." She eyed me suspiciously, per-haps because she suddenly saw me as a member of an enemy group that she was going to be unwillingly forced to join.

"Does he want you to be a surgeon, too?" I asked.

"Certainly not a psychiatrist," she said, and I detected the begin-ning of a smile.

"Why do you think you're here today, Maura?" I asked.

"I was just here for a physical, and then the nurse and the doctor freaked," she said quietly.

"Freaked over what?" I asked, trying to get her to talk about it.

"These," she said, and she shoved her wrist close to my face.

I looked at her forearm and then directly into her eyes. "Are you trying to check whether I'll freak out when I see your cuts by shoving them in my face? I know all of my questions are a bother, but it's important to figure out why you keep doing this," I said gently.

She lowered her arm. "How did you know I've done this before?" she asked suspiciously.

"The other doctor noticed some scars when he was examining you, but it was largely a guess on my part. Most of the girls I've worked with who cut themselves have done it more than once," I said.

"You've worked with other girls who've done this?" she asked, somewhat surprised.

"I have. Did you think you were the only one?" Then, sensing that for Maura the cutting might have earmarked her identity, as it does for other girls who are unaware that others do it, I added, "All kinds of teens cut themselves, but it means something special to each of them. How did it happen today?"

"I'm not sure. I was unhappy after the soccer game. I hadn't wanted to go." She looked at me for some understanding. "Four soccer practices a week is a lot. I wanted to finish my homework—start it would be closer to the truth. There's a paper I've got to turn in for my writing class that's already three days late. But I guess I really began feeling upset when my dad arrived forty minutes late at the game. I was sitting out, resting. I had actually asked my coach to let me sit out so that I could rest. When my dad saw that I was sitting out, he started yelling at the coach to put me in the game, so he did. It just went from bad to worse. I was really tired, but my dad started screaming at me from the sideline, 'Get in there, Maura. Don't just stand there!' I ran, but I wasn't into it. I could tell he was disappointed in me. After the game he went back to the hospital to see his patients, and I cut my arm in the school bathroom."

After a pretty animated description of what had happened at the game, Maura said this last part very matter-of-factly, in a tone of voice that made the event seem very ordinary. It has been my experience that a considerable amount of ritual, even passion, is involved when teens cut themselves, although they are often reluctant to discuss it. I mentioned to Maura that her description of cutting herself sounded dull, and I wondered whether she was leaving something out.

Now she started developing an interest in my curiosity. "You're not grossed out? You actually want to hear more about how I do it?"

"Yes, I want to hear more about how you cut yourself," I said. "But I also think it's important that you start to wonder about it, to try to figure out why you do it."

Angrily she said, "I don't wonder. I know. I was so depressed after the soccer game. I hadn't even wanted to be there in the first place. It helped that my coach let me sit out when I asked. Then my dad comes, and I end up going back in the game. I was mad at Dad, but I was even angrier at myself. I couldn't tell him to back off."

Gently I asked, "So how did the cutting figure into it?"

Staring off into space, her speech changed again, once more becoming more mechanical. "So I go to the school bathroom. It's like the only space that I've got to myself all day, the only place where I feel like I've got some control. I lay out a white paper towel and tear the wrapper off the razor blade, keeping it sterile the whole time. I pick up the razor blade and watch myself in the mirror, cutting my arm very carefully until I see the blood. It makes me feel alive."

"What makes you feel alive?"

"I'm not sure. The cutting, I guess. I think all I know is that I feel kind of dead before I do it, then, immediately after, I feel better."

Maura's story of cutting was familiar to me, yet I was still curious. Why young girls and boys would injure themselves was perplexing to me when I first started working with teens. I am still interested, but no longer surprised.

Self-mutilation occurs when teenagers injure their bodies on purpose, most commonly by cutting or burning, and do not intend to kill themselves. It frequently begins in adolescence and can continue for decades if untreated.[1] It is dangerous, with risks of permanent scarring, blood loss, infection (including HIV), and even death (by accidentally opening up a large vessel). Although a teen often begins by experimenting, often using his or her own body in an effort to end psychological pain, resolve a conflict, or even, ostensibly, just to "see how it feels," it can evolve into a repetitive pattern, a habit, becoming one of the risk behaviors that is most difficult to stop. "Cutters," as they are known, carve words, pictures, and, most commonly, delicate slashes into arms, hands, legs, chest, face, stomach, or genitals using razors, knives, paper clips, bobby pins, pens, scissors, combs, pieces of glass, and fingernails.[2] The teen who cuts often has experiences of depression or a history of sexual abuse.[3] Self-mutilation is part of a continuum of activities that involve scarification and the body; activities defined as "skin art," which can include branding, artistic scarring, body piercing, and tattooing, also fall along this continuum. Certainly not all tattoos or piercings qualify as risk behaviors; it is important to understand the reasons behind an adolescent's choices before designating any particular activity a risk behavior.

By many cutters' reports, the act of self-mutilation provides relief, albeit short-lived, from intense feelings of anxiety, anger, emptiness, and depression. Many who mutilate themselves also suffer from dissociation, a numbing defense common to victims of trauma, including sexual abuse. Dissociation is an altered state of consciousness, a feeling of being outside of one's body, of being unreal. It can be a way of "leaving" an unbearable situation, at least psychologically. Children who are being repeatedly sexually abused learn how to leave their painful reality and retreat into their own world. What works as a coping strategy during a traumatic event can become a habitual response to stress.[4]

Maura was not a victim of sexual abuse or any other trauma, but like other cutters, she used her self-mutilation for several purposes—to purge her body of the angry feelings she was "feeling" for her father, and to reclaim and punish her body, which had betrayed her by playing soccer for her father, by doing what he wanted and not making her own choice. It gave her back control, but at the same time she lost control to the process as it became an ugly habit she could not stop.

Maura's self-mutilation had begun as experimentation. She was playing around with a nail file one day when she was feeling particularly angry with her father, and she "accidentally" cut herself and found that it helped to relieve her anger. Although currently there are only theories about why this activity succeeds in alleviating a teen's psychic pain, it is likely that biological factors contribute to the reduction of pain, most probably hormonal or endorphin pathways that, over time, yield a type of physical "rush" when the skin is cut.[5] Maura also told me that cutting wasn't the first dangerous risk she had taken in response to the situation with her father. Before she had tried cutting, she would angrily smoke cigarettes or sneak shots of whiskey from his liquor supply.

After I felt that Maura was calmed down, I told her some of what I knew about self-mutilation and encouraged her to take this opportunity to get help. Although it was just a beginning, that first hour I spent with her in the emergency room accomplished a great deal. I was the first person she had ever spoken with about her cutting. Knowing that she was not alone, and that I had seen and helped other girls who self-mutilated, reassured her. And knowing that I was not totally disgusted by her raw wounds, or by what she herself viewed as shameful behavior that deserved to be hidden, helped her to be more open. The road ahead of us was going to be difficult, so the success of our early bond was vital.

The Other Side of the Knife

Edward and Sarah, Maura's father and stepmother, were waiting outside when I stepped out of the exam room. I knew that I had taken a lot of time with their daughter and realized that the delay might be upsetting to them, but I was not prepared for how angry Edward was. Placing a firm hand on my shoulder, he stammered, red-faced and obviously very angry, "You know, the plastic surgeon came down, and they wouldn't let him see Maura. They said that the time with you was more important. I don't know if he'll be able to come back."

Sidestepping the question of relative importance, I told him that I hadn't realized that the plastic surgeon had come and, after volunteering to repage him, did so immediately.

While the surgeon was meeting with Maura, I found a quiet spot in the yard outside the emergency room to talk with Edward and Sarah. "Edward, I'm glad that the plastic surgeon is here." I was being more than a little insincere here, but I didn't want to appear too oppositional. Plastic surgeons are increasingly called in by parents of cutters who want more than anything to make any signs of trouble disappear, quite literally. I knew the surgeon would ultimately evaluate against the necessity of any procedure for Maura. I went on. "I think your daughter is going to need a lot of help. This isn't the first time she's cut herself. She told me that it's happened more than several times before, so it's already become a dangerous pattern. I'm also worried that she has a serious depression and, although she denies it today, may be at risk for suicide sooner or later. It is very important that she get psychological treatment."

"Then give her meds," said Edward, not missing a beat. "That's what you shrinks are good for, treating depression. It's a biological illness. I'll sign for it, just get it started."

"You're right that depression has a strong biological basis, and I do treat many adolescents I diagnose as having a major depression with antidepressants, but it's very important that I do a complete assessment first. Not all girls who cut themselves are depressed. I'm not convinced yet that Maura is, although I suspect so. You want the plastic surgeon to do a full evaluation; I hope you'll agree the same thoroughness is important in this area, too." He seemed agreeable enough at this point. "Maybe we can begin by you telling me how you think things have been going with your daughter recently."

"She's a great kid. She's the highest scorer on her soccer team. She gets excellent grades in math and science and English. She has been confused recently about college and career choices, but I don't understand this. I just can't believe it, these gashes. When I picked her up at the clinic after they called me and brought her over here, she wouldn't talk to me about it. All she said to me was, 'Don't worry, Dad, I used sterile technique.'" Edward's voice was no longer raised; in fact, he was almost whispering as he stared off into space.

"You seem struck by her comment. Do you have any ideas about it?" I asked.

"No," he said, and then, after a long pause, "I use sterile technique every day. I'm a surgeon. I cut things every day. It came to me right away, then I thought it couldn't be directed at me. Nobody would do something so horrible because they were angry with their father, would they?"

"Edward, I don't know yet why your daughter cuts herself. Usually it's fairly complicated. She could have angry feelings toward you, and toward herself, and be very confused about it. Cutting can serve many purposes. It's important that we work together to help Maura figure it out." Then I asked who else was in their family.

"Sarah and I have been married five years," said Edward. "I have two other daughters who live near their mother in Los Angeles. They're older, both out of college, working."

Quiet up to this point, Sarah's gentle voice surprised me and, I think, her husband. "They're both coming up here next weekend for a short visit."

Looking thoughtfully at his wife, Edward spoke again. "My two oldest daughters and I had some hard times. They sided with their mother after the divorce and didn't talk to me for two years. Maura, I guess you could say, sided with me. At least, she stayed here and lived with me. It hasn't exactly been easy."

Edward's comments were sobering, revealing a divorce that appeared to have torn a family in half, and I was impressed with his honesty about what had happened with his three daughters and himself. Although he was aggressive a lot of the time and appeared to lose his perspective when in that state, he also revealed some awareness that there were problems under the surface. I saw his comment as an opening for me to begin building an alliance with him, maybe the best opportunity I was going to get. Following up on Sarah's comment, I suggested that it would be helpful to meet with everyone, including his two older daughters when they came up, in order to better understand what was going on with Maura. I sensed that Edward was starting to waver in the face of this prospect—a family meeting with Maura and his two formerly estranged daughters didn't exactly fit with the idea he'd already expressed about how this problem should be treated. After all, I was a psychiatrist, trained to push pills; how did this family meeting business fit in with my job, and perhaps more important, how was it going to affect his life?

I had already met with Maura twice during the week before I saw her on the weekend with Edward, Sarah, and her two older sisters, Kathleen and Christine. Those two visits had given me time to better assess Maura's mental state. Although she had not cut herself since the episode after the soccer game, she continued to feel sad every day. She also was having significant difficulty concentrating on her schoolwork, had lost much of her normal appetite, was losing weight unintentionally, and was having trouble sleeping every night. With these ongoing problems, she fit the criteria for a major depressive disorder.[6] Although she told me that she did not feel like cutting herself, she was having suicidal feelings on and off again during the week. I anticipated that the scheduled family session on the weekend would bring up even more complex and difficult feelings for her. I considered all of these factors and decided to suggest beginning an antidepressant medication.

I have prescribed medications for depression to teenagers for twenty years, and I have seen many excellent responses: the symptoms of depression improve remarkably and the adolescent reports a significant change, both of which responses enable him or her to address more easily, and work toward resolving, other problems he or she is facing. Medication for an adolescent is never a simple procedure, but one that requires consent and cooperation from the patient and his or her parents or guardians. As I usually do before beginning a medication with any teen, I gave Maura, Edward, and Sarah several articles to read about the diagnostic condition we were treating and about the specific medication we would be using to help.

Medications often prove very useful but do not take the place of spending time with a teenager to talk about the problems he or she is having, clearly outlining how I see the situation, and, in a case like Maura's, coming up with some ideas about why the teen is experiencing a depression at the time. Having worked as the assistant director and then the director of an inpatient psychiatric unit for eight years, I've had many opportunities to talk to many teens and parents about such treatment questions. It has been my experience that adolescents are no more resistant than adults to this type of medication if they are given both an explanation they can understand and a choice they feel they can participate in. Parents are just as likely as the teens to have questions. They, too, need a similar educational approach and time to think about the choices and ask their questions.

With Maura's family, Edward had already demonstrated sufficient, if not excessive, willingness to have his daughter medicated. He accepted the articles I handed him, but I immediately sensed that he wasn't going to rush home and read them. Sarah was quite a bit more interested. She gave me the family history, indicating that both she and Maura's mother had suffered from depression, although neither had taken medication. Sarah had recently read Peter Kramer's *Listening to Prozac,* and asked several informed questions.[7]

Maura's response was similar to those I've had from other teenagers. She readily agreed with me that she was depressed. After talking with me about it, she believed that an antidepressant would be a good idea and probably would even help her, but she was very worried that the medication would dull her feelings and that she would no longer feel like herself. Although the feelings of anger toward her father and the complex feelings of self-loathing that surrounded the mutilation episodes were intensely uncomfortable for her, she accurately recognized them as part of herself; in some ways she saw them as defining parts of her identity.

I told her I believed that her overall sadness, low energy, and problems with eating and sleeping would probably improve and that the feelings she saw as defining herself would still be there, although I was honest with her and said that I wasn't 100 percent sure. Would her anger toward her father be diminished after taking an antidepressant? One of the important questions raised by Peter Kramer is, Just how much does a medication like an antidepressant alter what we know as character, or what individuals perceive to be their core identity?[8] This question is particularly relevant to adolescents, who are locked into the developmental task of discovering their identities and are almost always unsure of themselves on some level; the idea that a medicine can sweep away some of their hard-won self-knowledge is frightening.

I worked hard to allay Maura's fears, but I did not falsely reassure her. I believe that teens need to be active and well-educated partners in any treatment endeavor. With Maura, who agreed to give the antidepressant a try, taking the medications proved to be less painful than the family meeting only a few days later.

Gathering the Tribe: A Visit from Distant Daughters

The outward appearance of Maura's family during their first session told me a lot. Her two sisters, Christine and Kathleen, sat on the couch so close together that their legs touched. Sarah and Edward sat in the two largest chairs in the office, also next to each other. Maura was sprawled on the floor in front of my largest bookshelf and immediately pulled out a pile of books and began shuffling through them, searching for a readily available distraction if things got tough.

She was right to be prepared; this was not going to be easy. Her two sisters began jointly voicing the complaint that they didn't see why they had to be present: they didn't live with their father, in fact hadn't lived with him for more than five years, and at this point they had very little relationship with him. I told them that I had asked Sarah and Edward to have them come to the family meeting because Maura had recently been having a very difficult time and I thought they might be able to provide some insight. Although the two sisters gave each other sidelong glances, they stopped openly glaring at the other members of the group.

I noticed that Edward seemed intimidated by his two oldest daughters. Seeing me speak to them directly, he added, "I realize, Kathleen and Christine, that I don't have much of a relationship with either of you. I am very sorry about that and would like to help make that different. Right now I need your help. At first, when the doctor suggested that the two of you come to the meeting, I thought it was crazy considering the state of our relationship, but then Sarah and I talked, and I realized that some good might come of it. I don't want to make the same mistakes with Maura."

Kathleen, the eldest, responded, her voice filled with anger. "Why would we want to help you help her? You've always spent your extremely limited free time with her. You've ignored us for years."

His own anger growing, his voice rising, Edward turned to face his daughter. Being familiar with Edward's temper from our first meeting in the emergency room, I decided to intervene again and asked Kathleen whether she had ever considered the possibility that things could get better. Maybe she could tell me why she was here visiting her father?

My question clearly surprised Kathleen, as my interruption and silencing of Edward had surprised him. Both were tensely quiet, leaving an awkward silence in the room. I was left to consider whether I had made a good decision in stopping what would have been an explosion between oldest daughter and father. I decided to share my dilemma with the family and admitted that I might not have made the right decision in interrupting their argument, but that I didn't see how it would have helped anyone.

Kathleen gave me a weak smile. "It hasn't helped anyone yet, but this is the only way I know how to talk to my father. I'm not even sure that he hears me when I scream back, but at least I feel better."

Christine, who seemed connected to her older sister in ways other than just physical proximity, added, "I get angry with my dad, too, but I don't scream. I guess I just watch Kathleen go at it with him, but the same feelings are inside me, too."

Maura's gaze had shifted from the pile of reading material on the floor to the faces of her two sisters. She was watching them intensely but was unable to speak.

Again, I asked Kathleen why she was here. She answered slowly, this time turning to face her father fully. "I'm here because I am still angry with you, Dad, and want you to know that. I am also here because I want it to be different with you somehow. When I heard that Maura was cutting herself, I wasn't surprised. I tried it once, years ago, with a bobby pin. No big deal, but still, I did it to myself after a fight that you and I had." Pausing, she added, even more slowly, "For me, there has never been a way to tell you who I am and what I want."

The faces of his three daughters upon him, Edward appeared lost for words. Sarah spoke. "Kathleen, your father struggles a great deal with this. I know there are no excuses, but I think he is trying to change."

Gaining courage, Kathleen said, "I need to hear it from him, Sarah, though I appreciate your help."

Maura spoke for the first time. "We all need to hear it from you, Dad. Kathleen, Christine, and me. I haven't had the same struggles with you that Kathleen and Christine have had. In lots of ways you've been a great father to me, but I still need you to be able to listen to me. You have so many ideas for me that I can't focus on my own. I need to be able to have my own ideas. You're always trying to confuse me."

"I don't know what to say," said Edward, again left speechless by the comments of his three daughters.

"Edward, I don't think that they're asking you to say anything. They're asking you to listen to them," I said.

"So that we can hear ourselves. I don't know why I think it would help so much, but I believe that it is important for you to listen to us," added Christine, now moving a little away from Kathleen to sit more evenly between her two sisters.

Edward survived that session, but it wasn't easy for him. He actually took two breaks and walked around outside, talking quietly with Sarah, but he was starting to hear *and understand* what his daughters were now able to tell him. Kathleen and Christine told him how they had resented his "suggestions" that they apply to medical school. Each, in turn, had refused to comply with his recommendations or expectations; now both of them described how they felt he had turned his anger on them and eventually rejected them because of the decisions they had made for themselves.

Edward looked genuinely shocked when his daughters described their perception of what had taken place. Yes, he had expectations for them, but then, what father doesn't have expectations for his child? Yes, he believed that medicine had been a good career choice for himself, so why not let his daughters know about this opportunity? I asked Edward just what he had intended to accomplish with his suggestions about medical school. Was it possible that Kathleen and Christine could have experienced his suggestions as pressure? Had he talked with them about their own ideas for their careers? Did he know what their ideas were? Edward admitted that he could now see that maybe it wasn't that they hadn't had any of their own ideas, but that they had had trouble talking to him about them. This small acknowledgment changed the expressions on Kathleen's and Christine's faces. Maura's face lit up, too, and she said that now it was she who couldn't articulate her dreams whenever her father outlined what she called his "oh so reasonable plans" for her.

In that single session Edward was able to begin to listen to what his daughters had to tell him. He agreed that it was possible that he had heard them before without really listening, possibly because he automatically translated what they had to say into something he could understand. This was a small step, but it was a start.

Fathers and Daughters

Of the four possible parent-child relationships—mother-son, father-son, mother-daughter, and father-daughter—the last one is the least written about. Fathers and daughters also spend the least amount of time together. Several studies describe fathers as having emotionally "flat" relationships with their teenage daughters in comparison to mothers and underscore how few activities fathers and daughters share.[9] The father-daughter relationship has been described as unique among the four parent-child combinations in both its emotional blandness and low levels of interaction.[10] In examining father-daughter relationships in sessions like the one with Maura and her sisters, I also take into account some of the more recent information we have about how adolescent girls develop socially.

As described in chapter 5, Carol Gilligan has noted that the outspokenness of young girls and awareness of their authority in the world changes in adolescence so that by the age of fifteen or sixteen they become less able to speak out, less sure of themselves, and less willing to discuss honestly their feelings and observations.[11] Gilligan believes that girls at this age undergo a crisis in response to both adolescence itself and to the culture's demand that they learn to keep quiet. This crisis begins slowly during the early years of adolescence when girls attempt to speak out, discover that it is not as acceptable (to teachers, parents, and the culture at large) as it was when they were younger, and alter their behavior accordingly.

Gilligan has also examined moral development.[12] In her observations, adolescent girls report that "not hurting others" is a major factor in both their determinations of how to act when faced with a moral dilemma and in their decision-making. Although it misses the point to infer from this that girls use less abstract thinking than do boys, she says, adolescent girls do make moral decisions differently from adolescent boys. Gilligan postulates separate and distinct pathways of moral reasoning rather than a hierarchy that judges the moral reasoning of adolescent boys to be superior.[13] She distinguishes between a justice orientation and a care orientation toward the conception and solving of moral problems. A justice perspective draws attention to problems of inequality and oppression and focuses on reciprocity and equal respect. A care perspective highlights relationships and focuses on balancing responses to different needs. Gilligan's work raises the idea that, at the very least, adolescent girls consider different factors in making their choices.

In parenting adolescents (and in doing psychotherapy with them), it is vitally important to be aware of differences in male and female decision-making. Maura's father had a great deal of trouble both listening to and understanding Maura's ideas, and he repeatedly insisted on comparing her thought processes to his own, using his way of thinking as the baseline. Maura, on the other hand, had trouble holding on to her own feelings, particularly when confronted by her father's ideas.

When I met with Edward and Sarah alone several days after that fateful family meeting, Edward mentioned that each of his daughters had changed her way of thinking in her teens and that he could no longer understand them after that had taken place. Kathleen's career choices became focused on taking care of children (for example, as a day-care worker or play therapist); although her choices were consistent with her own goals and expectations, Edward felt that she was "selling herself short." Yet Edward had no idea how her career choice reflected her values, interests, and sense of her own skills. In talking with Edward alone, it became clear that he had considerable difficulty not only in listening to his daughters but in understanding and accepting that their decision-making processes and priorities were different from his. I shared with him some of the ideas of Carol Gilligan, mentioning the high value many adolescent girls place on relationships and fulfilling needs. In this context we talked directly about Maura's goals.

Maura had expressed to me her desire to become a writer. One of the reasons she had been so upset the day of the fateful soccer game was that she hadn't been able to spend time on an essay she'd wanted to submit for a writing competition. With Maura's permission, I brought up her desire to be a writer with her father and stepmother. The discussion that followed was interesting. Edward had read a lot of Maura's writing but focused on specific pieces, some years old, that reflected his goals for her. Several years earlier Maura had written an essay that indicated a strong interest in medicine. Edward kept a copy of that essay in his desk at work and mentioned proudly to me that he still referred to it often. Over time, however, Maura's interests had changed. So had her writing. She had written the school play the year before—a spoof on a horror story with a lot of blood and guts but not much medicine in it. What had Edward thought of that? He admitted that he couldn't see "medicine" in that play, and maybe I had a point, maybe he screened out those things she said or did that didn't fit with his dreams for her.

Having been quiet up until that point, Sarah finally spoke. "It is very hard for anyone to tell you anything, Edward, me and your daughters included. So one of the things you lose out on is that we stop trying. Until this week Kathleen and Christine had stopped completely. Maura and I are still trying, but there is so much that you don't know about us. Either we don't tell you because we're afraid of how you'll react, or we try to and you mold it into something else. We lose, but so do you."

Although Sarah spoke very quietly, there was a force in her voice that Edward heard along with her incisive and honest message. At that moment she was successfully working to close the gap not only between Edward and his daughters but between Edward and herself. Although he truly listened to Sarah in this session, Edward—no surprise—was slow to change. Learning to listen to what you've screened out for a lifetime is not an easy task.

Discovering Healthy Risks, Discovering a Healthy Self

Not long after we began working together, Maura quit both her soccer teams. That lasted about a month; then she made the decision to rejoin one of them, at least until the season was over. Sports offer both boys and girls a wonderful opportunity to participate in positive risk-taking. They can challenge themselves by taking chances, learning about winning and losing, giving their bodies a full workout, and, at least in group sports, learning how to work together. Opening up sports activities for girls has—to use the phrase in a perfect context—leveled the playing field in many ways. It helps girls feel better about their bodies, encouraging them to focus on being healthy instead of being thin.[14] Coaches can also act as important mentors, showing girls how to practice taking positive risks.

I've learned a great deal about positive risk-taking in sports from watching my daughter's soccer coach work with her team. Jaime Howell is something of a legend in San Francisco girls' soccer; he voluntarily coaches up to four girls' teams at once, teams usually identified by the names of flowers (African Violets, Texas Bluebonnets, Trolley Roses, etc.) and characterized by the good sportsmanship he has taught them. Jaime emphasizes that soccer is a game, not a competition, and that it offers many opportunities to try again. For the girls on his teams this approach seems to take the pressure off, and they are willing to try because they see the game as one of continuous opportunities to try and fail, as well as to try and succeed.

Jaime's coaching strategy is in sharp contrast to the interest that Edward showed in Maura's soccer game on the afternoon before they ended up in the emergency room, when he had pushed her to play even when she was exhausted. Maura had told me that first day that when her father shouted at her it made her feel even less like competing on the field. She'd also said that she believed that his shouting played a role in her cutting herself. When she brought it up again, with weeks of work together behind us, I asked her how she thought that might happen. She said that his encouragement, specifically when he had shouted at her to "kill" the other team, exhorting her to be aggressive, had backfired, and she had ended up taking it out on herself.

She and I talked about how she could handle her own aggressive, angry feelings in ways other than cutting herself. Although she blamed her father for making her angry as well as for her cutting herself, she was also starting to recognize that not everything came from him and that she had to understand her own feelings and actions better. Here the antidepressant was particularly helpful. Rather than robbing her of her feelings, she found that the medication helped her not only to continue experiencing them but to talk about them more easily; she also no longer felt controlled or overwhelmed by them.

In one of our sessions she brought in a copy of the school play she had written, her "spoof on a horror story" that she'd described as full of blood and guts. The play did have a lot of blood and guts in it, but reading it I discovered that it also had a lot of Maura's soul in it. In the lone medical scene a surgeon is working on a patient, singing and listening to rock music on the radio. He has been up all night and sings about having no choice but to keep working—in Maura's words, to continue "cutting."

Maura and I spoke about how cutting had become part of her life. She remembered that when she had written the play she hadn't felt badly about herself. She'd known that her father wanted her to be a doctor, but she still felt as if she would be able to choose her own path. Slowly over the next year her feelings had changed. She wasn't sure what she wanted to do with her life. She had an excellent English teacher who worked with her individually, critiquing her writing and encouraging her to try new things—a poetry reading, the essay competition. Maura had discovered that when she tried to speak with her father about her developing interest in writing he wouldn't listen to her; he even tried to reshape what she was saying, pointing out how useful writing would be in her future medical career.

Maura wasn't exactly sure how the cutting had started. She vaguely remembered that one weekend afternoon she'd had a fight with her father. He had wanted her to do something immediately, and she had gone along but, in doing so, had felt that she was squashing her own desires and thoughts—she felt alienated from herself. In anger, she'd plunged her nail file into the palm of her hand and discovered that the sharp pain made her feel like herself again. Recalling that first incident, Maura remembered that Sarah hadn't been there that afternoon, and she told me that she felt that her stepmother's absence had made a difference. Maura often felt that Sarah at least understood her, and that she had a quiet ally. After all, Maura's mother was almost totally absent from her life, and her older sisters lived far away; her stepmother really served as her only older female role model. Sarah was thoughtful and supportive, but quiet.

Maura's family helps us to better understand what can happen when a father looms large and isn't able to hear what his children have to say. A mother doesn't have to be absent or even soft-spoken, and the children don't have to be female, for this dynamic to work in oppressive ways. Still, a father like this can perhaps more easily, however unintentionally, silence a daughter if she is also in the midst of the crisis Gilligan describes, when everything and everyone around her seems to be encouraging her to lower her voice until even she can't hear herself anymore and she has to communicate nonverbally—in some cases through her body, via cutting.

I became aware of how easily things evolved into a struggle between Edward and Maura. Edward wasn't alone in it; Maura played a role, too. Edward continued to believe that Maura should become a doctor, while Maura was now sure that she should be a writer. Initially, and somewhat simplistically, I encouraged Edward to take an interest in Maura's writing, indicating how important I believed it was to her. Following my suggestion, Edward tried. He asked to read her work and then expressed some genuine interest. His interest, however, frightened Maura. How could a man she had always seen as trying to control her life and the lives of her sisters now suddenly change? He had to have hidden motives. Deep down, surely he still wanted to control her life, only now it was more subtle, hidden behind supportive words and carefully chosen compliments. Maura believed this, and it frightened her. She told me that she was worried that her father would somehow take over her writing in the same way that he had claimed her other dreams. We talked about how she could hold on to her dreams in light of her father's interest. Could they share an interest in her work and life without it becoming entirely his, or at the very least, without Maura feeling like it was entirely his?

For many months Edward and Maura walked the precipitous edge around her dreams for herself. I encouraged Edward to support Maura's risk-taking and, in light of her fears, to back off from the topic of her writing, since she found his interest so threatening. At the same time Maura and I worked together to help her believe that her work was her own and could not be stolen by anyone, including her father.

The edge that Maura and her father walked is something I've seen many fathers and daughters struggle with. Fathers need to be there to encourage their daughters to take risks, particularly when a mother is either absent or unable to do so, but they need to remember who is actually taking the risks, and for whom. All adolescents need parental support and encouragement for taking their own risks *for themselves*. Many fathers recognize the importance and necessity of assisting their daughters with positive risk-taking. It is vitally important that they also remember that their daughters' choices have to be discovered in their own time, and that quiet or weakened voices can be easily drowned out by stronger ones.

Not surprisingly, Edward is still struggling with this issue. Maura is in college now and calls me every few months to let me know how things are going. She hasn't cut herself in the past year, although her left eyebrow is pierced with a small hoop ring. She hasn't made any permanent decisions about her career yet, but she knows that she has choices and is enjoying figuring out what they are.

Chapter Nine

Divorce Wars:
The Buddy Dilemma

It's all in my backpack somewhere . . . my whole life.

—Jenny

Jenny and her parents, Jonathan and Sarah, discovered together how much teenagers notice their parents' risk-taking patterns. Following their divorce, Jonathan and Sarah both seemed to have difficulties with their roles as parents, and both modeled unhealthy risk-taking, with serious consequences for their daughter.

H aight Street, which captured the world's attention for a few months during the "Summer of Love" in 1967, dead-ends into Golden Gate Park. The grassy slope there, shaded by eucalyptus trees, is still a mecca for adolescents visiting from all over America and for San Francisco's own teens who come for a few hours after school, some to escape from their parents' watchful eyes, others just to hang out. Like other parents of San Francisco teens, I look out the window of my car as I drive past this historical gathering place and wonder whether either of my daughters will ever spend an afternoon here, drawn to the crowds of kids who lie on the grass staring up at the sky. Many parents are fearful of their children's friends, worried that buddies will lead them into risks they wouldn't take otherwise. I have learned, however, that sometimes the identity of the buddy worth fearing can be surprising.

When Jennifer, the fourteen-year-old daughter of two divorced architects, arrived for her first session, I was startled not only by the many belongings she brought with her but by how she managed to cover the waiting room with them. Jenny had plugged in her portable tape player and was listening to the Doors. Jim Morrison was asking his baby to c'mon and light his fire while Jenny used my teapot to prepare hot water; she was just finishing a Cup o' Noodles. Her tiny kitten, introduced to me as Angel, had escaped from one of her three backpacks and was playing in the center of the room, where Jenny had spread her science project—a collection of the diverse fungi of California—all over the carpet. Wearing wire-rimmed glasses and a tie-dyed T-shirt, Jenny jumped up to greet me, shook my hand enthusiastically, and apologized for dimming the lights in my waiting room.

The contents of two of the backpacks had spilled out onto the carpet and chairs. Angel had overturned the wastebasket and was quickly advancing to my bookshelves. Jim Morrison was now passionately insisting, "You know it couldn't get much higher." At that time, I shared a tiny waiting room with a group of obsessive doctors, and I found myself wondering what any one of them would think about its current state. None of them even liked teenagers, and one had complained that the muted Sony Walkman of another of my patients had bothered a patient of his, disturbing her serenity.

As I surveyed the mess I thought back to the phone messages about this case that had been left for me earlier that day. Jenny's parents were in the middle of a nasty custody battle, each claiming to be the more fit parent and decrying the other as unfit. And although neither accompanied Jenny to this session, they had both left lengthy messages with my assistant supporting their own position and vilifying the other.

Jenny and her parents had already participated in a court-mandated custody evaluation conducted by another child psychiatrist. This doctor had recommended that Jenny—who was living with her mother but had found a stash of marijuana in her mother's room and proceeded to smoke it by herself—spend more time with her father. The doctor also had guaranteed me that her initial evaluation was airtight, with clear recommendations for both therapy and custody, and that there would be no room for contest. So although I would be meeting with all three family members individually, I would not fall victim to the frequent pitfall in custody cases of getting caught in the middle. The initial evaluation was in no way final, so I had only half-believed this, but I agreed to begin therapy with Jenny anyway. The evaluating therapist had also mentioned that Jenny was a survivor of a very difficult situation and had both determination and a sense of humor. I always admire these traits; in my work with teens, they can make the journey much easier.

Jenny's determination was immediately visible in our first encounter. In less than half an hour my formerly tidy waiting room had been transformed into a teenager's room with a unique personality. I could feel myself being transported back to the late sixties — the tie-dyed T-shirt, the granny glasses, the mushrooms, maybe "magic," all over the carpet. How had she ever managed to carry everything?

Jenny attempted to "bag" Angel so that we could move from the waiting room to my office. Scooting under a couch and skillfully managing not to knock over a Monet print, Jenny finally scuttled a mewing Angel into one of her bags. I grabbed the other bags — one of which was so heavy it nearly caused a muscle spasm — and the mushroom collection, and we proceeded into my office.

Jenny demonstrated a certain therapy savvy, indicating that she had been in this setting before. She spied my analytic couch and asked whether she could forgo lying down on it this first time because she had just finished a Cup o' Noodles and might throw up. Guessing that she was joking but aware that she could be at least partly serious, I asked her how she was feeling. She was very quiet for several minutes before she picked up the heaviest backpack, the one I had carried in, and painstakingly laid out on my office floor a complete collection of Grateful Dead records.

"Do you know anything about them?" she asked sharply. Behind her glasses I could see frustration in her eyes.

"It looks like you've got a complete collection," I said. "They must be very important to you to carry them around. They're heavy."

Jenny's face relaxed as I spoke. I had resisted sharing with her what I did know about the Grateful Dead because I had perceived that she was near tears and imagined that an in-depth conversation about the group would have distracted us. I also knew that she had brought this collection to my office for at least one reason, probably several, and I wanted to start talking about that if we could. Jenny told me that when her family had been together, mother, father, and Jenny listened to the records together. Now, since the divorce, neither parent wanted them, and Jenny carried them from her mother's house to her father's house and back again, playing them wherever she was. "It's all in my backpack somewhere," she said. "Not just the records—my whole life."

We then talked about how the records made her feel safe, and she asked me whether I would like to keep one. I said that I would. Jenny then pulled out her appointment book and asked to schedule the next meeting with me.

The Buddy Dad: Part 1

The first time I met Jonathan I could see traits he shared with his daughter. When his wire-rimmed glasses slid down his nose, they landed at the same point Jenny's did, and his red hair—on the long side for a man over forty—framed his face in the same way Jenny's did. In place of Jenny's tie-dyed T-shirt he wore a baggy sweater with leather patches at the elbows. His hazel eyes were kind, and he appeared to be fully comfortable with himself and his surroundings.

Whereas my task in sessions with Jenny was to provide therapy, my meetings with her parents were intended to provide them with support and information about handling their daughter in the context of their recent divorce. Jonathan had left a message on my answering machine filled with stinging comments about his ex-wife, but he brought none of this up during our first meeting together. Instead, for forty-five minutes straight, he talked with enthusiasm about his fascination with Jenny and described her physical attributes, athletic skills, facility and ease with relationships, and intellectual and artistic accomplishment. I've found that I can learn a lot from the first session with a parent or parents just by listening, and this information can help me to help them with their child in subsequent meetings. Single parents especially seem to hunger for the opportunity to talk about their children.

After listening to Jonathan's glowing description of Jenny, I asked him about his relationship with her.

"Our relationship is wonderful, truly wonderful. It's the bright spot in my life. How could anybody have any trouble with a daughter like her?"

"Good question," I said. "But she's here in my office about her drug use."

He then looked straight at me and asked whether I had listened to his phone message. I told him that I had, and that while I appreciated his alerting me to concerns about his ex-wife's mothering ability, I was also interested in his role as a father. He looked surprised and spoke again about his ex-wife.

"Sarah's always saying bad things about my role as Jenny's dad. Jenny says only good things. Of course, she only says good things about Sarah, too. I know there are problems, though. Jenny's the person that I care about the most in life. I sometimes think that she's the only person I've ever cared about. She's my buddy. After the divorce, in some ways I feel like I'm married to her. It's really never been that way with anybody."

Although Jonathan was not the first parent I had worked with who saw his or her adolescent child as a "buddy," I asked him what that phrase meant to him, especially given his description of his relationship with his daughter as being like a marriage.

"Good question. You're asking me why I feel like I'm married to my daughter when I never felt like I was married to my wife."

"Well," I said, "I'm not sure that's what I was asking. I wanted to know what you think about what you just told me."

"I'm real lonely right now. That's part of why I spend so much time with Jenny. It makes me feel good, and I really didn't feel that way about Sarah. Or anyone else. Maybe my daughter isn't the person I should practice feeling married to, though."

I then asked Jonathan about his relationship with his parents. Although this topic seemed difficult for him to discuss, he did.

"I couldn't stand my father. He was horrible. He beat me all the time and threatened to beat me even if he wasn't going to follow through with it. I guess I wanted to make sure that I didn't have the kind of relationship with Jenny that my dad had with me. I mean, of course I've never hit Jenny, but I can't even remember saying an angry word to her. I don't think I've ever had an angry thought about her. Of course, she's an easy kid. You'll see that."

I smiled, thinking of Jenny's possessions scattered all across the waiting room. Engaging, yes, but not so easy.

"It might be me, too," continued Jonathan. "Jenny and I seem to resonate together. But if you're asking about problems, you know, I wonder about our relationship, if it's not too close. And I also think maybe I'm too permissive. All that sixties stuff. What do you think about smoking dope with your fourteen-year-old daughter?"

Like Jenny, her father was a master of surprise, and I hadn't expected this question. I also wasn't certain where he was coming from. It was Jenny's mother who'd had the stash in her bedroom. Was he keeping drugs, too? Or was he asking this now to see whether I, like the evaluating therapist who had recommended a change in custody, found such behavior objectionable? I probably did look taken aback at his question because he didn't pause for much of a response.

"I can see from your face that it kind of puts you off. You have some of the sixties touches here in this office, but you really don't look like a sixties person."

Now I smiled, and we laughed together. "Well, I lived through the sixties, too," I said, "but that doesn't always mean we all think the same way about smoking dope with a fourteen-year-old daughter. Jenny is participating in some unhealthy activity, and how you act with her is very important. You and Sarah are key role models for her."

Jonathan now stood up and said, "You know, I think I do have things to work on here. I also know that the divorce hasn't worked out well for Jenny. Maybe my response to it has been to hold her very close."

This first session with Jonathan was particularly revealing about some of the difficulties in Jenny's life—such as her relatively recent declining grades in math, and money disappearing from his wallet that he thought Jenny might be taking to buy marijuana—but also indicated that her father was able to begin to look at his own behavior. For any parents the ability to look at their own backgrounds and actions and see how these affect their relationship with their child is vitally important.

I remained suspicious, though, wondering about his question

about smoking dope with one's fourteen-year-old child. I also remembered that we were all caught in the midst of a custody struggle in which both parents most likely were telling only part of the story.

"Just Like a Sister"

The day after I met with Jenny's father, I had my first meeting with her mother, Sarah. I knew from listening to Sarah's phone message that she was quite upset, probably because the court evaluator had recommended that Jenny now spend more time living with her father.

If there is continued animosity between two parents following a divorce, a court recommendation for a change in the amount of time spent with either parent can cause old battles to flare. Generally it's the parent losing time with the child who will be angriest.

Sarah arrived in a beautifully designed gunmetal gray silk suit and flashed a smile at me before she began to talk. When I heard her voice, I was instantly reminded of the tone in her phone message — rapid-fire, and full of instructions.

"First of all, Dr. Ponton, you will be denied access to the evaluator's report. There are certain papers that you will be able to read, of course, if proper requests are made. I view this custody change as a temporary situation, and it is that message that I expect to be communicated to Jennifer when and if you ever discuss this matter with her. I also expect that equal amounts of time will be spent with each of us."

Well, I thought, at least she's direct and, unlike her husband, isn't going to try to charm me first. "When you say 'each of us,' you're referring to yourself and Jonathan?"

"Yes, yes, of course I'm referring to the two of us. I presume that you will spend more time with Jennifer." She faltered some here, and I wondered whether I was seeing a tear in the corner of one of her carefully made-up eyes.

"You seem worried that things aren't going to be kept equal."

"No. No, I presume that you are a professional and you will conduct yourself as one."

"But equal between you and Jonathan with Jennifer — it seems that you're afraid that it's going to be unfair."

"Well, of course the evaluator has made that temporary recommendation regarding increased time with Jonathan, which I think is unfair, but Jennifer actually wants to spend more time with me."

"I've heard that from Jenny," I said, "but you seem worried that others are going to unfairly take away your time with her."

"Yes. Maybe so." She looked unwilling to continue talking, and I commented that it seemed hard for her to talk with me.

"Things actually are not the way they used to be with Jennifer. We used to be inseparable. We were just like sisters. Always together. It's not like that anymore."

Sisters, buddies . . . where were the parents in this family, I wondered. As I had done with Jonathan the day before, I now asked Sarah to say more about what she meant by being "like sisters."

"Well, we were a team. You know, after the divorce. Jenny would make dinner at night, I would come home, and she'd listen to me talk about my day, I'd listen to her talk about school. It was wonderful. I really miss that, I guess. All of this going back and forth and spending more time with Jonathan, you know, we don't have that anymore." She paused for a second. "Jonathan's so charming. He'll do anything, and he fools people."

"You're worried that he's going to fool me, or, more importantly, Jenny?"

Sarah's rapid-fire style had not only ceased, she was clutching her briefcase, staring at the floor. Children are not the only victims in a prolonged custody battle; the lives of parents are profoundly affected. I could see that Sarah, too, had lost out. In a muted voice, she continued talking about what it had been like with Jenny several years before.

"Right after the divorce it seemed okay for a while. Jonathan and I were still speaking then. He hadn't turned his seductive charm on Jenny, planting ideas in her head about me . . . a snake."

In the middle of one of these battles it seems like any discussion with a parent can lead to angry comments about the other parent. Being caught in the crossfire is one of the hardest pitfalls for me as a therapist to withstand, but it also teaches me a lot because in some ways the experience parallels what the children of many divorced parents report they go through at home. Much of what Sarah was saying was true. Her former husband did have a kind of charm, mixed with a certain audacity. But Sarah was totally caught up in it and fearful that she would lose her daughter to it.

I decided to take a risk with her by asking a pretty straightforward question. "Do you really think that he can charm your daughter away from you?"

"What do you mean 'think'? He already has! She's spending more time with him." Tears were running down her cheeks.

"Sarah, you know that Jennifer told the courts she wanted to live with you. They made the decision to give him more time based on only two reasons that I can see."

Sarah had stopped crying and was looking straight at me.

"First, they generally recommend more equally shared time between parents when a child becomes a teenager, and second, they are worried about Jenny smoking marijuana, and they think that you haven't been able to help her with this."

"Just because she found my cache of marijuana in my underwear drawer and smoked it one time. You think that Jonathan doesn't smoke dope? He's a pothead."

Carefully I asked, "What do you think about Jenny smoking marijuana?"

"Everyone does in California," she said pleasantly.

I figured that there was no response to that I could make that would not make me sound like a preachy doctor who didn't believe that children should smoke dope. Again I wondered whether Jenny got embroiled in these discussions, and how she handled it. I also wondered again about Jenny making dinner for Sarah every night while Sarah talked about her day. It was a pleasant-sounding scenario, but it wasn't the whole truth about the situation. Sarah had described it all so nostalgically; helping her to understand that in this setup Jenny was acting in the role of mother to her mother was going to be crucial.

Alone Together, Alone Apart

The three backpacks had been my first tip-off that Jenny felt painfully pulled between her parents—better to carry her entire life with her than to be caught without some part of it. The initial focus of Jenny's therapy was working together to find "a port in the storm" of her parents' bitter divorce where she could feel safe.

I also knew, based on the precipitating events leading up to the evaluation and my first session with each of Jenny's parents, that marijuana was going to play a large part in the therapy. Were either or both of the parents "potheads"? More important, what attitude about smoking marijuana did they communicate to their fourteen-year-old daughter? How severely had their parenting skills been affected by the divorce?

Jenny spent the afternoon before her fourth session wandering around Golden Gate Park with her friends. By the time she arrived at my office she was late for her appointment and very high. Explaining the delay, she said that she and her friends had become lost in the park after they all smoked pot together.

Some therapists who specialize in working with teens recommend not allowing adolescents to stay for the session if they're drunk or on drugs of any type. I always consider it a difficult test posed by the teen, one that reminds me of the ways they constantly test their parents. I decided to let Jenny stay but insisted that we talk about what was going on. First, I shared with her my dilemma: if I let her stay in the session after she had smoked marijuana, I was worried that I would be giving her implicit permission to do this. If I told her that she had to leave, I would demonstrate through my action how I felt about it, but we would lose the opportunity to talk about it. The alternative was that she understand that I didn't think it was okay for a fourteen-year-old to smoke marijuana at any time, and that she would work with me to try to understand why she was doing it.

Glaring at me, Jenny demanded to know more. "Do you think it's okay for parents to smoke dope with their kids? No, let me put it another way: do you smoke dope with your kids?"

I sighed. "The answer is no to each question, Jenny." Just then I felt like I was losing my temper with the whole family. So I took another breath and tried again. "Jenny, I'm not a perfect parent, or a perfect person—I've made a lot of mistakes. But our job is to figure out a better answer for you in your life. Spending your afternoons wandering around Golden Gate Park stoned is not the answer. How did you spend your time after school before you started doing this?"

Slowly Jenny answered. "Was there a before? I feel like I've smoked dope since I was nine."

"The time of the divorce," I said, and we looked at each other.

"They, my parents, both do it. You know that."

I hadn't known that for sure until this point, but I had guessed it.

"What's that been like for you?"

"Just fine. Everyone does, you know." Her mother had made the same observation.

"It must seem like the whole world does if your parents do," I said.

"It isn't like they offer me dope all the time. It's actually different with each of them."

"Tell me about it."

Quietly Jenny began to talk about what happened with her parents and drugs, and through her description I began to understand more about what it was like to be the child of this divorce.

"They didn't smoke it much when they were married. At least, I think it was that way. They may have hidden it from me. They listened to the Grateful Dead." She patted her largest backpack, home of the family record collection. "They fought a little bit. Mostly they were going to the university, studying architecture, so there was no time to fight, I guess. It was okay when they first separated. I'd spend most of my time with my mom, but I got to see my dad a lot.

"I'm not sure when I noticed that my mom started staying in her room a lot, with the door locked, but that's when I started smelling it. The dope, I mean." In a very quiet voice she added, "I also think she was crying."

"It sounds lonely for you," I said.

"Exactly. I'm there alone, sitting on one side of a locked door with my mother getting high on the other. It happened a lot. I don't know when I got the idea to go through her drawers and look for it. I was with a girlfriend. We found it right away. Then I sat on my mom's bed, turned on her music, and smoked away. When she came home from work that night, she guessed what had happened and got mad at me. I bet she smoked dope at least twenty-five times with her door locked. I smoke once and she's pissed."

"How did you feel about your mother smoking?"

"You ask a lot of dumb questions for a smart doctor." Jenny

looked away from me, grabbing a stuffed elephant that I keep in my office. "At first I thought it was cool, lucky me to have a mom so hip, but she doesn't notice me much when she's stoned, whether she's locked in her room or sitting in the living room watching TV."

Holding the elephant, Jenny continued to describe how it seemed that she had lost her mother even though she was right there on the other side of a bedroom door. It felt to me like she was still searching for her.

"Does your mother seem a little closer when you smoke marijuana?"

"A lot closer. If it works for her, I assume it'll work for me." After a long pause she said sadly, "We *are* alike—both potheads, and both depressed."

Jenny hugged the stuffed animal now and spoke slowly. "You're right that part of the time when I smoke dope I think about my mother—maybe trying to get close to her, to be like her. But I'm not sure that I could end up a pothead. It's scary either way, though."

For several months Jenny talked about her feelings for her mother. She began to feel better and stopped spending her afternoons cutting classes, getting stoned, and wandering around Golden Gate Park. She'd also given me permission to talk with her mother about her drug use.

Eventually Sarah and I also made some progress in our sessions together. In my most straightforward manner I told her that her pot smoking was directly harming her daughter: not only was Jenny left essentially unattended when Sarah did this while Jenny was home, but she was imitating her mother's behavior in an attempt to be close with her. Initially Sarah hadn't believed me when I told her that Jenny knew a lot about her regular smoking, but after I revealed specific details and descriptions of where her caches were stored, she was embarrassed and agreed not to smoke when Jenny was home.

This work with Sarah took a while, and it was not easy. She was often angry with me and claimed more than once after "lapsing" around her pot smoking that no psychiatrist, and no child, could tell her how to behave. At this point she was still dependent on the drug. I had leverage, though: her time allotment with Jenny. There were several showdowns between us, but slowly Sarah began to modify her behavior. The change in her really started to stick after

Jenny refused to be with her if she smoked. I encouraged Sarah to join a support group and to seek individual therapy. Eventually she was able to admit she had been extremely depressed.

Too Close for Comfort

In many ways Jonathan's continued use of marijuana was an even stronger threat to Jenny's well-being. After his initial provocative question, and after realizing my stance, Jonathan clamped down and mouthed slogans about a drug-free America where it would be safe for his daughter and other teens. And for many weeks after initially acknowledging it, Jenny stopped mentioning her father's drug use. It's possible that she did so at his urging, but more likely that she was choosing on her own to protect him. Over time, and as things improved with her mother, Jenny began to talk more about her father.

Rarely do the seductive feelings that some adolescent girls feel when they're with their fathers come up directly, but Jenny, like both her parents, could be fairly direct when she wanted to. When we were discussing her reluctance to spend more time living with either her father or her mother, Jenny said, "Well, I want to be emancipated. My best friend tells me that my dad is a really nice guy but he is too passive for me to live with."

"When we've talked in the past, you've said your dad was easier to live with, but you've also gone back and forth."

"Yeah, he is," she said softly, "at least in some ways. But I can't stand his sexual obsession with cats. He purrs over Angel. I wonder what you do with your husband."

"What do you wonder about?"

"It's like, I was sitting watching TV, and my dad sat on my bed. He put his arm around me and said, 'You're a great daughter.'"

"If things were going on with my husband . . . "

"It would be a healthier environment here, sexual things, I mean."

"It would be safer?" I asked.

"A lot safer," she answered.

Questions from adolescents about what I do with my husband are not unusual; they're rarely about whether or how I'm having sex with my husband, but more about how the patient feels about adults having sex. With Jenny, it became pretty clear that if she could know that adults were having sex together, she might feel less pressured to perform as an adult in their world. This could leave her safely outside the realm of adult sexuality. If, on the other hand, adults were not having sex together, then she might fear being drawn into an intimacy, sexual or otherwise, that she was not ready for.

"It hasn't seemed very safe with my dad since the divorce," she went on. "We're too close. I don't know if I wish he was with someone else. I just wish that it didn't feel this way. I've always been closer to my mom. She's missing out on a lot."

"Do you mean your living with your dad more of the time now leaves her out more?"

"Yeah, I feel like I've got so much now—my dad, school, therapy. It leaves her out."

There was a long pause, and then Jenny said quietly, "My mom is right about him, too. He doesn't play fair. She's already admitted with you that she's smoked dope. I mean I found her stash, so what could she do, but she doesn't hide things the way my father does." Sounding miserable, she added, "On camping trips he's offered me joints. I've smoked dope with him lots of times. He thinks it's cool. I guess I did, too."

Although I offered Jenny support around this situation, underscoring that she was caught in the middle, not feeling comfortable with either parent, I communicated clearly to her that everyone in her family was responsible for his or her own behavior, and that included her.

Jenny and I also began to talk about what it was like to have a father who was her "buddy." It seemed pretty clear that sexual undertones were a part of their relationship. Jenny was able to talk to me directly about the pressure she felt from Jonathan to be his partner. And, as I'd guessed, she, like most teens, felt much safer when adults were partnered with adults. Jenny's father, on the other hand, had not yet recognized the pressure he was placing on his daughter. Part of my job was to help him see this.

A case such as Jonathan and Jenny's, in which there is no overt sexual contact but rather a "sexualized" relationship between a parent and child, is challenging for a therapist. I had to evaluate my legal responsibilities and consider whether I had heard of or witnessed any sexual activity between Jenny and her father that constituted abuse and would have mandated reporting. At this point I didn't see evidence of that. What I did see was a lonely, charming father reaching out to one of the few people he felt close to after a bitter divorce—his child. The problem was that he was reaching out with inappropriate offers to share marijuana and a certain degree of sexually tinged intimacy that was frightening to her.

Jenny's mother, too, had been acting inappropriately with her child in the area of intimacy. The many nights when Sarah had encouraged Jenny to behave as the parent had also taken a toll on Jenny's emotional well-being. Helping both of these parents to understand that they were making mistakes was a challenge.

Just as the negative impact of Sarah's pot use didn't become clear to her until Jenny threatened not to come home if Sarah smoked, Sarah could not understand how their sisterly intimacy was hurting her daughter until Jenny herself told her that she found their evenings together uncomfortable. Was Jenny going to have to make the same sort of effort to get through to her father, or was there something I could do to help him understand?

The Buddy Dad: Part 2

Although I felt empathy toward Jonathan, I also knew that I was angry with him. As a younger, less-experienced psychiatrist, I used to get angry with parents all the time—how could they act so stupidly with their kids, especially their teenagers, making mistakes that were obvious even to a thirty-year-old, childless psychiatrist? Fifteen years later my perspective has changed. I've struggled with raising my own children, and I've worked with a lot of parents and teens. I've come to realize how difficult it is to parent a teenager.

Even bearing this in mind, I was pretty angry with Jonathan. When he arrived for his next session, however, I decided that I'd better bite my tongue and pay close attention to my own reactions. I remembered that this was still a custody battle, with angry feelings flying back and forth and a child caught in the middle, but a child who was surprisingly adept at maneuvering through it.

Jonathan surprised me by beginning with a fairly straightforward approach. "I know that Jenny told you about the camping trip. I know that there is no excuse for smoking a joint with your own teenager. I'm here to get some help for me, too. You've helped Sarah and Jenny a lot. I tried to ask you for help the first time we met, but I thought if I came out and told you right away, I was worried I would lose more time with her like Sarah had. I guess I thought there was no one to talk with about it. When Sarah and I were married, even when it was bad we could talk about Jenny. I got some good ideas from her. Now there really hasn't been anyone to talk to about these things."

Notwithstanding the fact that I was suspicious of Jonathan's behavior with his daughter, and with me up until this point, what he was saying was true. Parents try to make themselves look good in the middle of a custody evaluation, and in this process they often lose each other as valuable resources around parenting strategies.

"You're right. I'm probably not the best person to talk with under the circumstances. But you need some guidance about your parenting of Jenny. And you're also right that you shouldn't have offered her the drugs. It has raised a lot of difficult questions in her mind about herself, you, and your relationship with her."

"I'm beginning to see that. My own dad would hit me whenever I took a drink or drove the car too fast. I didn't want it to be like that with her. I wanted to be friends with my daughter. Now I'm worried she's going to be a pothead at fourteen."

"You could tell her what you think now about what you did, and what you think about her smoking. You also need to find someone to talk to besides Jenny," I added.

I told Jonathan that I had worked with parents who relied too heavily on their children following a divorce, frequently sharing ideas or affections that were not healthy for the child or, for that matter, the parent. I described how a child might feel overburdened by such a relationship, perceiving it as too intimate; sexuality was just one component of it.

Jonathan sounded genuinely sad when he responded. "So it's not only the marijuana, is it? It's got more to do with the fact that I've pushed her to become my little buddy."

I asked him to talk more about what he saw as his "little buddy" relationship with Jenny, and slowly we began to work together to change it.

He shared his loneliness following the divorce, as well as his feelings of neediness and rejection. Jenny's love and admiration had helped to fill a gap in his life, but he understood now that he had used her inappropriately; she was a young woman in some ways, still a girl in others, and she was his daughter. She needed a father, not a buddy, friend, or lover.

Diana Baumrind's work emphasizes the importance of adhering to a code of values when parenting a teenager.[1] She reports that often parents who tend not to fulfill their own responsibilities are lax in enforcing a code of values, often being too permissive with their children. Parents can also fail by being too strict; they may seem to express a code of values but often fail to communicate the reality of choices and, perhaps even more important, fail to demonstrate how to make choices. Jenny's father fell into the first category. He was trying hard to not be like his own father, who failed as a parent by falling into the second category—he had beaten his son for any disobedience, causing Jonathan to lose respect and love for him. In choosing to be too permissive, Jonathan was more like his father than he knew. Each man failed to communicate to his child the importance of well-considered values that respect the individual, and each failed to demonstrate how to make choices.

Communicating values is an important part of parenting a child during the teenage years, particularly in the area of risk-taking. Risk-taking is partly a process whereby adolescents set up and test their own boundaries while negotiating their parents' boundaries. It's important for every teenager to know that his or her parents *have* boundaries; a task of adolescence very similar to those of certain stages of earlier childhood is rediscovering where those boundaries are. Often a teen does so by trying to discover, directly or indirectly, what he or she can "get away" with. No matter how well parents demonstrate and communicate boundaries, values, how to make decisions, and how to take risks, adolescents will still explore and take their own risks—and will make mistakes in judgment along the way. But they will ultimately have a much better chance of cultivating healthy behavior if healthy behavior is modeled for them by their parents.

After our discussion Jonathan apologized to his daughter for smoking marijuana and acknowledged that he had a problem with it that he was going to work on. He also told her that he didn't think that smoking marijuana was healthy. He believed that it had already affected Jenny's performance in school, and he described several instances of this. He then told her that he was ready to help her with her problem with it.

At first Jenny was angry and called him a "doper," adding that no pothead could make rules. Jonathan agreed with her that he had made mistakes, but his job was to be her parent, and part of that was to guide her. He managed not to get into an immediate fight with her about the rules, and they pounded them out together over the next few months. Among others, a few important ones included no smoking marijuana in the house; no smoking marijuana on weekdays; and grounding (which precluded going to Golden Gate Park and smoking marijuana with friends) if her grades fell below a certain level.

Remembering Your Role:
Parenting Teens During and After a
Divorce

Family systems are changing. The increased frequency of divorce means that almost half of our children will spend some of their childhood and adolescent years in a family where the parents are undergoing a divorce. Although divorce has been associated with higher rates of a variety of risk behaviors in adolescents, including drug abuse, delinquency, and precocious sexual behavior, it is important to remember that each teenager is unique, and no two sets of parents are alike either. Divorce initiates a chain of events characterized by the child's and parents' immediate reactions, frequently followed by periods of grief, anger, depression, and anxiety.[2]

Factors that affect both immediate and long-term reactions include a child's character before the divorce, each parent's ability to cope with the divorce, and the characteristics of the particular divorce, such as extreme conflict. The periods immediately before and after a divorce are commonly full of conflict, but this usually diminishes after some time passes.[3] High-conflict divorces in families with children are those that involve continuous fighting between the parents, often for years; false allegations of child abuse, either physical or sexual; unnegotiated moves by one parent to another part of the country; and frequent attempts by one parent to alienate a child from the other parent.[4]

When I began my work with Jenny, she had already been exposed to several years of her mother and father bad-mouthing each other. They were also locked in a legal struggle, each trying to prove that the other was an unfit parent. This prolonged struggle, as well as their own needs, had seriously interfered with their ability to parent. They blamed each other for Jenny's problems with marijuana use instead of being willing to examine their own parenting and the examples they were setting, especially when their own risk-taking behavior escalated during this period.

While parents are often worried about their adolescent child succumbing to peer pressure, parental patterns of risk-taking are also important. Jenny had smoked her first joint well aware of the fact that each of her parents smoked marijuana. When she was caught smoking dope at either house, she blamed the other parent for "allowing" it, and because her parents weren't communicating, there was no way to check up on her. Jonathan and Sarah actually used marijuana in different ways and for different reasons. Sarah was extremely depressed, smoked marijuana while locked in her room alone to take away the pain and loneliness, and was caught in her own experience. Jonathan liked to smoke dope with others, "a social thing," and stated that he enjoyed sharing this experience with his daughter. Jenny felt neglected and ignored by her mother when she was smoking. On the surface, Jonathan appeared much less depressed and better able than Sarah to cope with life after the divorce; however, he, too, was demonstrating some deficient parenting skills in using a "buddy" model and was getting into some serious trouble with his fourteen-year-old daughter, who felt that he was trying to get "too close" to her and wasn't able to act "like a dad."

Many parents are stimulated when they see their adolescent child take risks. It can awaken a desire to be an adolescent again themselves and to try all of these exciting things—the romance of risk revisited. If this is happening, parents need to be aware of it or they may escalate their child's dangerous risk-taking and place them in jeopardy. Both of Jenny's parents were oblivious to the impact that their own behavior was having on their daughter, and the end result was very much the same with each of them: neither was able to be an appropriate parent to Jenny, to function as a guide and role model for her adolescent years. Their conflict with each other, and the needs each was left with following their divorce, were important factors in their detour from the road of "good-enough" parenting.[5]

Parenting, especially with adolescent children, requires an ability to look at your own behavior and, if needed, to modify it. When parents always blame the other instead, then adolescents will imitate their parents' poor strategy and fail to learn how to take responsibility for their own actions.

Again, Jonathan's and Sarah's adoption of the "buddy" or "sister" model is not unusual for a parent, especially a divorced parent. And being friendly with your child at the same time that you fulfill your parenting role can be invaluable. A teenager listens better to parents who are available, kind, helpful, and respectful of his or her changing life and different views—parents who really listen to their child. So the model of the "good listener" who also spends time with the teenager includes many aspects of a good friendship. But teens also rely on parents to be their guides for the future, to communicate a clear set of values and expectations, to look ahead and help them scope out future problems, and to provide both knowledge and experience. Following their divorce, Jenny's parents found themselves forgetting this primary aspect of their roles as parents. Jonathan knew that he didn't want his teenage daughter to smoke marijuana, let alone be one of the people who would provide and share it with her. But after the divorce he was lonely and "paired off" with her. His need for Jenny to be his friend took precedence over Jenny's need to have a father she could rely on. And Sarah's need to talk to someone at the end of a long workday took precedence over her daughter's need to have a mother she could rely on.

After working separately on their own issues, Jonathan and Sarah were better able to work together to coparent Jenny. First they decided to develop a method for communicating about their joint parenting responsibilities. Initially short phone calls worked the best, and then they were gradually able to increase their length. They agreed to stop bad-mouthing each other in front of Jenny and to support each other as parents. These steps, by no means simple, were among the most important they would ever take for their daughter. Modifying their own risk-taking patterns, clearly voicing values, and setting limits around Jenny's risk-taking were important components of these changes. The conflict diminished remarkably. Jenny, after years of her parents tugging at her, still found it difficult to get out of the middle, but at least her parents stopped giving her daily fuel to maintain the fire. Jenny was then able to see that she had trouble getting close to either of her parents, let alone anyone else, because she didn't trust them to not campaign for their own platforms.

In *Second Chances*, Judith Wallerstein describes the potential in divorce for setting the stage for other relationships to develop.[6] Certainly that's true for parents, but it's also true for teenagers in their current and future relationships. They don't have to make the mistakes their parents made in their marriage. Change, however, requires hard work. After the divorce, Jenny's parents had continued an ugly war with Jenny caught in the middle. With assistance they were able to change this pattern, allowing Jenny the opportunity to see how she, too, had participated in and perpetuated it.

Once her parents returned to their job of parenting, Jenny was able to stop carrying it all in her backpack. She could relax a little and know that both she and her family's Grateful Dead collection had homes—two of them.

Part III

The Outside World: Risk-taking and Society

Chapter Ten

The Wild West Lives

The only way to fit in at school has been to drink.

—Joe

Joe, a high school senior, spent his afternoons renting western movies and watching them with his buddies while they learned to drink beer together. It wasn't long before Joe developed a serious addictive alcoholic pattern. Sometimes an adolescent lifestyle like Joe's—adopting certain behaviors in the social peer group and having minimal contact with parents—can foster risk behavior. So can the role models he finds in the media.

Seventeen-year-old Joe strode into my office two days after his parents called asking me to see their son, who had just been arrested for drinking and unruly behavior. Joe's tall, lean frame was only partially obscured by the baggy, oversized clothing he wore. He looked me right in the eye with an engaging smile. I asked him why he was in my office. "No reason, Doc. My parents just thought it would be nice if I talked to someone."

I asked him what he thought about that idea. "No need, everything's okay," he said, giving me another prime example of that winning smile.

The rest of the first session with Joe continued along that line. Arrest? He was just at a party, a lot of his friends got arrested, too. Anyway, everyone drinks, no hassles. Grades falling? Yeah, but everyone's grades fall senior year, it's just "senioritis." In other words, nothing was wrong.

Adolescents can be as challenging for therapists as they are for parents. Joe's attitude in the first session was not unusual. Initial refusal to see or admit that there is a problem is common. I try to stay calm and, most important, not give in to the teen's resistance by giving up. Calm and persistence are two keys to spending time with adolescents. At the end of the first session I thanked Joe for coming in, told him that I had learned a lot from him, and wanted to see him again. He appeared surprised; after all, he didn't have any problems, did he? But then, he was a "no hassle" kind of guy and that applied to his interactions with me, too. Shrugging his shoulders, he agreed to come back, nodded, and calmly strode out of the office.

The first session with Joe's parents was anything but calm. The family lived in Menlo Park, a suburb south of San Francisco with single-family homes and good schools; it was a pleasant community without the overwhelming wealth of nearby Hillsborough or parts of Marin County. Joe's parents, two solemn-faced accountants, told me immediately how hard they had worked to obtain this life for their son, a life that now appeared to be in ruins. Joe was arrested at a senior party but had apparently been drinking heavily for months, maybe even years, before this happened.

Sitting in my office, Jennifer and Jack said that they felt "shell-shocked." They had been proud of their son—a good athlete, a B student, outgoing, popular. Up until a week before there hadn't been a sign of trouble. Or had there been?

I felt their genuine surprise and total upset. They both described themselves as "linear thinkers"; this series of events didn't fit with the way they thought of their child or their world in general. Jack spoke first, nervously moving the handle of his briefcase. "I've been working a lot the past few years. I took on a lot of other accounts trying to save money for Joe's college education, and I haven't been home as much."

"Ditto for me," said Jennifer. "We've each picked up a lot of clients, many more the past two years. We were really proud of our firm. Jack and I built the business together, and it's really growing, but Joe—I feel like he's telling us something."

"What do you think he's trying to tell you?"

"At the very least, to pay more attention to him. Jack and I have only had dinner with Joe one weekday night in the past month. It's our busiest season, but it leaves me feeling like I don't have a handle on what's happening with him."

"How does the dinner hour usually work?" I asked casually, but listening carefully for their answer after Jennifer's last comment. How families with adolescents handle the dinner hour tells a lot about how they work together or fail to work together with their teens.

"Well, it doesn't go well," grumbled Jack, at which Jennifer flashed him a look of some resentment. "We fend for ourselves now. Joe usually eats early with some of his buddies, pizza, pasta. He's becoming a reasonable chef, at least by his friends' reports. He's the only one of us who usually eats with someone. Then Jen and I, well, we'll each nuke a Lean Cuisine when we get home, or get carryout at the office. Not too appetizing, but it helps us stay thin. Then there's the not so healthy part, but we do it together, at least Joe and I, snacking on Häagen-Dazs ice cream before we go to bed," he said sheepishly. "I saw your brochures in the waiting room on a healthy diet for teens. You probably think our diet's crazy."

Sidestepping his last comment about diet, I asked him how he thought the dinner program was working.

"It's funny. We only started this plan—if you can call it that—about six months ago. As Jennifer said, our business has really grown, and we realized we could make extra money that would be helpful with the college expenses. Of course, most of the clients can only come in late. One of us gets home early, at least by our standards, around seven-thirty or so, and the other usually after nine."

"How has it changed things?" I asked.

Wornout-looking and guilt-ridden, Jennifer now spoke. "I think it's changed everything. I just couldn't do it anymore, though. Before we started this, I'd get home every night by five-thirty or six at the latest, and then I'd have dinner on the table by seven. We all ate together every night. It's just that I was becoming too exhausted. Working late and ordering carryout is a break for me. Working all day, coming home, cooking dinner, and dealing with the high energy level of a teenager, I felt like I was going insane. I fantasized about running away, not to some fancy spa but to one of those old sanitariums this country doesn't even have anymore, where you weave baskets. I guess I can see we're going to pay for this now. I'll go back to making dinner," she groaned, looking like she was being sent back to a chain gang.

"Things are pretty rough for your family right now. Communication has clearly broken down, but I'm not sure that this is the best solution. We don't really understand the problem yet; the dinner hour changed—disappeared really—but is there anything else?"

After several minutes Jack spoke thoughtfully. "I know Jen blames herself and me—the increased work, decreased time with Joe, and most of all, our lack of energy—but there are other things, too. The high school, Joe's social life. He's in with a real popular crowd, has been for years. Every weekend at kids' houses there are parties with kegs of beer." He paused, then added, "And probably hard stuff, too. It's unbelievable. Two hundred kids at a house all at one time. At first I told him that he couldn't go, but then he got on me: 'Dad, what about my social life?' So I let him. Maybe I even stopped talking about it. I thought about calling other parents about it—all these underage kids drinking, sometimes drinking and driving. I guess I just gave up. What are parents supposed to do? It seems like all of the kids are doing it."

Gently I said, "It is a big job if you look at all of the kids, taking more energy than you, Jennifer, and I have, but if you focus on your child and try to help him figure things out, you just might manage it."

"I see your point. By turning it into a monster task, we won't get anything done, and I guess you're saying that this job is big enough already."

I agreed with Jack and asked them to come up with a plan for the dinner hour and return with Joe the following week.

The Old West in Today's Living Rooms

Risk-taking, both in fact and in mythology, played a unique part in the development of the American West. During the nineteenth and early twentieth centuries this region of our country was portrayed as a land of challenge and opportunity, unhampered by the traditions and social hierarchy of the East. Not only was risk-taking permissible in this rapidly changing area, it was solicited and encouraged.

Reading the journals of those who chose to settle in the West, it

is clear that much of this risk-taking was a quiet process, with
courageous individuals confronting challenges, developing creative
solutions, and slowly changing the course of their own lives and history.[1] This is not the West that has been immortalized in legend,
however. Brash decisions, a quick hand with a gun, and large quan-
tities of alcohol color the mythological landscape of the American
West, particularly in Hollywood's version. Most of this celluloid culture portrays the West as a young and largely male culture, one
dominated by risk-taking, violence, and alcohol. Above all, it is exciting. This tradition, whether realistic or legendary, has not been
lost on successive generations of American teenagers.

Joe knew this culture well. He had watched thousands of westerns on cable television. Mostly he watched alone or with his buddies, sitting around in their houses after school. Slowly, smoking
and drinking became a part of this picture. Joe and his buddies
would have a beer or two just to take the edge off things after their
hard day at the local high school. After a couple of beers and a pack
of cigarettes, homework was often forgotten.

"Latchkey" children are those between the ages of six and thirteen who go home after school and are left unsupervised until their
parents return from work. There are 450,000 latchkey children in
America today.[2] Adolescents are not even counted in this number; in
fact, there are no estimates on how many latchkey teens there are in
this country. At a time when 75 percent of mothers are working,
there are also very few after-school programs for them. For years
Chicago television would flash the question, "Do you know where
your teenagers are?" every night at ten-thirty as the hour of curfew
approached. That same question could now be addressed to parents
as they sit in their offices in the middle of the afternoon.

Jack and Jennifer knew where their son was, they just didn't
know what he was doing. They didn't know that Joe was drinking
every day, sitting in a smoke-filled room with a few buddies, watching old westerns. Clues existed, but Jack and Jennifer were busy,
extremely tired, and didn't want to believe that their son had a serious problem. Once Jack found an entire bag of beer cans by the
garbage. Joe lied about it, telling his father that he and his friends
had cleaned up the neighborhood. Jack found it hard to believe
that his son was spending his afternoons scouring the streets to
work on neighborhood environmental improvements, but after all,

the family did recycle and, more important, Jack wanted to believe his son.

Drinking after school was reinforced by the large drinking parties Jack mentioned during our first meeting. Joe confirmed that the parties were attended by two hundred or more high school students and were generally held on Friday or Saturday nights at different homes. He talked freely with me about the amount of alcohol consumed at these parties. Joe had begun to drink when he was a freshman, and he was proud to be invited along with the senior guys. For the first year he had been able to consume only three or four beers before he had to disappear into the backyard and throw up. Gradually his tolerance of alcohol increased to the point where he could drink four or five, then seven or eight, and finally eleven or twelve. By the time he came to see me he was drinking fourteen beers at these weekend debaucheries. Unbeknownst to his parents, somewhere along the way he had also acquired the exalted reputation of "best partier" in his high school.

Easily acquired and frequently addictive, alcohol and cigarettes are the most commonly used and abused substances among youth today.[3] In addition, both act as "gateway" drugs, paving the way for further drug use and other risk behaviors. Of the different theoretical models used to understand adolescent risk behavior, the "lifestyle" model is particularly useful in trying to understand what is happening with a boy like Joe.[4] Using this approach, one can see how a variety of behaviors work together to support and develop a pattern of alcohol use slowly, over years. Joe had considerable social reinforcement for his risk behaviors. At first, seniors encouraged him to drink, then gradually he achieved the status of top "partier" himself. He quickly fell into a pattern of binge drinking, defined as drinking five or more drinks consecutively on one occasion.[5] Binge drinking should be an important signal for parents and adolescents both. In teens it is associated with problems with parents, school, and the legal system. Daily drinking and smoking usually lead to addiction, biologically reinforcing a pattern begun for social reasons. When Joe came to see me, he was not only addicted to alcohol, he had developed a number of alcohol-related problems, including falling grades, blackouts, and unnecessary fights with his friends and parents. Changing an addictive pattern that offers so much positive reinforcement and has become so entrenched is difficult for anyone;

adolescents are no exception. To make anything happen, Joe had to be motivated to change. So far that wasn't happening.

A Wake-up Call

Two weeks later, at six o'clock on a Sunday morning, I received a phone call at home. It was Jack. He told me that Joe had totaled the family car the previous evening. Driving home drunk after a late-night party, the car had "slipped" off the road. Joe had left the car in a eucalyptus-filled ravine and walked home. He appeared to be physically okay except for cuts and scratches, but he was shaking, and Jack said that his son couldn't stop crying. He apologized for calling so early but said that he really didn't know what to do.

I reminded him that he would have to call the police, adding that I would like to see him with his son as soon as possible. How about 8:00 A.M.?

As I showered, made coffee, and watched the fog lift off the redwoods in the backyard, I thought about Joe on the slippery California roads alone that night after an evening of heavy partying. He had been driving along Skyline Boulevard when the accident occurred. At certain points Skyline offers amazing views of the Pacific Ocean and the San Francisco Bay, but it also has some tortuous turns, blind spots, and sections that should be only one lane. It is a road I drive on only during the day, without fog, and even then I'm extra careful.

Injury is the leading cause of death, hospital admissions, and emergency room visits for adolescents in the United States.[6] Although "injury" is a general category representing a number of causes (e.g., drowning and unintentional death from a firearm), motor vehicle injuries outstrip all others. The pattern of motor vehicle injury among adolescents over age fifteen reflects several factors generally associated with higher risk of collision and injury: driving at night and on the weekend, drinking and driving, and driving smaller cars. Sixty percent of the deaths occur on the weekend between the hours of 9:00 P.M. and 6:00 A.M.[7] Joe fit the pattern except that the car he crashed was a Volvo. Safe cars help save lives, but the outcome also depends on the driver.

Joe and his parents were at my office by 7:30 A.M. Joe had an ugly red scratch on his face. The engaging smile and "no hassle" appearance had disappeared. He was chewing on a styrofoam coffee cup, leaving a rim of red blood from a small cut on his lip. Jennifer was standing next to her son, and I noticed that she didn't stop looking at him, even to greet me. Her reddened eyes highlighted by dark shadows revealed the fears of a mother whose son had nearly died alone on a highway.

Jack appeared the most together of the bedraggled family group. He was pouring cups of hot coffee and let me know that I was out of both sugar and artificial sweetener. It was only when I noticed that he had poured six cups of coffee for the four of us that I realized how shaken he was, and how hard he was fighting to stay in control.

I began the session by thanking everyone for coming and noting that I didn't usually see teens or families at 7:30 on weekend mornings, but I thought we needed to meet as close to the time of the accident as we could. I let them know that I saw the accident as an emergency akin to other ways that teens unfortunately end their lives.

Appearing somewhat insulted that I had linked his "accident" with kids who died by their own hand (although I hadn't mentioned the word *suicide*), Joe let me know that this had not been his intention.

I asked him whether he had been drinking, to which he answered yes, but I noticed that the sheepish grin had returned and I could feel an encroaching atmosphere of denial moving in to replace the morning fog.

"So just what was your intention?" I asked.

Jennifer, who had been crying softly, now spoke, and her usually calm voice was filled with anger. "Joe, I thought you saw it clearly for the first time—you were crying when you told me what it felt like when the car dropped into the ravine after you lost control. I felt like I was there with you when you told us how it felt like you were going to die as you sped toward a tree. Then the car stopped because a boulder got in its way! You told us how you crawled out of the car through the window and kissed the ground, saying you would never drink again. Have you forgotten it all already? I felt like I was there with you. Over the past six hours I have watched you die over and over again in my head. Don't sink back into hiding

things from us and pretending like nothing is wrong!" Then she
added, "We're going to help you with this."

Overwhelmed by his mother's clear expression of her feelings,
Joe began to cry. Between his sobs I could make out pieces of what
he was saying. "I feel like I've had to be so strong. The only way to
fit in at school has been to drink. It's never worked for me. It got me
sick at first, and then when I got good at it I felt trapped, like I
couldn't relate to kids without it. You and Dad were working so
hard to get money to pay for my college. How could I let you down
by telling you that your perfect son was such a screwup?"

"Joe," said Jennifer, "it's okay to make mistakes. We all do it.
Part of the problem with our family is that we just haven't been
able to talk about them. I've been doing a lot of thinking about last
night. It reminds me of another night five years ago. Do you remember? The night that I packed you into the car and was going to
leave?"

"What are you talking about, Mom?" Joe asked, even paler now
than he had been.

"It's okay, Joe. Your father knows about it."

Joe looked over at Jack, who said quietly, "Look, Joe, your
mother and I haven't been perfect. We don't expect you to be either."

I asked Jennifer to tell me about that other evening. What had
reminded her of it?

"Seeing Joe scratched, bruised, and unable to stop crying reminded me of it," she said. After a long pause, she explained. "Five
years ago I was miserably unhappy with my marriage. Jack and I
weren't talking at all. He was working all the time, but it was much
more than that. We were never good at communicating. He was
drinking but not talking about it. I had fallen in love with another
man but wasn't talking about that. That evening it was also foggy,
raining. Jack was working late. I couldn't sleep and was pacing the
house. I woke Joe up and put him in the car with suitcases I'd
packed. He was so kind, gentle. I started telling him about everything, his father's drinking, my love for this other person, mostly my
unhappiness. Once I got started talking, I couldn't stop. I drove and
talked for hours." Jennifer was crying softly as she recounted what
had happened. "That night I burdened our son with the problems of
an entire lifetime."

"Mom, don't . . ." Joe's ashen face looked much younger suddenly.

"Joe, I have to finish talking about this now. You and I never discussed it after that evening."

In spite of her comment, Jennifer appeared to have run out of steam. She seemed surprised that she had said so much and sat back, clutching her coffee cup. Hearing now about Jack's drinking problem and the troubled times he and Jennifer had had in their marriage was helping me develop a fuller picture of all the factors contributing to Joe's behaviors.

Jack, although still silent, seemed quite moved by what his wife had said. When I commented on that, he was able to voice his support, saying, "Our family needed help back then. The problem has just been buried. I think that you've learned from us, Joe, not only from me about the drinking, but how it's not okay to talk about things."

With the support from her husband, Jennifer, who had regained her courage, was now able to finish her story.

"What really made me think about that night wasn't only the obvious similarities of the rainy roads, a long night, scary thoughts. It was how you came home, hurt but more open, honestly able to look at what was going on in your life. You saw what the drinking has done to your life. I don't want you to close up like I did after that night. But telling you my secrets, I felt so ashamed that I had burdened you, a twelve-year-old child . . ." Jennifer was sobbing openly now.

"Mom, you didn't do anything wrong. You're too hard on yourself," Joe said.

"Joe, you're right that your mom's too hard on herself, but equally important, she's telling us about things that she wished she had done differently," I said. "It seems that she opened up all these things for you—her desire to leave, your father's drinking, and her depression—but then finished it off by closing up. What did you think about that conversation with her later?"

Surprised by my question, Joe stared for several minutes. "I used to think about it. About how if we had run away, Mom and I, what our life would have been like. About what would have happened to Dad. Then things changed. Mom went back to work, was gone all the time with Dad. I guess I just thought things were work-ing out better for them."

"How were things for you?" I asked.

Some of his bravado returning, Joe laughed. "I guess I watched a lot of movies. I tried not to think about it."

"When did the drinking start?" I asked.

"It started at the parties, but it was also the same year that Mom went back to work so much," he said slowly.

At this point Jennifer began to blame herself again, beginning with a moaning refrain about how it was all her fault.

Not wanting her to lapse into self-blame after she had coura-geously confronted both her son's behavior and her own, I spoke. "Was the need for extra college money your fault? Was your fam-ily's inability to help with the countless chores your fault, or maybe your husband's or son's drinking?" I asked. "Jennifer, you are right to accept responsibility for part of this, but nothing is all one per-son's fault. A few moments ago you were trying to get Joe to see that he doesn't have to be perfect, that he has to look at things hon-estly. Yet you expect yourself to be perfect."

"So you're telling me that I'm either in denial or see it as totally my fault," she said a little defensively.

"I didn't say that, Jennifer."

Then Jack said, "Whoever's saying it, it says something about how our family operates. There are the quiet times when we don't talk about stuff, like my drinking. Then there are the not-so-quiet times when we blame, usually ourselves. I see it with Joe now. He's not much different from me or Jen. Like him, I drank during the quiet times."

"How did you stop drinking?" I asked.

"I really don't know. When Jen came back early the next morn-ing after packing up and taking off, I realized what I could lose, what I'd nearly lost, so I stopped. But I've never stopped the denial. I've pretended like I wasn't a drinker, like it never happened. That made it easier to ignore Joe's problem. I saw the beer cans. I knew, yet I decided not to know."

That session proved instrumental and powerfully demonstrated the problems of substance abuse and the denial that is so often its partner, but it was just a beginning.

Not all families are given the opportunity that Joe, Jack, and Jennifer were given. Joe's narrow escape on the highway gave them the opportunity to examine their lives and how they coped with their problems, largely through self-blame or denial. Drug and alcohol use is not the only type of unhealthy risk behavior that lends itself to these coping styles. Jill's running away was accompanied by a certain amount of denial, as was Hannah's disordered eating. What is important is that the denial has to be recognized and confronted if the teenager is to get better and change. Lucky families are given, or find, opportunities to do this.

From Posses to Teams

This session with Joe and his parents offered us a place to start, but it was just that. If we had stopped there, I have little doubt that Joe would have ended up in a rainy ravine on another night. One result of that early morning session was that Joe agreed not only to come but to participate more actively in the sessions with me. I told him that his "no hassle" style wasn't going to work for our time together. Immediately blaming himself, he said, "Well, I can see how I've turned this Sunday into quite a hassle for you and my parents."

"You're not the hassle, Joe, the problems are the drinking and the way you've tried to cover it up," I said.

Joe seemed relieved. Of course, acknowledging all the "hassles" in his life was going to be no easy task. One of the first things that Joe and I talked about was the conversation with his mother on that first memorable rainy night. Although I hadn't said it in the family meeting, Jennifer was right about her confessional conversation with her twelve-year-old son: it had placed a great burden on him. Many things can motivate a parent to confide so emotionally in a child; loneliness is just one. It is understandable, yes, but never appropriate. To hear an adult's feelings about deeply personal matters can be titillating for a young person, making him or her feel special and grown-up for having been chosen as a confidant. But no child, not even an adolescent, should be asked to serve in this role for a parent, particularly if what has been shared is a "secret," something not to be spoken of. (And certainly no parent should put a child in the position of hearing private information about the other parent or information that cannot be shared with the other parent.) In this reversal of roles, the child is being asked to provide emotional support to the parent. Parent-child relationships are usually not reciprocal until long after the child has become an adult, if then. Children — and in this context adolescents are still children — should never be asked to "hold" a parent's problems.

In the next sessions Joe began to talk about some of the changes he had made after that conversation. At first he remembered only that he was worried about what would have happened to his family if his parents had separated, but as we talked about it more, he remembered other feelings — shock that his mother had these feelings, and a sinking realization that his father wasn't able to share any of his feelings, spent his time either working or drinking, and was generally unavailable. Joe also recounted the very painful feelings he had had when his mother returned to work. For a brief period she had shared her deepest feelings with her son, and then she had disappeared to rejoin his father, leaving Joe without answers to piece together what had happened. Alone, he tried to do that. He concluded accurately that things had improved between his mother and father, but he never knew whether his mother had told his father about her feelings. Sometimes he thought about what it would be like if his father never knew about it. It would remain forever a secret that Joe and his mother shared. These thoughts were exciting for Joe, but at the same time they frightened him. Perhaps most important, there was no one to talk to about any of this. Instead, Joe was left alone after school for hours each day.

He was lonely. The context had been disturbing, but Joe had also loved it when his mother talked to him in such an adult way; when she stopped, he missed feeling "like a man." Now, years later, he was modeling his behavior after the male heroes of the westerns he watched, men of few words who could handle anything, men who certainly didn't need their mothers. Gradually his buddies, often other boys without parents at home, would congregate at his house, and they would watch the films together. Joe would cook for them. There was a friendly atmosphere to it, almost like a family. How the beer had become part of it, Joe wasn't sure. First they smoked cigarettes out in the backyard so that there wouldn't be traces of smoke in the house. Then they began smoking in the house, and finally they added the drinking.

Several weeks after the car accident Joe was able to talk about how angry he felt about what had happened in his family. The way he saw it, his parents had backed away from being parents. As mentioned, Jennifer had made her son feel like an adult by sharing her deepest feelings with him. The secrets were meant for an adult, so he concluded that she saw him that way. His parents' disappearance into their office only fostered that idea. Leaving him alone at home, they were now treating him like an adult. Although Joe was able to bring up some of his anger with me, most of it remained hidden. The pattern of silence he had acquired was proving difficult to change. Slowly, though, he was beginning to recognize his feelings.

As part of our treatment, I recommended that Joe and his family attend Alcoholics Anonymous meetings. Joe and his father decided to go to AA together, and his mother went to Al-Anon. At first Joe didn't like the meetings. The horrible stories others had to tell about what alcohol had done to their lives frightened him. He told me that he didn't see his own life that way at all.

Things started to change for Joe when he heard his father share his own story at one of the meetings. Jack described how he had really wanted to be close to his own father but always felt put off because his father was always either working or drinking. Searching for companionship, he had turned to his high school peers, among whom he found both friends and alcohol. By the time he went to college he was locked into a pattern of weekend drinking that gradually expanded to drinking every night. This pattern had continued, slowly escalating, for twenty years, until his wife said that she would leave him if he didn't stop. That had scared Jack. He felt as if Jennifer was the only person he was able to talk with. He agreed to stop, went through some difficult months kicking his habit without any assistance, and then "forgot" about it all — his own drinking, his father's drinking, and the risks his son was facing. At the AA meeting, for the first time, Jack was able to admit to his tremendous struggles with alcohol and loneliness. He was able to see how his own denial ("Alcohol's not a problem for me anymore, I've been able to stop") had blinded him to his son's problem. Painfully Jack could now see Joe as the lonely kid who had waited until nine-thirty at night to talk to his father, wearing a half-dazed expression, sometimes slurring his speech, hiding beer cans in his closet and his unhappiness behind the "no hassle" veneer. Jack could also see that this was just what he had been wanting to avoid—sharing the legacy of alcohol and loneliness from his own past with his son, whom he loved so much.

Joe was deeply affected by what his father was able to share that night. Hearing how much Jack had tried to reach out to his own father for years, finally turning away, helped Joe to understand what was happening between himself and his father. Jack had been able to stop drinking, but he hadn't been able to change the type of father he was, at least not until the consequences of Joe's drinking— the arrest, the car accident—woke him up. Our family sessions together, the AA meetings, and the car rides back and forth gave Joe and Jack time to talk about all of this.

In this book I repeatedly stress working as a team with a teenager who is trapped in negative risk behaviors; for Jack, Jennifer, and Joe making a commitment to attend meetings together was one key aspect of such an effort. When a teen is locked into a pattern of risk behavior associated with addiction, team efforts can be even more difficult. But self-help groups such as Alcoholics Anonymous and Narcotics Anonymous are familiar with addiction and its frequent companion, denial. They have successfully worked with teens like Joe and fathers like Jack and are an important part of the treatment effort, offering a peer group, education, and a place where stories can be both told and listened to. Therapy with a teen who is struggling with alcohol offers some of the same benefits, most obviously education and a place to tell his story, but groups and individual work are not mutually exclusive. In fact, as different components of treatment, they work together to promote recovery.

In addition to individual and family therapy and Alcoholics Anonymous, I spoke with Joe's counselor at school to help develop a large-scale prevention effort that would help target drinking among the students. The administration knew that the school was recognized in the community as the high school with the wildest parties and the biggest drinkers. They were able to put together a special program for their students that focused on drinking after school and highlighted ways to avoid it. Jack and Jennifer also got on the telephone and called other parents, letting them know what they had found out about the kids and the drinking. They invited parents to an informal meeting at their house.

Alone, any one of these efforts to help Joe would probably have failed. An entrenched drinking problem is hugely difficult to conquer. Like Jack, many are able to stop their drinking but don't take a good look at what is behind it so the problems show up in another form within the family or community at large. Enemies such as boredom, loneliness, and addiction are powerful, so the treatment effort has to be strong.

Meeting at the OK Corral, Living in Front of the TV

Unfortunately, Joe's problem is not unique. Across the United States boys and girls come home after school to empty houses. No surprise, they are lonely and don't want to be alone. Friends join them, but even together they are often bored. They watch endless television and music videos or cruise the Internet looking for excitement. Smoking, drug use, and drinking can easily become a part of this picture. Teenagers do not need to be supervised all of the time, but they do need to be supervised some of the time. More important than constant supervision are parents who keep lines of communication open with their teens and remain educated and alert to the pitfalls of negative risk behaviors, parents who don't ignore the beer cans and who marshal a treatment effort when things start to get out of hand.

Boys today spend much more time in same-gender peer groups than girls do. This has distinct implications for boys who participate in gangs (see chapter 11), but it also affects all boys.

I teach a course that covers the development of adolescent boys and girls. Teaching this course has been an eye-opener for me mostly because, as the mother of two daughters, I have learned more about how we are raising our sons in America today. Only one hundred years ago adolescent sons were encouraged to take on adult roles. Much of their time was spent in apprentice-like situations in which they were certainly learning about work but were also spending time with adults, learning how to interact and behave responsibly. This apprenticeship pattern, once so common in adolescence, no longer exists. Opportunities for teens to have contact with adults in one-on-one situations have virtually disappeared. Today's boys spend more time with their peers, whereas girls spend more time with older females.[8] Mothers and other women, even when they work outside the home, are still the primary caretakers for both boys and girls. And working women still have enough in common with girls, and vice versa, that they seek out each other's company. Boys, in contrast, learn from each other. Sometimes they also find nearly constant companionship in the media.

One focus of my work with Joe was to help him understand why he chose to spend so much time sitting in front of the television watching westerns, either alone or with a small group of friends. Although there is much opinion about the long- and short-term effects of mass media on adolescents,[9] there are surprisingly few studies.[10] The studies that do exist show high levels of media use by adolescents, something any parent is aware of. Small-scale investigations show that teenagers typically spend one-third or more of their waking hours with one or another form of mass media (e.g., television, music, music videos, radio, film, computer-related materials), either as a primary activity or as background.[11] In contrast to popular belief, the time an adolescent spends using mass media does not displace more valuable activities such as homework. Rather, it occurs during what is called "unmeasured time"—the time teenagers refer to as "hanging out." It is also important to know that studies have not shown that large amounts of time spent on media activities result in poor grades.[12]

So just what are the dangers to adolescents from the growing amount of media pursuits available to them? First, it is important to understand the media as sources of information available to teens. The mass media are no different from other information sources in that there are tremendous variations in what adolescents attend to, in what sense they make of it, and in how it affects their actions.[13] Attempting to understand the role that media participation is playing in a particular teenager's life is a job for his or her parents. What is appropriate, or even desirable, participation for one teenager may be damaging to another.

A look at Joe's constant viewing of westerns interspersed with listening to music says a lot about him. One of the most obvious ways that it affected him negatively was that it increased the amount of time he spent engaged in a passive activity. Joe was aware of this and in fact raised it as a topic of discussion with me. He realized that as he became more and more passive over time, it was easier to keep drinking and harder to take risks, at least positive ones. And by this point Joe did not see his habitual viewing of westerns as positive. He now readily admitted that he had begun watching them in the hope of not only figuring out what "real men" do but also being able to do it himself. It hadn't exactly worked out that way. He had imitated the drinking in those movies, but not the more positive activities; he was the popular one always hanging out at the saloon, not the one stopping in on his way to drive cattle, settle land, or right some grievous wrong.

It's worth noting here that positive risk-taking requires a certain amount of energy. And certainly it's important to acknowledge that some educational and informative media activities can present adolescents with opportunities for positive risks. But when fictional characters are more present in a teen's life than real role models, and when passively watching or taking in begins to replace actively doing or putting forth, the role of media can be powerfully detrimental.

Some adolescents are able to pursue positive risks without engaging in negative ones. Others are fortunate to discover that positive risk-taking can help break negative patterns and even come to replace them. For Jack, facing his addiction and working on real recovery, without denial, was a huge positive risk. For Jennifer, attending Al-Anon meetings was a courageous step to help break her own patterns of silence and self-blame. Jack and Jennifer not only undertook the work of the family's recovery through meetings, they changed their schedules at work to be home together for family dinners at least four nights a week, and they alternated late nights at the office so that at least one of them was home with Joe on the remaining three nights.

So Joe, who had in many ways lost touch with his parents, finally had his real-life role models back in the picture. After school he still watched westerns, but with an eye to how they're filmed, written, acted, and directed. He began to read books about Hollywood and planned to enroll in a film theory and criticism class as his freshman elective at college. He also learned how to be around his friends without drinking. The battle with alcohol would be ongoing for Joe, but it had already begun to get easier—not drinking gave him more energy to pursue other activities. That his parents were more present in his life, both physically and emotionally, continued to help.

Chapter Eleven

Acting Tough

Look at us — it's like we're speaking two different languages. Our family's been in San Francisco for generations, and my parents act like they just stepped off the boat.

— Evan

What can I say? It feels safer to hurt others before they hurt me.

— Cecilia

Evan, a boy who participated in illegal gang activity, and Cecilia, a girl who victimized her peers at school, both illustrate what can happen when an adolescent engages in behavior that is directly destructive to his or her peers. Their stories also illustrate what can happen when parents fear, sometimes rightfully, that their child has befriended a "bad apple," fallen in with "the wrong crowd," or become involved with gangs. Their confusion and distress over the apparent descent of their child can leave them passive just when their children most need them to take an active role.

San Francisco's Chinatown occupies only fourteen square blocks. At one point the growth of this neighborhood was limited by city edicts in order to prevent the increasing "Asian menace" from having too much economic influence and power in the city. Famous for the many excellent restaurants and grassroots businesses that import Asian products to the United States, this maze of San Francisco streets also houses the headquarters for many Asian gangs, which control large amounts of gambling, especially mah-jongg and poker.

I've been fortunate to have the opportunity to work with a number of adolescents from Chinese families, mostly referred by other families in their community whom I've worked with in the past. Several years ago Evan, a sixteen-year-old Chinese American boy, was referred to me because his parents were concerned that he might be part of an Asian gang. Evan had recently been arrested by the police for being caught with a stolen car, and the police had told his parents that they believed it was a gang job, although Evan was left alone holding the car.

Evan's parents, Mary and Richard, had grown up in old Chinatown. They were the first generation to leave, in their words, the "Chinese ghetto" and move to a middle-class neighborhood in another area of San Francisco. They were also members of the first generation in each of their families to attend college and were proud of the education and career status they had achieved; Mary was a teacher, Richard an accountant.

With assistance from their parents and grandparents, they had enrolled Evan, the oldest male grandchild on both sides of the family, in one of the premier private elementary schools in the city. Great things were expected from Evan. When he was about to enter the sixth grade he told his parents that he had never felt accepted by his peers at this school and asked to transfer to the public junior high. In his own words, there was "no room" for him in any of the cliques. When his parents asked Evan whether he thought he was excluded because he was Chinese, Evan said he wasn't sure, that he just felt different. After the public junior high he went on to the public high school, where he gradually began to skip more and more classes and his grades began to fall. When he was referred to me, shortly after his arrest in his sophomore year of high school, he had missed more than one-third of the previous school year.

I began by seeing the nuclear family—Evan, Richard, and Mary—as a group. Several people influenced my decision to work with the family in this way, including one of Evan's teachers, his parole officer, and a therapist who had tried to work with the family by

seeing Evan and his parents individually and told me that the therapeutic work had failed miserably.

My first meeting with Evan's family was an experience I will
never forget. Often there is a visible contrast between different generations within a family. This was perhaps never so apparent as in
my first observations of Evan and his parents. Evan bounded up the
stairs to my office wearing very baggy black jeans, a semilayered
haircut with a ducktail, sunglasses, and a bold black leather jacket.
He grabbed my hand and shook it with enthusiasm and more than a
little bit of sarcastic charm. "Dr. Ponton, this is a pleasure I have
truly been looking forward to." His appealing bravado reminded me
of Marlon Brando in *A Streetcar Named Desire*.

Approximately twenty paces behind, his parents followed. Although they were dressed in conservative, casual clothes with button-
down broadcloth shirts and creased khaki pants and were clearly
attempting to assimilate into conventional American culture, they
conveyed many signs of another culture: their voices were very low,
and I had to bend my head to hear them. They followed their son
from the waiting room into my office and stood in a corner, whereas
Evan immediately found the most comfortable chair, propped up his
feet, and pulled from a nearby shelf several toys that he began to take
apart right away. After I bowed to the parents, I pointed to other
comfortable chairs and suggested that we all sit down and begin the
meeting.

I have learned a great deal about working with Chinese American families, most of it from early blunders. Each family brings its
own background, pattern of immigration, structure, and family
roles to the sessions. These are often diverse, unique patterns, and I
may need to spend quite a bit of time educating them about how to
participate in this thing we call "family therapy." In general, I have
found that Asian families with a more formal, ritualized style respond best to a cautious, respectful approach that acknowledges the
importance of the family structure.[1] Still, it is this ritualized family
structure that many of the adolescents I have worked with are attempting to rebel against. Their families tend to be resistant to psychotherapy and at least initially think of me as a medical doctor.
Although I use a similar approach with all families I see as a group,
with Asian families of this type I try to offer more information about

the techniques I use and make an effort to modify my personal style to fit better with their cultural style and background.

In this initial session with Evan and his parents, I dutifully spoke first to the father, welcomed his family to my office, and mentioned our mutual acquaintance. We began indirectly by discussing several points of common interest related to the Chinese community. I turned to include the whole group to describe my approach to family therapy and then, in an indirect manner, stated that I understood that they had come to see me because of their concerns about some recent events. I asked each family member to think about what his or her own plan might be for family therapy and also asked them how they thought they could benefit from working together as a group in order to attempt to solve some of the problems they were facing.

Richard nodded and thanked me for seeing his family, again referring to our mutual connections. He began by talking about his father and his father's adolescence and moved on to talk about his own adolescence, alluding very briefly to difficulties he had experienced. Then he said that he believed that he and his wife were not working very well with their son, describing the "giant river" growing between them.

I asked Mary to speak next. She appeared to be very angry, although she was reluctant to show it. Without looking at me, she said that she was worried about the impact of Evan's problem on their entire family—aunts, uncles, cousins, and grandparents. She hoped that we could all work together to change Evan's behavior, but added somewhat bitterly that she and Richard were strongly considering having Evan leave home.

During the lengthy amount of time his parents were talking, Evan repeatedly decapitated and reattached the head of one of the dolls I keep in my office. I complimented him on his adept maneuvering of the toy but said I would appreciate it if he would reattach the head, adding that I also appreciated his remaining quiet while I talked to his parents; I recognized that that wasn't an easy thing for him.

"Yeah, you caught on, Doc," he said. "I can't listen to them, and they're always talking about this disgrace business. I just don't get it. I mean, I guess if you asked me what my agenda is, I think they really don't know what's going on here in San Francisco. I would like a larger allowance, later hours, and more money for clothes.

They don't buy me cool clothes. Just look at the two of them. Look at those button-downs they're wearing. They just don't know what's really cool out there. It's impossible to have parents like this. Maybe I should leave. You know, maybe it would work better if I had an apartment and lived alone or with a group of guys."

Evan's words don't relay his persuasive charm. He had a certain suave manner and appearance that seemed to leave his parents in the dust. I commented that I very much appreciated that he had an agenda and that I would pay attention to it—cool clothes, larger allowance, later hours—but I also told him that I was curious about his ideas about living separately from his parents. His handsome face clouded, but only for a moment, and he said, "Well, I just don't think we get along very well. I mean, they're very angry with me. I'm angry with them. We can't talk at all. Look at us—it's like we're speaking two different languages. Our family's been in San Francisco for generations, and my parents act like they just stepped off the boat. Where do they think we live, Shanghai?"

I said that San Francisco had more than a little bit of Shanghai about it, but I could understand that he felt frustrated by the fact that they really couldn't talk as a family, and it also seemed like he felt that he might be asked to leave at any moment.

He nodded to that. "Well, they've already asked me to leave. You know, before they came here, look, they thought it was either you or tough love, and they were planning to kick me out." Drawing himself up to his full height in his chair, he said, "I've been arrested, and in my family that doesn't happen."

"Unfortunately, that does happen to a lot of kids from a lot of families," I said, and then asked him to tell me about the events leading up to the arrest.

"It was just a group of guys. We were hanging out on Geary Street at night, pals and all, and then it kinda happened. You know, I was stuck with the car, and the police were all around. It was really something."

When I asked him what he meant by "really something," he gave me details. I took notes as I listened to his description of a fight with another group of boys on the Geary Street bus. "We pounded their faces until they bled." This was followed by the car theft and arrest. One thing became very clear: Evan was part of a gang. He also had been left holding the car and was taking the rap for his buddies. It was also clear that his friends meant a lot to him; it was from them that he was getting new ideas about the sort of person he was or wanted to be.

Adolescents test out new roles with groups as part of their search for individual identity. Evan clearly wasn't happy with his familial identity and was out there searching for another one. These kids helped provide it. He made several references to other groups of kids in the city, describing how they looked different from or similar to his friends. He now felt that he fit in. This was very different from his years in the private school, where he felt totally cut off.

I asked Mary and Richard what they knew about Evan's current friends, whether they had made any attempt to talk with Evan about them or to investigate. It became obvious that Evan wasn't talking with his parents about these friends. They had come to an early conclusion that these boys were gang members but they were unsure about what they could do without more information. Helping his parents to understand that they were going to have to get more involved and curious about their son's behaviors became the major task of this first session.

I began by identifying and defining Evan's behavior as risky. To do this most effectively, I referred to the notes I had carefully taken when he described the night on Geary Street that had included the fight in which a boy was badly beaten up and a car was stolen—two violent acts. I then highlighted this as very negative risk-taking with serious consequences. He grunted as I said this, but he eventually agreed that he was taking risks and said that he was proud of it. I pointed out to him that my job was to help him take risks in a more successful way, so that he wouldn't end up paralyzed by the negative consequences—dead or in jail. He conceded, though not in so many words, that this was a goal he could share.

I also told Mary and Richard that I hoped that with their wealth of experience they would be able to help their son learn how to assess and take risks in a healthier way. Part of that would involve examining why Evan had so much trouble talking with them about these issues. They nodded together at this point and said that they would like to do that, but they were unsure about how to proceed. What could they offer their son other than the exhortation to stay away from bad kids? I acknowledged that this was a good question, and said that I wanted them to think about what they had to offer Evan, particularly in terms of the formation of his identity. I also reminded them that they had known Evan his entire life and had very important relationships with him as parents. Although their influence with him was under attack, this powerful relationship gave them both knowledge and leverage with Evan, and I cautioned them not to discount it. This statement alone seemed to reignite their pride in their son and in what they had already been able to do as parents. Both of them looked at me thoughtfully.

"You Can Be One of Us, and We'll Be So Cool": Guys and Groups

Evan was very clear with me that he had never really felt like he fit in, and certainly not in the private school he had attended. Although his public school in San Francisco had a majority of Asian American students, Evan still felt "different," like he had "landed on another planet." Then guys from the Geary Street gang had reached out to him, offering him an identity that included a sense of membership and belonging that was "cool." This was a powerful magnet to a kid who felt not only different but weird.

In San Francisco in the 1990s gangs perform several functions for teenagers. Adolescents from vastly different cultural backgrounds with different beliefs, physical traits, religions, and social groupings are meeting on the streets and in the schools. Many of the once-unique cultural groups are changing, adapting to this new location and looking quite different than they did a generation, or even a decade, ago. Two or more cultures join to form a blended culture that looks very different from the original cultures. An example can be seen in kids who mix the dress, language, and attitudes of the Filipino and African American cultures. Such blendings have some unique effects on adolescents—all of whom are engaged in a search for their individual identities—and on how they take risks.

Erik Erikson introduced the concept of identity formation for teenagers, broadly describing adolescence as a developmental period when young people are struggling to shape a focused, personal identity.[2] In trying on or experimenting with different identities, adolescents may accept their parents' identity, choosing roles and values prescribed for them by parents and, by extension, society. They may search for their own identities elsewhere, trying different options and checking the personal fit. Or they may choose to remain in a more childlike state, neither accepting their parents' choices nor making their own. Children or adolescents who have begun this search early may possess values and have developed a course of action that are uniquely their own.

Mary Jane Rotheram-Borus, an investigator with many interests in the field of adolescent risk-taking, has focused a part of her work on the significant role that cultural background plays in an adolescent's search for identity. She describes how teens search for their identity in many different areas or domains—among them, sexual identity, work-related or occupational identity, philosophical or religious identity, and cultural or ethnic identity. In one of her studies she found that adolescent ethnic minorities, including samples of African American, Hispanic, and Asian adolescents, were undergoing longer periods of struggle before they made their choices, specifically in the area of ethnic or cultural identity. She believes that exploring and defining one's ethnic identity is an important developmental task for minority youth that may take more time and involve more struggle than the identity quest of an adolescent who is part of the majority culture.[3] Although this idea is somewhat controversial, other researchers have supported Dr. Rotheram-Borus's conclusion, reporting that teenagers from minority ethnic backgrounds participate in a more complex identity search that focuses on understanding their ethnicity, and that the development of their self-esteem is related to the degree to which they have thought about and resolved issues related to their ethnicity.[4]

Evan was certainly confused about his cultural background. He put part of the blame for this on his parents by suggesting that because they didn't fit in very well (at least by his perception, one that is not unusual for teens regarding their parents), he couldn't be expected to. From another perspective, his parents had worked hard to find a place for themselves in this culture, but they were afraid to look at other choices and were fearful when their son started to do so. They brought these fears to their next meeting with me, but they were already working to change them.

The Family Takes a Risk

I could tell something was different at the start of the next session with Evan and his family. First of all, they entered the room differently. Mary and Richard entered first, together, and as Richard waited for Mary to be seated first, they carefully chose the best seats before Evan could be seated. Evan appeared not to be upset by this and was smiling. He did insist on grabbing his familiar toys. When I asked how things had been going, Richard began the session by pulling out a list. Nodding carefully to me, he asked whether it was acceptable to begin immediately by talking about the work they had done. He said that they had taken to heart what I said in their first session and had tried to make some changes, beginning with an agenda, and he thanked me specifically for this idea. "First of all," he said, "we recognize that the family issue has been a problem. We have not been able to talk to our family members because we felt that they had not experienced a situation like this. This has robbed us of one of the major supports that we have."

Mary nodded and said, "I began by talking with my father about this. He suggested that it was a family problem and said to me that my brothers and sisters actually admired the way that we were raising Evan. He also mentioned that if there was a problem, that everybody in the family would be willing to help."

Richard continued. "So they have all volunteered their time, and we have come up with activities for Evan that we think will encourage healthier risk-taking in the family. First off, Grandpa is going to paint his house with Evan. Second, Evan will be going away with me. We are planning a ski trip in the mountains."

"Third," added Evan, flashing me the Marlon Brando smile, "I am going to take my dad water-skiing and teach him how to do it."

Mary then began to express some fear about her husband's health, but Richard said that he was sure that he and Evan could handle it. Everyone laughed. Their laughter illustrates an important point: a parent's physical abilities often decline as an adolescent's abilities increase. Parents who recognize and accept this process learn how to share leadership in risk-taking.

"Fourth, he is going to go with his uncle, and they are going to do some work up in the mountains on one of the family homes, maybe burning some brush and things like that. Everyone seemed to want to participate and get involved," said Richard, "once I mentioned that it was a problem. It's also surprising to me that this is a problem for my nephews, too. It hasn't just been our immediate family.

"The other thing," Richard continued, "is that I really didn't talk to Evan about my own problems when I was growing up. I was late in starting my college education because I got off track for many years, unsure about what I wanted. I hadn't told him that."

Evan then said, "When my dad started talking with me about how he got off track when he was younger, I realized I might be more like him than I thought. I told him that the Geary Street gangs are different than the old Chinatown gangs were when he was my age. I guess I hadn't really felt like I could talk to my dad about that. I felt like he didn't know anything about my problems and I didn't realize that he had been through stuff when he was young, too. I mean, the Geary Street gangs have a lot of kids who just want to be part of something. They want to be part of a group. I mean, I've been in that group. I'm actually kind of a leader there. That's why I go for it. That stuff with the car—yeah, we probably shouldn't have been doing that kind of thing. I know that. And yeah, there were older guys involved. But most of the time we're hanging out on Geary Street just riding the buses. It's not like that's the usual thing. We get involved in all kinds of other activities. It started at a Chinatown youth center actually. Most of the guys were involved there."

Richard said, "But you've got to remember, Evan, that this kind of thing just grows, it takes over your life." This comment wasn't made with reproach; Richard was just sharing information. "I guess that's what I learned. That I've been hiding stuff from Evan about my own past problems, trying to protect him, but it really wasn't working at all."

Evan then said, "And once he got started talking about this stuff, I felt like we could share information."

Mary then said, "I think we had given up. I mean, we felt like we were going to have to send him away. We were ashamed of what had happened. We weren't using the strength that we really had—I mean our family and our brains—to figure this out. But we have to thank you, too. It's just a start, and we really didn't know if we would be able to figure it out and work together."

"It is a start," I said, "but you've made a lot of progress already. I really want to hear from you, Evan, about how you see things, because I still am concerned about the whole incident with the police and everything."

"Yeah," he said. "I'm confused about it, too. I mean, I don't know how I got pulled into all that kind of stuff. I haven't felt very good about myself. I didn't feel very good about my parents then. I never felt like they really fit in here in the United States. I felt like I had a couple of dorks with me." Looking at his parents, he added, "I guess I still sometimes feel like that, but I think they're listening to me, and I realize now that they don't want me to be a dork, and that they're willing to try to make some changes, so I guess that's been the thing I've learned from them—if they can change their patterns, it makes me feel like I can, too."

This was an unusual, and unusually rapid, turnabout for beginning therapy with a family, but it demonstrates how powerful family interventions can be. (This is true in all areas of family work, not just in examinations of risk behaviors with adolescents.) Mary and Richard did not want to desert their son, but they did not feel that they had any other options. Encouraging them to use their supportive family structure and to look to their own resources led them to talk to other family members and come up with a home-therapy program for the problems they were facing. Evan, however, was just beginning his changes.

Many months of arduous therapy followed, during which Evan slowly extracted himself from a pattern of fighting and stealing, eventually leaving the Geary Street gang. It was a pivotal moment for him when he saw a member of another gang get shot and killed on the bus. What he gained over this period, though, was significant. The men in his family learned ways to provide leadership to their sons, helping them solve not only questions of ethnic identity but basic questions about identity and masculinity. Evan himself became a real leader in the family, helping his younger cousins. What Mary and Richard did as parents was get involved. Richard's fatherly input was very important, specifically because he acknowledged the attraction of engaging in risk behaviors and revealed that he had experienced problems during his own adolescence. He and Mary were willing to discuss the problem with their son with less blaming, and together they worked out a plan that would not only provide support but serve as a model for others in the family.

Many parents are afraid to interfere with their adolescents' choice of friends; a question of gang involvement can make them feel both wary and powerless. Parents can end up expressing fear or disapproval without knowing the facts. Finding out about a teen's friends is part of a parent's job. There are many ways to do this, but perhaps most important is to use the already existent relationship with their child: listening to what the child says about his or her friends, and asking about them as well. Richard shared some of his current problems with male buddies and admitted to Evan that he was still learning about friends. Parental curiosity and candor can open the door in this area, letting the teenager know that the parent, although in a different capacity, is still available.

Often parents hold back when it comes to discussing with their teen his or her relationships with friends. During the late 1960s — by which time the myth of the all-powerful teen culture had been developed — youth was characterized as part of a subculture that was strongly opposed to adults, even hostile.[5] This concept of adolescents and adults as groups in conflict has been promoted by the media and by advertisers, and many parents take the message to heart. They believe that they can no longer understand the child at thirteen whom they understood so well at ten. Instead of conceptualizing the adolescent experience as one in which very curious young people try a whole range of new ideas and behaviors, testing out what they might want to be and bringing some of these new ideas back to enrich the family, they believe that their child is joining a foreign group and will no longer want to spend any time with them or listen to their ideas. Evan's parents were paralyzed by this notion. Yet studies indicate that teens are still very attuned to parental influence and values.[6] Teens may rely on their friends regarding matters of music and entertainment and clothing, but they weigh their parents' opinions much more strongly in the areas of vocational choice and moral and social values.[7]

The amount of time that teens spend with their parents is particularly important during this period of development. Teens who spend less time with adults rely more heavily on peers. Many turn to peers because they lack a closeness with adults. It is particularly important to be aware of this tendency in boys, who spend more time in groups of same-gender peers than do girls.[8] If parents believe that their child's friends are playing a negative role, they can spend more time with their child, although this time needs to be spent doing something the teen will be interested in, specifically something that provides challenge. Danger signals in their child for parents to be alert to include both keeping friends entirely secret and suddenly losing interest in friends altogether. Even though teens may deny or minimize parental support during a period of painful rejection or unhealthy gang activities, they never forget it.

It is important for parents to remember that peers can also be a very positive influence for adolescents.[9] During their children's adolescent years parents need to serve as guides or consultants rather than autocratic limit-setters. Helping an adolescent learn that relationships are dynamic and that they change constantly is invaluable. Parents and teens can even look to their own relationship with each other as a demonstration of how relationships change over time, with circumstances, and because of individual development.

Leader of the Clique

Fourteen-year-old Cecilia was one of my best teachers on the inextricably linked power and control that operate in cliques. Cliques exert power over those they exclude, and control over those they include. Perhaps nowhere has the message of control been illustrated more clearly for me than in working with girls who are leaders in a clique.

Cecilia's parents brought her to see me because she was making or receiving roughly ten phone calls every evening and often moaning that she didn't want to go to school, that her "friends" were going to kill her. One night her parents unplugged her telephone and she threatened to kill herself, resulting in the visit to my office.

Cecilia, who had a waif-like appearance and a particularly angelic smile, began the session by tearfully pleading with me to have her parents reinstall her telephone, claiming somewhat dramatically, but with conviction, that she couldn't live without it. Gently I explored with her what she couldn't live without and in that process discovered what the phone calls were about. Cecilia would call Anne, who would call Jessica and then Mary and so on, extensively discussing their plans for the next day—what they would wear, where they would eat lunch, who they would talk to, and, yes, who they wouldn't talk to, or more forcefully exclude. After an hour and a half on the telephone all the girls knew the game plan for the next day; in effect, they had their marching orders. Cut off from the exchange because of her disconnected telephone, Cecilia was right to be worried. She was no longer in the loop. Forget about making the rules, she might not even know the rules. Her position in the clique was very much in jeopardy. How could her parents do that to her?

From Cecilia and similar patients I have learned that what kids eat, wear, say, and even think is the topic of hours of conversation. To listen to incredible minutia about groups of friends and still provide a supportive, if sometimes challenging, perspective is not easy. During my early years as an adolescent psychiatrist I often found myself becoming bored or condescending with the repetitive nature of an adolescent girl's conversation (white blouse, blue blouse . . .), but gradually I saw it as an opportunity to see what the inner world of a teenage girl really looks like. Indeed, enduring the boring, repetitive details allows girls to hold on to a tenuous identity and to avoid taking risks outside the group. Cecilia, for example, wasn't willing to take any risks, even those with obvious positive consequences. She continued to need the clique for several years to bolster her limited self-confidence. My work with her parents also took a long time, partly because they failed to see the extent of her problems—one of which was tremendous insecurity.

Confronting a Bully

Cecilia was the oldest of three daughters of two schoolteachers. Her father taught shop, and her mother history. When I first met with them, I noticed that they were kind and loving toward Cecilia, but that they were exhausted from working, ferrying their three children to after-school activities, and paying special attention to their second daughter, a child who had serious learning problems. Cecilia, their "golden girl," had never caused any problems until she started staying up until all hours to talk with her friends; after several months of this, her grades had started to drop.

During the parents' first visit with me there were several signs that all was not well. First, Cecilia's mother, Alison, fell asleep in my waiting room before our session even began. Noticing how relaxed she looked and guessing how much she needed the sleep, I was re-

luctant to wake her up. It was also apparent during this first interview that Cecilia's parents wanted me to tell them that everything
was okay.

Parents often want my reassurance, and often I am able to tell
them that things are fine; sometimes I even use that old expression
learned during my pediatric training, "Don't worry, she (he) will
grow out of it." With Cecilia's parents, I was tempted to say this. The
grades weren't too bad. I was sure that I could help the family work
out a compromise around the telephone. Then Cecilia's teacher
called me and left two messages asking that I call her back. With Cecilia's and her parents' permission, I did so. What this thirty-five-year
veteran of middle school had to say was disturbing.

"I wouldn't have called, Dr. Ponton, if it had just been all of that
stuff that girls go through with cliques, but Cecilia's always putting
herself down. At first I thought it was something that she was trying
to do to get other girls to like her. I've seen other girls do that—pretend to be dorks just to get others to like them. Then I noticed that
there was more to it. Cecilia puts herself down, but she also puts
down other girls. It's usually pretty subtle, but I saw it in a bigger
way at lunchtime yesterday, and then again today. Cecilia was encouraging two girls to make fun of another. They were shouting
some song at her. The girl was crying, and Cecilia was smiling."

"Did you talk with Cecilia about what you saw?" I asked.

"No, and I should have. I'm not sure I would know how to go
about it. I mean, this innocent, blue-eyed angel with the low self-
esteem is torturing other girls. It's not that easy to observe, let alone
confront her about it. Maybe I'm also a little afraid of her."

I agreed with her that it could be painful to watch such behavior.
"Angels" like Cecilia are not supposed to torment other children. I,
too, had been fooled, and Cecilia certainly wasn't talking about this
bullying behavior in her sessions with me. After I hung up the
phone and thought more about it, I realized that Cecilia had been
giving me hints that I had overlooked. In our last session she had
talked about a girl who was a bully and had to be shown how to act
on the playground. Cecilia and her friends (the telephone army) had
told the girl that they wouldn't be friends with her if she acted like
that. Acted like what, I now wondered.

In our next session I asked Cecilia about the "bully" on the playground and what had gone on there. Very reluctantly she told me

that this girl still followed her and her army of friends around, constantly asking them why she was no longer their friend. Who would want to be friends with a girl like that, she again asked rhetorically.

"Yes, who would?" I echoed. I then told Cecilia that her teacher—whose permission to discuss this I had obtained—and I had spoken, and that she was very worried about how Cecilia was feeling about herself and the way she was acting with the other girls at school.

"Did she say anything more about it?" she asked quietly.

"What do you think she might have said?"

"I don't know," she said sadly.

My own feelings about what to do next were very mixed. I try to be straightforward with the teens I work with, letting them know where I'm coming from. Hiding things from them not only doesn't work well but adds to their suspicions about adults. I spend time obtaining permission from teachers and parents and informing them that I will use the information so that I can more honestly discuss important issues. At this point with Cecilia, however, my courage was slipping. Maybe I could get out of this situation by commenting on how sad she looked and hope that she would bring it up. Confronting bullies—children and teens who employ violent, coercive methods with their peers—is not easy. The bully can just as easily turn into a sad-faced child like Cecilia was becoming. However, if a therapist who studied teen risk-taking looked away from this, how would that leave Cecilia feeling about her behavior?

Slowly I said, "Cecilia, the problems you are having with the girls appear to be pretty complicated. You talk with me about the bullying things that you see other girls do, how you're afraid of them and try to stop their behavior, but your teacher also said that she's seen you bullying other girls."

"When? Who? Where?" she asked.

"Sounds like I'd be presenting courtroom evidence to you, and I'm not sure that I want to get into that with you."

In fact, at this point in our session I wasn't sure what direction I wanted to go with Cecilia. I had confronted her about the bullying; it was a first step, but I knew it was going to take a lot of work on both our parts. What impressed me was how much effort it had taken to get even this far with her. I decided to repeat exactly what her teacher had described to me, including the chanting.

"I suppose you want to know what the song was," she said bitterly.

"If you want to tell me," I said. "I think it's important that we understand it."

"We called her a whore and told her we didn't want to be with her because she was one," she said, stony-faced.

"What do you think about that now?"

"I don't know. Telling you about it makes me feel better somehow. I don't know why, maybe I hope someone will be able to understand why I'm doing this and why I feel so badly."

"Cecilia, it's not that easy to understand. It will take a lot of work, but it's really important that you told me."

What unfolded in the next session was exactly how Cecilia had tortured this particular girl and others, first taking away their friends, painfully isolating them, and then humiliating them with painful taunting. What was also clear was that Cecilia did not feel very good about herself. She described an episode years earlier in which she had been attacked by another girl and humiliated before several of her classmates, and said she had been shocked when none of her peers had helped her out. Afterward she felt terrible. Then she and her attacker became close friends, a friendship in which Cecilia learned the tools for scapegoating others.

The next part of the work with Cecilia's parents was also difficult. I told them what the teacher had said. They expressed considerable surprise, and it was only several weeks later in a different session that they were able to discuss it at all. Cecilia's mother appeared to have thought more about it than her father.

"What you said really surprised us," Alison began, "but then it was also surprising when she threatened to kill herself after we disconnected her phone. We know that Cecilia doesn't feel very good about herself and things can get twisted when that happens. I spend a lot of my time driving her around to activities to build her self-esteem, but I can see that there's more to it than that. How does that translate into hurting others? I feel like I've missed it somehow with her."

Alison's thoughtful comments have been echoed by scores of other parents over the years in my office. Not all adolescents with low self-esteem end up bullying other kids; why do some?

In general, the early teenage years are not a developmental period in which individuals feel good about themselves. This is true for both boys and girls, but boys are reported to recover their self-esteem more rapidly than girls do. Girls who experience early physical development are especially delayed in this recovery. Although Cecilia did not fall into this category, and she was not preoccupied with weight or suffering from a diagnosable eating disorder such as anorexia or bulimia nervosa, she was very concerned about her appearance. Unfortunately for adolescent girls, self-esteem is often significantly related to how they feel about their appearance.

Over time I learned from Cecilia that she didn't like many aspects of herself. She believed that she was dumb, ugly, and a poor athlete. She did acknowledge that she had some social skills, and this admission of strength gave us the opportunity to discuss her bullying behavior more directly. As she described it, she still saw herself as a victim, even when she was intimidating other girls. The victim attitude had somehow combined with the scapegoating skills she learned from her "friend," the one who had started out humiliating her years before.

"I realize now that I get carried away with it, but I know that they would get me back if I didn't do it to them first."

"So it's a matter of safety—do it to them before they do it to you?"

"Yes. No. What can I say? It feels safer to hurt others before they hurt me. It's also starting to feel pretty vicious to me. Honestly, I don't know if this is coming out of our talks here or is something that I've always felt."

She smiled when I agreed with her that it was probably both and complimented her on her ability to work on a part of herself that was both complicated and unattractive. Things were slowly starting to change for Cecilia at school. She realized that she had felt badly after she was humiliated in front of her class by the "friend" several years earlier. That episode had left her both angry and fearful, wanting to fight back. Now she was beginning to see that hurting other girls as a way to handle these feelings was harmful for both the girls and herself. One afternoon Cecilia refused to gang up with her bully friends and, when they turned on her, even told them to drop it. At first they made fun of her—the reaction she most feared—but then they let her alone, and she noticed that other girls started to speak up for themselves.

Cecilia's parents also stuck with it, coming to understand their daughter more clearly than most parents do and being supportive of the changes she had to make.

The boundary between the "abused" and the "abuser," illustrated here by Cecilia, is not always clear. Girls with low self-esteem may participate in either type of behavior. A girl who is being bullied and scapegoated can be doing the same things to other girls at the very same time. Children learn from other children, particularly if they don't have adult input. Parents need to understand that children and adolescents don't automatically know how to make and be friends with others. It is a gradual process, and many lessons are learned the hard way. Parents can be a tremendous support by letting their adolescents know they're available to listen and by encouraging them to try new relationships if current ones are painful. If parents observe severe scapegoating from either side of the fence, it is important to become more involved, helping their child to get the assistance he or she needs.

The School as an Ally

It is important for parents to realize that serious scapegoating that includes physical violence or sexual harassment can occur and that it can happen to any child. Episodes of sexual harassment, defined as unwelcome sexual attention,[10] are most frequently seen at the high school level, showing up in either physical activities, such as grabbing, or verbal or written activities, such as spreading rumors about topics related to sexuality. Such episodes are much more commonly reported by girls, and physical violence episodes are more commonly reported by boys. Still, teens of either gender may find themselves victims of either abusive activity. Education and prevention programs that address both violent and harassing behaviors need to be developed and individually tailored for several important groups, including teens, parents, teachers, and school administrators. Administrative follow-through on consequences is an important component of any school policy on harassment or violence. Making sure that a school has policies that address violent, harassing behaviors *and* follows up on them is an important role for any parent.[11]

Parents can take a role at the school or community level, but their most important role is to be available to listen to their own child. Teens don't necessarily talk easily about their friends, particularly when they are the brunt of painful attacks or are committing them. Here is where developing an ability to hang out with a teenager is important. There are many ways to do this, and an important one is nonverbal. It is necessary for the parent to spend some time when he or she appears essentially idle to the teen, sending the young person the signal that he or she is available for conversation. Lying on the couch in the living room or riding in an automobile together can provide such opportunities. If possible, that time should be essentially alone with the teen, with no siblings or friends present. Problems with friends are not something that teens want spread all over the neighborhood by a younger brother or sister. Parents can also promote discussions of friends by letting their teen know that they, too, have faced tough decisions with their friends or coworkers and have solved difficult situations.

It is often difficult for parents to believe that *their* child could participate in harming others. The expected parental resistance to such an idea makes it all the more important that parents listen when they hear even a small clue about this type of risk behavior. Initially listening can provide more information than confrontation does, but at some point parents do have to confront the behavior more directly, as I had to do with Cecilia. This is often a particularly difficult step for parents, but it can lead to important information about what lies behind the abuse of peers.

Getting Help for Abusers

Abuse of peers is an important signal that a teenager is having trouble. Disagreements with friends are not abuse. Dangerously conflictual behavior can be recognized by some of the following signals: physically or sexually violent behavior with peers; calls from teachers who have directly observed the behaviors; use of weapons; peer activity involving illegal substances and/or violent behavior, regardless of whether it is identified as gang-related; and any type of abusive behavior that results in trouble with police.

With this type of unhealthy risk-taking, I encourage parents to err on the side of being proactive because the consequences can be serious and sudden, occurring before a parent becomes fully aware of the problem. This is also an area that many parents cannot tackle alone; they need to get help so that they don't feel defeated before they've even begun. Parents with allies—teachers, counselors, family members—do better. One of the reasons Evan improved so quickly was that his parents were able to marshal the whole family as a resource.

Failing to assist a teen whose behavior has become abusive can have dire consequences. These kids can become permanent players in the legal system. Dangerous risk-taking becomes a permanent part of their lives, and a timely opportunity for intervention and assistance is gone forever.

Chapter Twelve

Fighting Back

I had a choice: go along with it all or not be popular.

—Eva

*Boys are supposed to be strong, tough, not stupid
enough to let this kind of stuff happen.*

—Jim

Both Eva and Jim were badly mistreated by their
peers. Whereas Eva's mother was overinvolved with
what was going on between Eva and her friends, Jim
never felt that he could even share with his parents
what had happened to him. Parents who make themselves available to their adolescents without becoming overly involved or identified with the peer
struggles their teens may have to face and overcome
can help their kids both to develop appropriate
strengths and coping strategies and to avoid seeing
themselves as victims. If such experiences and feelings go unaddressed, teens who have been abused by
peers are vulnerable to risk behaviors and a host of
other psychological problems.

In the winter of 1963 I was in the sixth grade, attending a small
public grade school in Cleveland, Ohio. I remember that winter
for two reasons: a giant storm kept my family and me, as well as the

rest of Cleveland, snowed in for several days, and my best friend Pam turned most of the girls in our sixth-grade class against me.

It began at a sleep-over at Pam's home to celebrate her twelfth birthday. Nine girls from our class crowded into a newly constructed and decorated family room—a design concept of the 1960s complete with television, stereo, and Swedish-style couches—for what I imagined would be the sleep-over of my dreams. It started out that way. Elvis was crooning "Blue Hawaii" on the record player, and we all started dancing. I was in heaven until I noticed that Sally, a new girl in our class, was practically swooning over Pam. After Sally had held her arms around Pam for several dances, I noticed that they were laughing, whispering, and pointing at me. At first I tried to shrug it off, imagining that I hadn't seen it, and went to the kitchen with another friend, Valerie, to make ice cream sodas.

An hour later I noticed that neither Sally nor Pam was talking to me. They wouldn't say why but continued to laugh and point at me. Again I decided to ignore it, but I was beginning to get worried. Pam and I had been friends for three years. We had transferred to our school together, and I believed that we had built this sixth-grade girls' clique together. We had fought a few times but then made up with long discussions on the telephone that ran late into the evening. Packing up my sleeping bag after the party, I was already beginning to wonder whether this "fight" wasn't going to be like the others. That Sunday evening I waited for an apologetic phone call from Pam, but it never came.

The next day at school was torture for me. Pam, Sally, and five of the other girls from the sleep-over weren't talking to me, but they were certainly talking *about* me to everyone else. I felt like I had entered the whispering gallery at the local fun house, where you hear voices mentioning your name and yet have absolutely no idea what they're saying. Pam, Sally, and the others organized into small groups that would sneak up on me when I was on the playground or walking home from school and point, laugh, and whisper. Valerie, who had made the ice cream sodas with me at the slumber party when Sally was dancing with her arms around Pam, stood by me, offering sage advice for a twelve-year-old. "Lynn, Sally is bad news. She turned Pam against you. I've heard she did that to a girl at her old school. It was nothing personal. It happens to a lot of kids. She wanted to be popular; Pam was the most popular girl in the class, so she needed her as a best friend. It's simple. You had to go."

Although Valerie saw it as a simple matter, and certainly not as a personal one, it didn't feel that way to me. My days were filled with visions of whispering girls who wouldn't talk to me, and my nights, formerly filled with long conversations with Pam and the other girls, now consisted of mysterious phone calls from callers who would either say nothing or whisper unintelligibly.

Ironically, this bitter experience with Pam and Sally marked the beginning of my own curiosity about how teenagers think, act, and feel. It was also as a result of this experience that I fell out of a trap common to many teens: searching for popularity. Many nights I lay awake thinking about Pam's betrayal, Sally's ability to woo her away, and the simple fact that my so-called friends, other than Valerie, had not stood by me. For a while I couldn't stop imagining what they might be saying about me. Then I started to learn how to look beyond the faces and the words searching for friendship and loyalty. These were difficult lessons in a painful time. At first I wanted nothing more than to be back in the clique, best friends with Pam. It was only much later that I realized what I had learned: I didn't need to be part of any clique.

Girls' cliques are small, tight groups of friends who generally share some expressed, mutual purpose. Cliques are common, beginning with the later years of elementary school and sometimes extending into the college years. Their popularity, however, seems to peak during the middle-school years—sixth, seventh, and eighth grades—and diminish in high school.[1] Many middle-school cliques are organized around the common purpose of maintaining the members' popularity. Some cliques are relatively harmless, and it is healthy and normal for kids this age to want to spend time with their friends. But cliques can have a darker side, introducing children and teens to power and pain, betrayal and exclusion. Those who are excluded may end up harassed. Those who give up their personal values in order to maintain their membership in the clique may lose their self-respect. Cliques are also vulnerable to coups and power plays; naïveté is generally not a long-lived trait in any member.

The role of parents in this process is a curious one. Often ignorant about the darker side of their child's involvement in a clique until it has developed savage proportions, they may become aware of it when their child is attacked on the playground by other children—for the third time, they discover. Or parents may hear on the family's answering machine the twisted voice of scapegoating, aiming strings of obscenities at their child. They may come to know about it from another parent who alludes to their child's rejection, unaware that the parent of that child is in the dark.

I have asked the children and teens I see who are scapegoated why they don't tell their parents. Many, particularly former members of a clique, still maintain the group's secrecy and power, declaring that it's personal business and can be discussed only with kids in the group. Of course, that leaves young people quite isolated if no one in their former group or in the classroom is speaking to them. A second reason given by adolescents for not telling their parents is that they worry about the impact their personal rejection will have on them. These young people feel that their parents will be badly hurt (as they have been hurt) by the news that their child not only is unpopular but is being openly scapegoated by other kids. A third reason to stay silent, kids say, is that they feel humiliated; even talking about the experience is difficult and reactivates their pain. Whatever its origins, their silence is unfortunate, because parents can offer their children much needed support. There are pitfalls, however, and parents do best by adopting a middle road between supportive availability and active intervention.

The following two cases illustrate how painful peer interaction can be for teens and inform us about the role of parents in these struggles. In addition, these stories underscore the dangerous risk in scapegoating, which can harm both the intended victim and the abuser.

Best Friends Forever: The Pain of Separating

Eva's mother was calling to request an evaluation for her fourteen-year-old daughter. She left a very pressured message on my answering machine: "Dr. Ponton, you've got to take us on. We're in deep trouble. She's been badly hurt. The whole school is against us right now. Please help." I was troubled by the message, but not totally surprised. Aside from my own painful experience, I have certainly become familiar with adolescent scapegoating through my work with its victims, and I partly recognized that this plea for help fell into that category. It was also not so surprising to me that the mother would initiate the call. Very few adolescents schedule an initial appointment with me on their own. What was particularly striking about Eva's mother's call was that she was so directly connecting her own pain with her daughter's. It was *their* pain; the whole school was against *them*. In some ways I was glad that this close identification was so explicit at the beginning of the request for treatment—I hoped that it would give us something to work with.

Eva and her mother Rachel arrived for the first session together. Eva was a very attractive girl with golden brown curls in a bouncy ponytail. Rachel was approximately forty years older than her daughter, but they were dressed in identical pale green sweaters. They laughed at the same moments and also began to tell me the story at the same time. Perplexed at first by the Doublemint mother-daughter combo, I began my meeting with them by commenting that I wanted to hear each of their stories but thought it was important that they tell them separately.

Eva began to tell her story of the rejection. She was a good storyteller and gave a painful, though somewhat dramatic description of coming to feel totally rejected by a group of girls at her school with whom she had been friends. The group had bonded together the year before and were a small clique that described itself as "Best Friends Forever." After a fateful slumber party (perhaps these are more common than any of us realize), Eva found that the girls were no longer speaking to her and that she was no longer included in their activities. Several weeks later she began to receive a series of hate letters that were particularly painful, making fun of her physical appearance and illustrated with cruel, sharply sarcastic cartoons. The hate letters were followed by equally cruel phone calls. Eva summed up her story by saying that she felt that she was "pretty much over it" but agreed with her mother that she would like someone to talk to about it. She seemed reassured when I mentioned to her that I'd seen many teenage girls who had been scapegoated. In fact, I was already sure—my own bias notwithstanding—that even at this first meeting Eva was on her way to recovery when she mentioned with a half-laugh that she'd become interested in the psychology of teenagers, at least in part to understand what was happening.

Eva's mother was at a very different stage of coping with the situation. Rachel happened to work with the mother of another girl in the clique, Jennifer, who was the most likely sender of the letters. Rachel felt that just as Eva had been very much humiliated at school, she now was being humiliated by Jennifer's mother. The women remained cool and cordial with each other in the work setting, but Rachel often found herself so angry at Jennifer's mother that she had to leave work rather than scream at her. According to Rachel, her anger was focused on the fact that Jennifer and her mother had "one-upped" Eva and Rachel. Rachel also mentioned that she had contacted the school after the first hate letters started coming but felt that that action had backfired: the school had done nothing to be helpful to Rachel and Eva and, if anything, had been more supportive of Jennifer and her mother.

I already knew that Rachel was too involved with her daughter. I wondered what could be behind it. Her concern and her interactions with the school were certainly positive on the surface, but I sensed that deeper down Rachel believed that the attack suffered by her daughter somehow had been aimed at her.

My first session alone with Eva was also informative. Although she was angry with Jennifer and with her school (for "taking Jenny's side," as she put it), she was successfully struggling to understand what had happened to her and to develop some perspective. "I felt betrayed, but in a way I'm glad it happened. I think for myself now. I had always relied on the clique. If they wore pink, I wore pink. If they didn't like a girl, I didn't like her. If they didn't like math, I didn't like math."

"It didn't leave you a lot of room, did it?"

She flashed me a big smile. "I had a choice: go along with it all or not be popular. I think I secretly hated it." She paused. "Yeah, I went along with it, but maybe Jennifer and the others knew how I felt."

"Maybe they did. What do you think they guessed about you?"

Her smile spread slowly this time. "You mean that they could have seen things inside of me that I didn't even know were there? I think you're right about that, because I think I was already starting to show them that I didn't want to be part of the clique. I mean, if they were all wearing pink, I would want to wear blue. I would feel myself beginning to like math even though the girls were all saying that they couldn't do it. It was tough—I was beginning to be different. I guess they saw that. I know they saw that before I did in some ways."

There was a long pause, and she slowly said, "I still wanted to be friends with them, though."

"Losing the relationships was hard for you," I acknowledged.

"Yeah," she said, "I really still don't know why it happened. I mean, it's the friendship thing I can't understand. You know, why did they stop being friends with me? Was there something wrong with me?"

"You talk pretty freely about knowing that you weren't following the rules of the clique, that you were slowly breaking away. And yet you seem stuck, Eva, on this whole friendship business, the 'liking you' part. Do you think maybe this wasn't totally about friendship?"

"You mean it could really be about the rules? That I wasn't following the rules? That I wasn't the clique member I had been before, and they were trying to get back at me for certain things? I've thought about that. I mean, my parents have a lot more money than Jennifer's parents. There was always a kind of jealousy there. Then when I started to not follow the rules, they kind of jumped on me." She was making connections pretty quickly. "So it's not all about friendship, this kind of thing. And if it's not about friendship, it's about something else. Control," she said slowly. "Who's in charge. That kind of thing."

"Power," I said.

"Yeah. It's about who's in charge and power. And it was kind of always about that. I mean, as long as we each followed the rules, we had the power. Maybe because I wanted to wear a blue sweater, I was affecting the clique's power. They didn't have control over everybody anymore because they didn't have control over me."

"So it's hard to be in a clique like this if you don't follow the rules," I said.

"And they're there," she said. "They're just kind of underground. They aren't called 'rules' either. But you have to go along with them."

Eva had already begun to be curious about the process and to not take it too personally. In this respect, she was different from many girls who have come to see me because of a difficult clique or experiences of being scapegoated. Two negative patterns commonly emerge. Many girls blame themselves and dissect their appearance, their background, and their family, searching for something they may have done to cause a situation that has brought them so much pain. They may also begin to see themselves as victims, subject to evil forces outside of their control. If they remain locked into either of these positions, it can be quite dangerous. Blaming herself gives a young girl the idea that something is permanently wrong with her and contributes to what is often a lifelong search for that damaging and damaged trait. Identifying herself as a victim can also be a serious problem, coloring the way she sees her teenage years and future.

It is an important first step to acknowledge that something outside of your control has been done to you. Eva saw that quickly — Jennifer had orchestrated something that Eva really had no choice about. In many ways Eva's mother was still taking the position of victim: "They did this to us." Because of her curiosity and a strong sense of herself, Eva was able to explore what had been happening with her friends.

With some assistance, Eva was able to take a second step, to stand back and try to look at what was motivating the group of girls. This wasn't easy. The language of girls this age can be confusing; it includes the following questions, asked silently or even aloud, on a daily basis: "Do you like me? Are you still my friend?" (Remember, Eva's clique called itself "Best Friends Forever"—pretty reassuring until it isn't true anymore.) But again, the language clouds the underlying issues embedded in the dual nature of cliques, the good and the bad. Cliques provide friendship, but they are not just about affection. They can provide both identity and a sense of power. Those on the inside may want to feel that they have something special; their subsequent behavior often makes those on the outside feel excluded and lacking. Cliques provide a place where girls are "known," but a price is paid to be part of them. Eva was able to see that although the language was one of friendship, the underlying message was about control. In many ways this is not so different from boys' gangs, although in cliques physical violence plays a less important role.

Mothering Beyond the Call

Rachel identified herself completely with Eva's rejection, which, from her perspective, had been directed at them both. The identical pale green sweaters purchased by Rachel were a sign of the difficulty she was having separating from her daughter, who, after all, was already able to wear a blue sweater on a pink-sweater day.

Eventually Rachel told me that she, too, had been scapegoated by a group of girls when she was Eva's age. It had been very painful. In fact, she still didn't trust groups of women together and worried that they might be whispering about her behind her back. In certain ways the clique of her own youth still exerted its power over Rachel, even four decades later. She still listened for its excluding voices and followed the unspoken command: twin-sweater sets for best friends.

As we spoke about her daughter's situation, Rachel could see that the clique was still a dominant influence in her life. She was still afraid of it. Although she was able to admit that it was mostly in her head, she was genuinely frightened by Jennifer's mother and described to me how she believed Jennifer and her mother together were attempting to destroy Rachel and Eva. She alerted me to a story receiving wide coverage in the media at that time, about a mother who hired someone to kill a girl who got to be a cheerleader when the mother's own daughter didn't. I told Rachel that I had seen mothers who were both overidentified with their daughters and extremely vindictive, but that it wasn't usually the case. It might be that Jennifer's mother was misinformed about the events. I asked Rachel exactly what had happened with the school.

Rachel had called them, describing how her daughter was excluded from the group by Jennifer, and then had sent them copies of the two hostile letters Eva received, supposedly from Jennifer. The school initially expressed support and called a meeting with both girls and their mothers to discuss the events. Rachel believed that things were somehow turned topsy-turvy at that meeting—that Jennifer had ended up looking like the victim, punished by the action Rachel and Eva had taken in contacting the school.

"How could that happen?" I asked.

She thought about it for a few moments and then said, "You

know, maybe it had something to do with the way we went about it. I mean, I don't think that either Jennifer or Eva was comfortable with the group format the school used to handle the situation. It might have been better if they had either met with Jennifer and Eva directly, or maybe with Jennifer's mother and me together, without the girls." She added slowly, "It does seem as if things have gotten blown out of proportion."

Maybe Jennifer and her mother weren't plotting against Eva and Rachel and were upset about the sequence of events, too. Rachel also admitted to me that information about the whole series of events had, of course, leaked out to other girls in Jennifer and Eva's class, and that there had been some negative consequences for both of the girls. I told Rachel that events like this were difficult to handle. Schools had experience with scapegoating, but even in the best-planned conference things can go wrong.

Rachel looked straight at me for a full minute and then said, "I was reluctant to go directly to Jennifer's mother. I mean, I guess I was afraid of her and saw her as the kind of scapegoating person that I had been exposed to as a teenager. I was sure she'd take her daughter's side under that kind of pressure. You know, now I'm not even sure that her daughter wrote the letters. I think so, but the truth is that I'm not sure about it. I wonder if I could try to talk to her again. A lot of water under the bridge at this point, but maybe I could try again, or ask the school for another meeting with just the two of us."

After that session Rachel was able to talk with the school, and they did support her suggestion to meet again—once with the girls, and once with the two mothers. These meetings went better than the first one had. At this point Eva and Jennifer were almost friends again, or at least uneasy admirers of each other. And Rachel and Jennifer's mother were able to sympathize with each other around the difficulties of parenting a teenage girl who is gripped by concerns about cliques and popularity.

At home Rachel was finally able to pull back from her overly close identification with Eva. Although the rejection by the clique had been painful for Rachel, it was Eva's rejection. Rachel was a strong mother, and Eva needed her very much at this point to reinforce the self-confidence that she had helped Eva build, to be a good listener, and to help her daughter think about and try out new solutions to this difficult situation. Gradually she was able to let go—not only of Eva but of fears from her own past.

As an aside, an "overly involved" parent is not the worst thing that I see in my work with teens and parents. Most such mothers and fathers need only a small amount of guidance to modify their behavior. As Rachel was able to step back, Eva found herself with the necessary room to separate from her mother and did not have to join a clique to break free. She had the self-confidence to be on her own outside a clique, independently choosing her friends. In contrast to Eva and Rachel, the following case demonstrates the problems that can arise for the victim of peer abuse when parents are too uninvolved.

"So You Want to Play Ball with Us?": Scapegoating and Boys

Although many girls have come to see me about problems with scapegoating—or at the very least, with feeling painfully excluded by friends—it is not a common complaint of teenage boys. Even in the context of groups of friends, or gangs in some cases, boys don't tend to see their lives in high school in terms of relationships or relationship dynamics.

Upsetting events with high school friends may haunt the adult life of anyone, and men, although reluctant and less familiar with the language, may seek answers in therapy as adults. Often initially bothered about something else, such as lack of energy, unmanageable anger, or an inability to perform at work, they will not take too long before expressing curiosity about a disturbing event in high school that they cannot forget. It is important to know about this "hidden" problem to be aware of the impact that cruel peer groups can have on boys.

Jim, a set designer in his twenties, came to see me about his difficulties completing his designs on the computer screen. He explained the problem concisely: "I start the design with a lot of excitement. Then the initial drawings are done and I'm usually pretty happy. I have only a few tasks left to finish, yet it either takes me a very long time or I can't complete it."

Jim and I had met twice before he mentioned that he had recurring daydreams that interrupted his work at the computer screen; he told me about them only when I directly asked him about what he was thinking when his work was interrupted. These daydreams, visions of men or boys engaged in violent physical altercations with each other, were sexually stimulating for Jim; some of the sequences would make their way into his artwork in the form of cartoonish drawings of men beating each other up.

After Jim told me about this, I asked some more questions about the content of the daydream, and before long he recalled an event that had occurred the summer before his freshman year in high school. He had been invited to play baseball with three boys who were athletic and popular and had never invited him to play with them before. Jim remembered himself as a stocky, uncoordinated child, but at the time the boys asked him to play ball he had been losing weight and gaining pride in his developing athletic skills. He recalled how much fun the ball game was, but when it was over and the four of them were hanging around the bike rack without a whole lot to do, two of the group jumped on top of him. One held him down and the other hit him repeatedly, a steady rain of blows lasting several minutes without a pause.

The third boy, with whom Jim had felt more friendly, watched and ignored Jim's pleas for help. Jim remembered that when the boy on top of him began to pull at his underpants, Jim pushed him off his stomach at the same time that he heard his underpants rip. He didn't remember exactly what happened after that, but he described running as fast as he could and getting on his bike and pedaling furiously, afraid to look back. Jim recalled feeling embarrassed, afraid to tell his parents about what had happened to him, sure that they would see him as both "a sissy" and stupid.

In fact, Jim never did tell his parents about what happened to him that day; instead, he hid the incident deep inside, hoping that he could forget about it. And though his daydreams were somewhat thinly disguised memories, Jim did forget most of the details of the incident until he was sitting with me in my office ten years later. At the time something strange began to happen. Just weeks after he was attacked, he found himself increasingly fascinated with men and boys beating each other up. He began to daydream about it, draw pictures of it, and attend movies that featured such sequences.

Years later he expressed to me his embarrassment over being sexually stimulated by these images.

When Jim talked with me about these images, he also mentioned that the person he identified with in the fantasy or movie fight sequence could shift. He could be the man lying on the ground, his arms stretched above his head, or he could be the aggressor, pummeling the weaker boy, the one who beats him until the blood runs out of the side of his mouth and then rips his underwear.

Until he came to my office Jim had never spoken about this event with anyone. When we began to discuss the day of the baseball game, he was shocked by the strength of his own feelings—the surreal sense that time had stood still and he was still being held on the ground and hit as he spoke to me, and the tremendous sense of betrayal by the boys, especially the boy he thought was his friend. But what eclipsed all other feelings in Jim's mind was the physical nature of the memory, the pounding of fists on his weak body, and the overwhelming sense of powerlessness. In his fantasies of physical assault, Jim relived these two sensations over and over again. His long-standing refusal to talk about the event with anyone had helped to keep it a frozen high-school memory, repressed, but preserved in an aberrant form, both in his fantasies and in his artwork.

Jim and I discussed why he felt that he couldn't talk to others about what had happened to him. He mentioned that he would have liked to tell his father at the time, but a couple of things had stopped him. First, he had felt that he should have been able to take care of himself. "Boys are supposed to be strong, tough, not stupid enough to let this kind of stuff happen. Telling a parent would have made me feel even weaker. Of course, now I can see it differently. Talking with people about something like this *can* make you stronger, but it's sure not the way that I saw it then. Telling my dad would have made me seem like a real sissy, and then, I think I was also protecting him. Having a son who gets beaten up even makes him look like a sissy."

Jim remembered his father as a kindly man, gentle and soft-spoken. Looking back as an adult, he was now sure that his father would have not only stood by him but even offered wisdom, helping Jim to understand what the other boys did and his own reactions to it, and providing supportive words that would have taken away some of Jim's shame. Again, the important question was why Jim didn't go to his father when it happened. Part of the answer began to emerge.

Jim remembered his father as a "Lone Ranger." He worked in New York City for one of the major newspapers; it was an important job that he did well, and a source of pride to their family. He left the house early in the morning, catching an "early bird special," and returned home at six, tired. Jim's father worked with men—aggressive, outspoken union leaders; strong truck drivers who distributed the papers; and persistent, independent "reporter types"—but Jim didn't see this side to his dad's life. He saw a tired, kindly man who fell asleep in front of the television, his newspaper fallen into his lap. Jim wasn't sure whether his father knew how to handle "groups of guys," let alone guys who would beat you up. Years later, when his dad shared some of the stories about the paper—strikes, lawsuits, and fights—Jim figured that his father actually knew quite a lot about conflict among males, but it was a little too late for the boy who got beaten up playing baseball that summer.

"If only we had talked more about this kind of stuff earlier—if only I knew that most boys get beaten up—then I wouldn't have felt like I had to hide it."

Jim described his hometown as one that a Marlon Brando character could have lived in, or Bruce Springsteen sung about—a man's town, at least in the eyes of an adolescent boy. Gangs of boys circled the middle school on their bikes and the high school in their cars or on motorcycles. Jim wanted desperately to belong, to be, in essence, what he thought of at the time as a man. Instead, he felt humiliated at having been a victim.

Boys as Victims

Jim is one of many men who have come to see me in their twenties or thirties and unfolded a story about being abused as children. Both physical and sexual abuse are underreported by boys.[2] Our culture does not look kindly upon "victims," whether male or female, but males who have been victimized may be even more prone to feelings of intense shame because our culture places such a premium on male strength and self-sufficiency.

Typically, girls are members of cliques and boys are members of gangs. Part of the difference is purely semantic, but there is also some real distinction. Both cliques and gangs are made up of groups of teens or preteens who engage in activities and hang out together. One gender difference between boys' and girls' groups is that male gangs may perpetrate physical violence against others or use it as a means of initiation, although that difference is slowly changing as girls form gangs and participate in groups characterized by violence.[3]

The use of physical violence clearly alters the scapegoating experience. Jim's strongest memories of the entire episode were of being held down and hit. The physical experience clearly intensified the scapegoating event for him. Because of his age at the time, the violence also affected his developing sexuality. Though certainly not pleasurable in any conventional way, physical pain can be strangely processed as a kind of "stimulation"; for both males and females, an experience of violence at an age when sexuality is emerging can become intricately interwoven into the sexual fantasies of the adult that child becomes. For many years after he was beaten, Jim "needed" the violent fantasies rooted in that event to have a sexual climax. It is also important to notice the type and amount of abuse that Jim was involved in. The boys jumped on him, held him down, and pulled down his underwear. This is all that he remembered later, yet it had a significant impact on his sexual experiences and self-esteem until he came for psychiatric treatment. Remember that he came to see me more than ten years after the scapegoating had taken place. This delay and the crucial time in his development at which he was beaten allowed the scapegoating to work its way into Jim's character. His case underscores the importance of early recognition and treatment of this problem.

Although men don't talk about abuse, it shows up in many other ways. Men who have been sexually abused as children have higher rates of drug and alcohol abuse, lower self-esteem, and increased depression.[4] They also place themselves in other high-risk situations. Mark Lodico, a psychologist who works at the Bayview Hunter's Point community research site in San Francisco, has studied adolescents who report being sexually abused. One of his most important findings is that those who have been sexually abused either as children or as teens are more likely to become involved in coercive sex, either as the aggressor (forcing someone else to have sex) or as the victim (being forced by someone else to have sex). Girls who have been abused are more likely to be victims but are twice as likely to force someone else into sexual activity as girls who have not been abused. Boys who have been sexually abused are four times more likely to force someone else to have sex, but almost six times more likely to be sexually victimized again, compared with a group of boys who reported no abuse.[5]

Dr. Lodico and I have also discussed the importance of abusive episodes, whether physical or sexual, as "initiators" into rapidly established patterns of abuse for boys or girls. His work has shown that physical or sexual abuse experiences not only can increase teens' participation in coercive sexual behavior but also can increase their participation in a whole range of potentially dangerous risk behaviors. For example, adolescents who have been sexually abused are more likely to practice self-mutilation (see chapter 8).[6] Whether the initiating experience was physical or sexual abuse—and even in those cases where no painful abuse episode lies beneath the surface—it is important for parents to recognize that when unhealthy patterns develop, a teen needs assistance.

Recognizing the Importance of Peers

Early recognition of the problems resulting for boys from experiences of abuse would not only reduce their pain and interrupt the disturbing sequence of symptoms and risk behaviors that can also follow, it would limit the therapeutic effort necessary to restore the boy to a happier life. Boys need to know that despite cultural stereotypes and expectations, if they are victimized, they can talk about it with their parents and that their parents will be supportive. Remember that Jim felt that he couldn't tell anyone: "These things don't happen to boys or men." It is also important that parents increase their awareness about the importance of peer groups to boys. Simply put, boys spend more time in peer groups than girls do. These groups perform a vital function in the socialization of all young boys, transmitting roles and values. Peer groups are even more important in the lives of boys whose father is absent.[7] Many boys have no one available to talk to about these matters. In contrast, adolescent girls spend more time with their mothers and other adult women; for example, girls are often directed in their after-school activities by women rather than directing the activities themselves.

The extended amount of time that adolescent girls spend with adult women has several interesting consequences (see chapter 9). Relevant to socialization, the time girls spend with adult women serves to decrease competitive behaviors. Jim's story raises serious questions about how our culture socializes boys. Jim spent very little time with his father and was hungry for any time with boys or men. But he was not able to recognize signals that violent behavior was about to take place, and when it did, he did not think that he could talk with his father about it. During an era when we are increasingly concerned about violent behavior among adolescent boys, knowledge about who they spend their time with during adolescence is crucial.

Joining a peer group also helps any adolescent, male or female, accomplish one of the developmental tasks of adolescence—separating emotionally from family members. This is one of the positive functions of peer groups. Participation in a group can also promote an adolescent's quest to develop his or her own identity, another task of the adolescent years.

It is now generally believed that Erikson's idea that adolescents "select" or "try on" different identities by being a part of different peer groups is not exactly how adolescents select a peer group. Many children have to wait until the peer group selects them. They can veto participation or say yes, but the number of groups open to them is limited by many factors, among them age, gender, cultural and socioeconomic factors, and teen labels ("brain," "jock," "nerd," "stoner").[8] Teenagers are not always aware of the important role that all these factors play and may blame themselves for not being in the "right" group. The limited opportunity to join a group is also one of the reasons young people become so upset when they are rejected by a group. Jim's understanding that there were not a lot of choices out there intensified his feelings of isolation.

Parents can perform a crucial role here by letting their teenagers know—frequently—that they don't expect them to be able to handle all their problems alone. They can let teens know that the world is difficult, but that learning how to ask for help when you need it is an important part of growing up. It is also important that parents understand the many ways young people can abuse others; spending a day volunteering in a middle or high school can be very illuminating. We all know that increasing violence in our society is paralleled by increasing violence in the schools. Recognizing the many ways in which children are frequently abusive toward each other, not all of them physically violent, underscores the point that all children are exposed to abuse, and many are directly involved, whether as victim or as abuser.

Children who have been victimized need special attention. They need support from concerned parents and sometimes medical and therapeutic evaluation to rebuild their injured self-esteem and begin to make the important transition from victim to survivor. Painful situations with peers can provide an impetus for adolescents to grow, wonder about their relationships with others, and acquire empathy and understanding, but not if they remain in the role of victim.

Chapter Thirteen

Risk-taking, Resiliency, and Responsibility

It's like I got faith back in myself.
It's the most important thing.

—Will

When I first met Will, a nineteen-year-old living and working on the streets of San Francisco, his shaggy black hair hung in his face and his emaciated body bore the signs of prolonged amphetamine abuse. He was a runaway, only days off the streets. Trauma and abuse had been a large part of Will's past; they were also part of his present. But Will's capacity to challenge himself and to overcome hurdles taught me more about resiliency and the need for all adolescents to accept responsibility for their actions, including risk-taking, than I had ever understood before.

J im Lees, a dedicated case worker and Will's personal guardian angel, first brought the nineteen-year-old to my office in a run-down van used by Project Ahead, a group that works with high-risk and HIV-infected youth in San Francisco. The Project is associated with the Larkin Street Youth Center in the Tenderloin area of the city, which is largely inhabited by a diverse, struggling population, including immigrants from the Far East, teenagers on their own, sex-trade workers, and unattended elderly, many of whom reside together in run-down hotels and overcrowded apartments. After introducing us, Jim articulated the attributes he believed might spark a connection, telling me about Will's determination to stay off drugs and to try to make his life better, and describing me to Will as a psychiatrist who especially enjoyed talking with teenagers.

At the time of this first visit Will had stopped taking speed for approximately nine days. Jim had told me on the phone that Will had been working the streets for a while. "But I like this kid," he added. "I've worked with him for a while, and I'm heartened by him. There's something about him, his energy level, that makes me think he can really lick this problem. He can certainly deal with it better than he is."

As I listened to Jim recount the events of Will's life, I was not so heartened. Will's past was disturbing, filled with traumatic events, and it sounded ominous even to me. "There's a history in the records of abuse," said Jim, "and probably at least twenty foster homes. What we know about his mother is that she beat him a lot. We think there was psychiatric illness there, too. I wonder if we could get the records about that. She seemed to think that he was crazy, too. It looks like the dad disappeared pretty early. Will was also badly abused in several of the foster homes, both physically and sexually. Not a very nice story. Following that, he ran away, got into drugs, and then got involved in the sex trade in San Francisco." I asked Jim what he liked about Will, and specifically what made him think that Will had a chance. He said, "I'm not exactly sure, but he is able to think about things and reflect on his life. Then he gets back into taking the speed again. But I think he's a fighter."

Will walked into the first session and slumped over in the chair. His eyes brightened when he noticed that I had a plate of Girl Scout cookies in the room. I normally have cookies in my office available to the teenagers who come to see me, but that particular month I had been barraged by neighborhood girls and had said yes to twenty boxes of cookies before I knew it; to say the least, I had a surplus. Will mentioned that chocolate mint and peanut butter were his favorites and proceeded to eat several cookies in a row. I asked him whether he had ever seen a therapist. "Sure, lots of times," he answered, and told me that he had been in a psychiatric hospital when he was younger and that everybody had thought he was crazy. In that first session he talked about his mother and told me about her emotional problems. He then addressed the topic of in-herited psychiatric conditions. "You know, I've read a lot about it, *Newsweek,* other things I pick up on the street, and I wonder about it. Am I destined to be like her with one of those serious illnesses? They say she had something like manic-depressive illness. What do you think about that?"

I told him that studies did suggest that many mental illnesses were inherited and that it was a serious problem, but the fact of his mother's disorder didn't automatically mean that he would be sick, too. He seemed satisfied with that answer. The things Jim had told me about Will suggested there might be a spiritual side to this young man. I decided to spend our first session looking for Will's strengths. After all, I knew that there were weaknesses, and I was pretty sure that if I went after those in a strict diagnostic style, I was going to find them. I was also hoping that Will and I could develop enough of a relationship during this first session that we could begin to work together to help him stop using amphetamines.

I began by asking him what he liked to do. He told me about a job he had working in an auctioneer's, where he moved furniture and artwork. He said that he liked the job because he made a lot of money, which he could use to buy things for himself. Will's attention flitted quickly from one topic to another throughout the session. He also seemed to be staring out at my backyard, framed by the win-dow in my office. I asked him about this, and he said, "Yeah, it's calm out there, I like looking out there. You can see a lot, the trees, all kinds of stuff. It's different, peaceful, the kind of place that I have in my mind."

I was interested in how the peace he saw in my urban backyard resonated with a "place" in his mind, and I asked him about it. He said, "I'm not sure, but I think that my mom's dad was part Chero-kee. That helps me a lot, to think about how he would have handled things, things like I've gone through. It seems to calm me down." I didn't get much out of the rest of the hour because Will quickly moved on to several other topics, and I couldn't get him to focus. But I told him that I wanted to see him again, and that it was impor-tant that we keep talking.

For a while Will showed up intermittently, between his bouts with speed highs. Some of the time I'd see him so down that he wanted to end his life, and at other points he was "flying," his attention span markedly diminished. In either state he was almost impossible to work with in a talking psychotherapy, which relies on the ability to discuss and reflect on one's life. He ate my cookies, though, and looked at my backyard; slowly we began to talk. The importance of this "bonding" phase of my work with drug-using adolescents cannot be minimized; it's often the attachment that drug-using teens make with a supportive adult or peer that helps them make the decision to control or stop their using.

It was several months later when Will made a real commitment to come in and talk with me. Meanwhile, I was absorbed in a search to discover his strengths, the advantages that would help us in this struggle. It was during this search that I began to think about resiliency, an idea that is often applied to children and teens having trouble. Resiliency in this context can imply that youth itself protects children and adolescents from the problems they encounter. Will was facing some powerful demons; his youth, by itself, hadn't really protected him at all.

Valuing Resiliency

In certain areas of child and adolescent psychiatry the work of a few individuals stands out. In the field of resiliency, Norman Garmezy from the University of Minnesota is such a person. He defines an adolescent's natural resiliency as the "ability to be aware of difficult realities in their life combined with their ability to conquer obstacles and to achieve goals despite negative circumstances in their lives, which were evocative of extreme sadness."[1] Understood in this way, resiliency can be appreciated as the capacity to *confront* hardships, or even traumas, rather than merely endure them, and to conquer and succeed rather than merely survive. Garmezy's idea of personal struggle and commitment characterizes the lives of certain adolescents who, despite profoundly difficult backgrounds, demonstrate an ongoing willingness to struggle against great odds and to recognize and attack problems they discover along the way. Taking on this type of struggle is a major risk, a positive challenge more consuming than most types of positive risk-taking. Will was locked into this struggle.

During Will's first visit I had already begun to examine his life for factors I knew affected resiliency. Those of us in close contact with teenagers know that a good relationship with a parent or the presence of a supportive adult is one factor that both positively affects their lives and promotes resiliency.[2] Yet this factor failed to explain resiliency in a boy like Will, who had had no relationship with his father, a seriously abusive one with his mother, subsequent abusive relationships with adults in caretaking and authoritative positions, and little support from any adults in his life until he entered the shelter for runaway youth. Clearly other factors had to have played a role.

Some of the positive factors that promote a natural resiliency are intelligence, social skills, a certain feistiness, and what might be termed luck—the sheer number of positive events in a teen's life. But nothing comes without a price, and teens from high-risk backgrounds who are most resilient and achieve the greatest success in their lives do pay.[3] No surprise, they are significantly more depressed and anxious than similar children from low-stress backgrounds.

Will was a case in point. When he entered my office for his first visit, he was one of the most anxious adolescents I had ever encountered; his anxiety was a powerful feature even when he wasn't using amphetamines. Amazingly, however, he was readily and courageously able to admit to the tremendous obstacles in his background and to acknowledge his own contribution to his problems. He wanted to work to improve his life because he believed that he could and because he liked challenges. And although Will had neither a supportive parent nor other relative in his childhood, his strong tie with Jim Lees seemed to have nurtured all of the positive traits in his character that were contributing to his willingness to stay in the fight.

The Role Risk Played

More than a case worker in Will's life, Jim was a linchpin in the coordination of Will's treatment. He was also an adult who told Will *strongly and repeatedly* that he believed in him and wasn't going to allow him to give up on himself. Like many others who work with high-risk youth, Jim is tenacious. He also realizes the limitations of the work. Mental health professionals can help high-risk youth, but there is an important piece that the adolescents themselves must volunteer. Some adolescents are capable of contributing that piece; others are not. Jim knows this, most of the time.

I like to think that I, too, know this most of the time. One of the dangers for those who work closely with or parent young people, especially those young people who may be in need of so much, is knowing when to step back, get a slightly different perspective on the situation with the teen, and make sure that you're not draining yourself. This is not always easy. Sometimes you get so deeply involved that you can't see your way out. Parents, of course, are especially prone to this pitfall. That's one of the reasons it's so helpful to have more than one person parent a teen. As professionals, Jim and I had lost perspective with teens before and had helped each other. We were working hard not to lose it with Will, and this was one of the reasons we needed a team effort. It worked better for Will and for us.

Jim's careful work with Will had set the stage for the therapeutic work with me. This isn't to say that Will was easy for me to work with. He wasn't, and I felt seriously challenged. He arrived at my office after taking amphetamines on several occasions. At these times he was extremely anxious and entirely unable to work as a partner with me. I repeated over and over to him during these visits that it was very important that he stop taking the drugs and recommended that he enter a special program for drug addiction. Both Jim and I supported Will in this endeavor by continuing to allow him to come to therapy if he was able. But we didn't mince words, clearly stating to him that the next step was to stop taking the speed.

Approximately ten months after Will and I first met he began a comprehensive eighteen-month program to stop his drug use. We continued our therapeutic work together throughout this period. Will's participation in the drug treatment program allowed us to discuss and work on other parts of his life that we hadn't been able to address previously. After Will began his work in the program, one of the first things we focused on in therapy was his history of being physically and sexually abused. Will had been physically and emotionally abused by his mother. By Social Services' report, she hit him repeatedly, believing that he was a "bad child." One period of sexual abuse was perpetrated by a foster father who took care of

Will in some important ways at the same time that he initiated very destructive episodes of sodomy. This complex intermingling of abuse and affection was extremely painful for Will, as it would be for anyone.

The episodes of sexual abuse surfaced easily in the therapy after Will had gone through the first fourteen-day drug-free period, demonstrating the importance of stopping his usage as an initial treatment goal. Shortly after he stopped he began one of our sessions by saying, "I just can't take it anymore. I mean, I know I've been off the drugs, but it [the abuse] is driving me crazy. It's all I can think about. You know, it seems like everybody else in the program was sexually abused, too. I just keep hearing about it. And all I can think about is the guy who did it to me. I want to kill him, and I don't think I can stay off the drugs. I mean, that's all I think about. It's better to be on the drugs than to feel like murdering someone all the time."

I agreed that these were terrible feelings. I was honest with Will and told him that he could anticipate tremendous anger and continued memories of abuse if he stayed off the amphetamines. This wasn't exactly a surprise to either one of us. I did think it was remarkable that the memories were so intrusive and affected Will's entire day. After Will and I talked, the group therapist from his drug treatment program called and told me that he was observing some of the same things I was. We discussed Will's need for support in order to deal with the memories of abuse that were surfacing in both the individual and group therapy, and I emphasized that the frequency and intrusive quality of the memories were typical given their traumatic content, adding that they would have to be dealt with so that Will would be able to manage them and continue treatment.

I was quite candid with Will about this discussion with his group therapist and suggested to him several ways that he could limit the return of these disturbing memories in his daily life while emphasizing the need for us to work on them in our sessions. My recommendations included not watching the television news or reading the daily newspaper; limiting how much he listened to other people's stories of abuse; and working to decrease the stress in his environment, including eating good food and getting plenty of exercise. Will listened and did everything possible to decrease his stress.

He and I also continued to discuss his strengths, one of which was his spiritual searching. We spent several hours discussing his personal quest, connecting some of this with what he knew about his Cherokee grandfather and noting how the traumatic events in his life had derailed him from his own path. This work brought up memories of conversations with several adults about conserving and developing spiritual energy. He recognized that this pursuit had not been possible for him during the years on the street. Now that his life was less difficult in a daily way—he was living in one of the apartments in the Larkin Street housing system, and he was staying sober—this endeavor not only was a focus in its own right but also served to help him deal with the memories of abuse.

Will's memories of his own suffering had surfaced fairly easily, but I began to notice other references to abuse during our sessions. During one session Will mentioned to me quite explicitly that he didn't want to get involved with a girl because he was worried that he would beat her up. I listened carefully and asked him more about it. He said, "I'm not so sure I really want to talk about it."

"Why not?"

"I don't think you'd like me very much if you really knew about me. I mean, honestly, Dr. Ponton, it's one thing if you think about me as this poor kid who was abused by all of those stepdads, but it's another thing if you really knew what I've done to other people. That's a big part of what's coming up—the stuff *I've* done to people." Then Will turned and looked out the window at my garden.

I told Will that he was right, it would be hard for me to listen to him tell me about how he had abused people. He had also mentioned the fact that I was a mother, and that he was particularly concerned about hurting me. Although I didn't comment on it at that point in treatment, this remark made me think about Will's experience with his own mother. I remembered the abuse by his mother reported in the records and wondered whether he might want to hurt women in particular. I said to him that although I was a mother, I was working with him as his therapist and didn't see any way to help him get better other than to talk about it so that we could work on it together. He agreed with me. "You know, I think that's probably true, because all this stuff is the other half of the story. If I don't deal with what I've done to other people, I'll always feel guilty about it. I mean, I feel guilty about it now. It gets so mixed up, though—memories of people doing stuff to me and me to others."

This conversation led to several sessions in which Will admitted perpetrating the sexual abuse and rape of young women. He had first done this while involved with the sex trade. It was clear that Will had become very psychologically involved in this abuse. He had enjoyed and was excited by abusing others. He acknowledged to me that it helped him manage his own anxiety. "I mean, when I'm with a girl and I'm hitting her like that, you know, I think about being beaten. It makes me feel better. It's not control, but I feel like somehow the whole thing that happened to me is okay then. It's a crazy thing. I mean, I can see it as crazy now, looking back on it, but when I was in that situation I really didn't know any other way."

One common observation of those in therapy with victims of abuse is that they often identify with the person or people who abused them (sometimes termed "identifying with the aggressor"), imitating and reenacting the experience by abusing others.[4] Very often as an abused child matures this protective mechanism develops into an identification with both the victim *and* the aggressor. Will initiated relationships in which he was the abuser so that he could feel the sense of power and control that he had not felt when he was younger. It's important to understand, however, that the one reason he stayed in abusive situations was that he felt a painful identification with the women he was abusing; this connection to his own childhood also provided familiarity and, thus, further unconscious motivation for remaining in an unhealthy situation.

This interwoven identification with both the aggressor and the victim is one of the unconscious behaviors that keeps an adolescent or adult in abusive relationships. When working on issues of abuse in a therapeutic relationship, it is important to be aware of the shifting identifications—Will's case clearly illustrates this point. Failing to acknowledge that a person is caught in such a cycle of abuse (once victim, now perpetrator, but identified also with the new victim) seriously limits the treatment. This cycle also plays a role in parenting teens who have been abused. When teens shift roles rapidly, first playing the part of the abuser and then the abused, parents, friends, and others can get caught up in this sad drama and find themselves being treated badly by the adolescent or wanting very much to treat the adolescent badly. Recognizing the disturbing patterns that abuse can provoke is crucial.

In keeping with this approach, it is important that a young person who is engaging in an abusive activity accept responsibility for his or her behavior and want to change the pattern. This is true for all teens engaged in any form of dangerous risk-taking—*they have to accept responsibility for their actions.* Part of Will's treatment with me included making restitution. He became very involved in treatment efforts to help others. In this undertaking he combined his spiritual life and therapeutic gains to construct a "payback" to others. This process allowed him to make a remarkable shift in how he conducted his life.

Abusive or violent behavior cannot be ignored by parents or society. Ignoring or minimizing sends a clear message to the teenager: either that such behavior is too shameful to talk about, leaving him or her with the idea that there is no possible resolution except to hide it, or that the behavior is silently condoned and so its effects can be minimized. Many parents are either shamed by it or unwilling to see it, unable to believe that their child could hurt others.

It takes courage to confront violent behavior and examine the pain and aggression that often lie behind it. This is not something that our society does easily, and many who choose to work with victims often either ignore or stigmatize those who victimize. Confronting and helping to resolve violent or abusive behavior patterns is a personal responsibility that both Will and I had to confront, but it is also a responsibility of parents and society in general.

The Broader Message

Teens who believe that the forces shaping their lives are largely within their own control do significantly better than children who believe that life's forces are largely outside their control.[5] A teen's ability to believe that he or she can determine in some measure what happens to him or her is an important coping skill that promotes active attempts to overcome stressful situations.

Successful risk-taking requires a persistent ability to believe in yourself even when others don't. This was a crucial factor in Will's life. Some of Will's major characteristics as a child were evident in vivid descriptions written by countless doctors, social workers, and other professionals: he was a feisty boy who expressed the belief that he did have some control over his fate. This sense of control and self-confidence (he believed that he should "try something at least once") had helped Will to survive the twenty different foster placements.

But Will's subsequent use of amphetamines seriously affected his sense of himself as the master of his own fate. He told me that he first tried the drug because he was confident, curious, and didn't believe that it would "get to" him. This kind of grandiose denial (drugs that harm others will somehow not harm me) is typical of many teens with or without parents, but the lack of adult guidance in Will's life was a real drawback. Once he began to use and became addicted, his entire drug-controlled lifestyle contradicted his belief in the importance of self-mastery because he was no longer in charge. Also important was the lack of adult input about his drug use.

In taking drugs, Will had lost the sense of control that had been so valuable to him earlier, helping him to surmount events that would have been catastrophic for others. The consequences of this serious risk behavior had robbed him of his main advantage. Life became drudgery. He was under the control of drugs, a developing depression, and a vicious lifestyle marked by extreme emotional ups and downs. He began to see himself as a victim at the mercy of others. Ending that cycle by stopping his drug use gave Will back some control over his life.

Once he began to feel this mastery again, he had ideas about how to make positive changes, and he set about doing so. He went back to school, found a job, and developed a healthy, nonabusive relationship with a young woman. Will made many of these important changes during the first two years after he first came to see me, but his work continues even today.

A turning point in Will's life occurred when he confronted his abusive treatment of women. Helping him to acknowledge his responsibility for his actions was quite important; so was communicating to him that his behaviors were serious but could be faced and handled better, and that in sharing this difficult information and choosing to work on it he had acted courageously. He began to understand that he could change his pattern of abusing others and make some reparation for his actions. Again, all of this served to give him back control over his own life, in which Will now accepted responsibility.

Risk-taking and resiliency clearly interface with the concept of responsibility, which parents, teachers, and other adults can promote in young people. Encouraging young people to stick with efforts they begin, and providing opportunities to meet real challenges that are not linked to self-destructive or otherwise violent activity, are crucial contributions. As adults, we can acknowledge our own struggles in life and examine and share how we gained perspective from them. Parents can also emphasize that the pursuit and development of responsibility is a lifelong activity. It is a *process* that begins with attempts that may result in either success or failure, and it includes preparation and planning. Adults must also emphasize to young people that acknowledging and confronting fear and anger is a big part of developing responsibility. And we must remain aware of how much work this process requires of both teens and parents, rather than assume that a "natural" resiliency will save a teen who heads too far down a dangerous road.

Will outlined this process when he described his outlook on life to me. "I keep trying now. When I was on the drugs, I couldn't do that. I'd plan to do stuff and then fall asleep. Now I really like my attitude. It's like I got faith back in myself. It's the most important thing." Will was right to value his faith in himself. This attribute, which he displayed even as a young child, had been lost somewhere along the way. The early Social Services reports on Will also indicated that even as a small child he would speak out when his mother hit him or his brother. He told me that he'd had to rely on himself when he was a child because there was nobody else on whom he could depend. "It seems like the adults were all messing up. One bad foster home followed another. I felt like I had to keep my attitude right and finally I had to get out of there—where the guy [the foster father] was really using me. So I ran away."

Will believed that he could make his own life better, but at the same time his appraisal of his situation was realistic. "The foster home situation isn't totally bad, but it wasn't working for me. The one good home that I was in I wasn't ready for, and then it's kind of like you go to the bottom, to placements for kids that are 'hard to place.' That's when the streets are better." Children in the foster system who have emotional problems and are hard to control become teenagers who are difficult to find a home for. Outreach programs for runaway teens, such as the Larkin Street Youth Center in San Francisco and the Greenhouse in Seattle, can make a difference by finding, promoting, and developing the strengths in young people like Will.

Will's story highlights two important themes. Promoting and developing an adolescent's ability to take on responsibility is one of the major tasks for those who work with young people. This was the most important part of the work that Will and I did in therapy, but it is also an important part of parenting a teen. I acknowledged that some individuals had let him down (the foster father who sexually abused him), but I insisted that he take responsibility for his own actions (sexually abusing women) and not see himself as a victim of "the system." Like many parents, I encouraged Will to take on new responsibilities as he was ready and praised him when he was able to accomplish goals (staying off the drugs, achieving other specific goals in his treatment program), but I called him on his failures to take responsibility (blaming friends who were still using drugs for his own behavior). Parents can and do accomplish this with teenagers. First, they define responsibility; second, they praise the adolescent's first steps; and third, they promote it. This is crucial.

For Will, accepting responsibility for his actions was a different type of risk-taking. With assistance from Jim, the staff and clients of his drug treatment program, and me, Will began to see that these new risks were positive. Priding himself on being a risk-taker, he now put this skill to work in a challenging new area.

Will learned about responsibility from watching and emulating adults in his life such as Jim Lees. Personal mentoring can be of value at any developmental point in a lifetime, but it is particularly important during adolescence, when role models mean so much.

At the end of his treatment Will invited me to lecture in a program he had developed for young people that focused on educating them about the risks in their environment—drugs and unprotected sex, among others. Will was a presenter at the program that day, too, and watching him speak to his peers and to many younger teens who clearly admired and emulated him illustrated clearly that responsibility and advocacy are learned first from watching others who respect them, value them, and carry them out, and then from being supported in your own efforts to do the same.

Postscript: Five Years Later

I have asked many of the adolescents described in this book to read their chapters and give me feedback. This has proved to be a very beneficial experience for me as well as for them, but it was to prove especially so with Will. I had seen him occasionally during the intervening years, most frequently at meetings where we both spoke about our work with youth, but I hadn't had a chance on any of these occasions to sit down and talk with him. On the morning we did meet I realized that I was extremely curious. How had things changed for him? Had he been able to stay away from dangerous risk-taking? What would he recommend to parents of teenagers?

The first thing I noticed about Will that morning was that he no longer rode a motorcycle. My home office is at the top of a steep hill in San Francisco, and I remembered hearing his large motorcycle take the turns slowly climbing to the top. On this particular morning there was no noise signaling his approach, and when he arrived he stepped out of a pretty mundane car.

This was the first of many changes I noticed. The next was his articulate manner. He confidently shook my hand and spoke right away. "I'm excited about reading the story about our work. I hope it'll help other kids. Parents, too."

"There's a lot to your story," I said. "I believe it will be helpful." I asked him what he thought teens need most from parents and adults when they're struggling with risk-taking.

Will looked thoughtful for almost a full minute and then spoke slowly. "I was going to say, 'Oh, that's easy—support and guidance, which includes structure, limits, and being a good role model.' But it's really not that easy. A lot of teens have trouble taking risks, but adults don't always do a whole lot better helping them."

"How could adults do it differently?"

"Well, probably most important, don't give up on kids. When kids get caught up in dangerous risk-taking, they need adults more than ever. I think about what would have happened if Jim had given up on me at the same time that I'd given up on myself. I know it was different for me because really, my parents had given up on me, and themselves, years earlier, but for kids who have parents, I see so many parents giving up when the going gets rough."

"Do you have any ideas about why?"

"Because it's not easy! Here you have to support your kid to take risks, that's scary enough, and then you've got to be real involved if it gets too dangerous. It takes courage—for parents and for kids."

"And work," I added.

Will left quietly, his car slowly rounding the corners of the hill. He'd given me a lot to think about. He knew what it was like to have parents who had failed; after his own left him, other "caring" adults had seriously abused him. Then he fell into patterns of abusing himself and others. On the surface his story doesn't look like the stories of adolescents with caring parents, but there are important similarities. Will's life was changed dramatically because during a period when he had lost hope for himself he received support, guidance, structure, role-modeling. Will knew from experience that these forms of love and discipline are not always easy to provide our adolescents, but they are crucial parts of what all of them need.

Epilogue:
To Risk Is to Grow

Adolescents take risks as a way of developing and defining themselves. They do this by taking on new challenges in areas that they often understand very little about, engaging in behaviors with results that range from devastating to extremely positive. *Risk-taking is the major tool that adolescents use to shape their identities.* Both directly and indirectly, risk-taking affects all aspects of development during this important period of life—physical, social, psychological, sexual, and cultural.

For many young people like Jill, risk-taking is powerfully attractive, offering a romance that their "boring" lives do not have. For Jill and others like her, risky behavior is imbued with aspects of heroism, adventure, and mystery. It is only much later that adolescents notice the not-so-romantic aspects of this behavior and become aware of the long-term consequences and their own responsibilities.

It is not only romance that attracts adolescents to risk-taking, however. Adolescents are sometimes drawn to take dangerous risks because they're following the examples of others. Peers provide the most obvious model to emulate; popular culture and the media are also influential. But parents and other adults also play a role, whether passive or active. Adults model how to take both healthy and unhealthy risks. Many parents would like to believe that biology, peers, and culture are the dominant influences on their child's risk-taking, failing to recognize the important role they play themselves. That point is highlighted by Jenny's parents, who failed to see the impact of their own marijuana smoking on their daughter's behavior.

Parents and other adults are more than role models, though. As many parents discover when they are forced to pick up the pieces after a teen has participated in some dangerous risk-taking, sometimes it takes bearing legal responsibility for the actions of a child before parents realize how much trouble their family is in. Parents need to find out about risk-taking before there are serious consequences. Adolescent risk behavior is not mysterious. Parents need to recognize that just as infants are bound to mature and one day start walking, adolescents are going to engage in risk-taking, an important, inevitable process through which they come to understand themselves and life. Parents need to understand that many behaviors can have either positive or negative consequences and begin talking openly with their teens about what they're doing in order to help them develop tools for risk assessment, including learning how to evaluate their own actions and anticipate and evaluate the consequences of those actions.

Parents also need to encourage positive risk-taking, seeking out and/or supporting opportunities for their teenagers to take on challenges in open and nondangerous settings. They may have to develop these opportunities if they do not find them ready-made. Evan's parents provided challenging situations for their son and called on family members to encourage his participation in various projects, and his father made a commitment to spend more one-on-one time with Evan. Ariel's mother Elena, a single parent, planned travel and other activities that she and Ariel were able to participate in together. Jill's parents were able to recognize their daughter's creative interests and talents and showed their support for her artistic endeavors and identity by facilitating her early graduation from high school and enrollment in a secondary fine arts program.

Perhaps most important, parents need to recognize the warning signs of dangerous risk-taking. Tumultuous upset accompanied by dangerous risk-taking is not a normal part of the teen years. Parents should be on the lookout for problems and obtain or provide help for their teens when they need it. All of the parents in this book were given warning signs that their child was developing an unhealthy pattern of behavior as a result of some conflict or upset. For example, Jill withdrew into her room and started using drugs before she ran away. Ariel got into fights that she seemed to have little perspective on before she put herself in life-threatening situations with others. Hannah developed odd eating behaviors, slowly restricting her food intake before her life became endangered. Joe had a couple of beers every now and then before he became addicted to alcohol. This book tells the stories of many parents who missed initial warning signs but who, once they saw their children were in trouble, took action. They learned about adolescent risk-taking; they looked at their own behaviors as well as those of their children; and they obtained help for their children and themselves. They show us that parents need not sit by and watch, filled with fear and impatience, when adolescents are in trouble.

A better understanding of risk-taking provides a better understanding of adolescence itself. Risk-taking must be placed in a developmental framework in order to see it for the vital tool that it is. The many complex developmental tasks of adolescence include: separation and individuation, developing a sense of oneself as a distinct person, separate from family members and others; identity formation; exploration of the biological, sexual, psychological, social, and cultural aspects of identity; learning how to develop close relationships with others; gaining control of one's impulses; and learning how to take responsibility for one's actions.

Risk-taking is one of the primary tools that adolescents use to accomplish these developmental tasks, which serve, in turn, to improve adolescents' risk-taking skills. Risk-taking is not completely explained by any one theoretical perspective, although theory may provide a partial understanding. For example, psychoanalytic thinking helps us understand how risk-taking behavior can enact or reenact psychological themes, traumatic experiences, or conflicts, as we saw with Ariel. It also helps us understand risk-taking as part of an adolescent's healthy struggle to separate from his or her parents.

Family systems theory offers a partial answer by suggesting that an adolescent's risky behavior may serve a specific function in a family. Joe became another "adult" out of necessity when his parents were hardly ever home, and he began hosting the afternoon parties to meet some of his own needs. Jenny carried in her heavy backpack the weight of her parents' divorce, while both of them chose to use drugs and their relationship with their daughter as sources of comfort rather than deal with their own feelings about the divorce and adjust to their new roles.

When parents can't or don't facilitate the adolescent developmental task of separation, their children will find ways to manage it alone. Maura's self-cutting revealed her anger toward her father and an identification with him, but she also used it to define herself as separate from him because he wasn't letting that process happen naturally. Eva's mother and Zoe's mother also had trouble letting their daughters separate and grow up. As adolescents are driven to take risks in the vital process of their own development, they do so both in the context of family *and* independently; it is important for parents to hear the truth in their adolescent's claim, "This is about me, not you."

Illnesses defined in part by biological factors, such as depression, eating disorders, and substance abuse, also interfere with an adolescent's ability to assess and take risks. A depression like Ariel's can intensify an underlying unhealthy pattern of risk-taking or promote a restriction of healthy risk-taking, as Hannah's eating disorder inhibited her sports activities. A serious addiction to drugs or alcohol affects both positive and negative risk-taking, as demonstrated by Joe's tale. Parents must also understand that it is crucial to get help for a teen struggling with mental illness or substance abuse so that his or her difficulties are not compounded by the consequences of dangerous or restricted risk-taking.

Another important biological factor is the timing of an adolescent's physical changes. For decades, around the world, the onset of puberty has been occurring earlier and earlier. For girls especially many of the physical changes of puberty occur before they even reach their teen years. This shift affects not only their appearance but also how they feel about themselves, and how the culture treats them. The trend toward earlier sexual activity may be closely linked to this biological shift. It is also important to remember that for many teens the changes they are undergoing are out of sync: they may be ready for sex physically but not emotionally.

Culture also plays an important role in how adolescents take risks. With their wide access to media, they see vivid demonstrations of all kinds of risk-taking right in their living rooms and bedrooms. Some of the risks they are exposed to in this way are dangerous for anyone; many others may be dangerous depending on an adolescent's level of maturity, emotional stability, physical development, family situation, school situation, and so forth. A risk that may be positive for one teen may be negative for another, and vice versa. Risk-taking needs to be tailored to the individual adolescent.

In addition, our culture has in one very real way guaranteed that teens remain dependent while simultaneously commanding them, through the media, to behave like adults (and not always sensible adults at that). As fewer and fewer teens and their families can afford college education, and as increasing numbers of teens graduate or leave high school in no way prepared to face the academic challenges of college, more and more of them are living with their parents in a kind of "holding" status while they wait for the limited number of available jobs. They have more time on their hands and will find their own challenges if their parents and the culture do not provide them.

Social factors continue to be important. As ever, teens look to their peers as they define themselves independently of their parents. It is crucial, however, for parents to appreciate how important they continue to be in their older children's lives, what they can contribute to their adolescents' continuing development, and how to remain actively, appropriately involved.

One Step Further: Promoting Youth Advocacy

As a society, we cannot ask our children to become more responsible if we, in turn, shirk our responsibility to expend energy and money on our young people. Recent societal emphasis on "family values" puts a tremendous burden on an overworked system—the family unit—by demanding that it take responsibility for many problems that are social rather than individual (e.g., unemployment, lack of adequate funding for education, and day care). But the importance of individual and personal values is lost when the responsibility for this activity is placed solely on families that are often over-burdened and underassisted. Will's story illustrates the need for both society —in legislation and policy—and individuals to take an interest in and responsibility for today's adolescents.

For adolescents who do live within a family structure, whether traditional or nontraditional, responsibility can be learned from a family member who teaches by example. My own interest in this area began on long walks with my father through desolate Chicago streets where he showed me more than twenty boardinghouses in which he had lived as a teenager; he never forgot what it was like to be an adolescent without a home or parents. He showed many of the characteristics of "resilient" children, including a belief in himself and the important presence of strong mentors who played an active part in his life. It was on those walks with my father that I learned how small the difference was between teens without homes and the suburban teenager I was. Being able to identify with adolescents who are struggling has been a terrific aid in my work, but this is only the first part of the story. The second part involves taking an active role, either by educating today's youth or by learning about and advocating for their needs. This, too, was a message in the conversations with my father: individuals can and do make a powerful difference in the lives of young people. His life was filled with children and adolescents he mentored. He also advocated for them, individually and as a group.

My father was remarkable in this way not only among the men in my family but among the other fathers in our neighborhood. He often assisted teenagers from other families with work on high school projects. And if there was a neighborhood crisis, such as a brush fire one summer weekend, he was the parent who was called by all the kids and who organized them into a well-supervised, effective fire-fighting team when the fire department itself was delayed. I remember his calm in the midst of this turmoil, as well as how constructive and complimentary he was with each young person who participated in the effort. After the fire was safely put out, he held a post-mortem with the kids and the fire department so that everyone could learn from the experience. One of the kids, clearly hungry for both the challenge and the supervision, stated that not only had he learned a lot from my father during the fire, but that my father had made him feel that he personally could make a difference.

Watching an adult interact with and advocate for youth serves as a powerful example to young people. It reaffirms their value, increases their self-confidence, and sets an example that encourages them to become adults who do not forget their own teenage struggles and who "give back." Tragically, youth advocacy has fallen out of fashion. Even child and adolescent psychiatrists are unlikely to know or mention child advocates such as Jane Addams, the founder of Hull House, a remarkable program for orphaned youth begun over a century ago; or Edward Zigler, a modern advocate at Yale University who was instrumental in the development of the contemporary Head Start programs.

Part of the problem is that today's youth advocates are not visible. How could this be changed? In my own conversations with Dr. Zigler, he makes the point that this country has not had a White House council on issues related to children and adolescents for two decades. This tradition, spearheaded by Eleanor Roosevelt, helped to focus the nation's efforts in this area, but it was lost to us in the 1970s and 1980s. Whether a consequence of such neglect or not, the fact remains that the dollars spent on programs for adolescents today are severely limited. Hillary Rodham Clinton's book, *It Takes a Village*, highlights the community needs of children, yet like other books on children, the specific needs of adolescents are rarely mentioned. In many ways adolescents challenge the community more directly. More than younger children, they are often outside the home interacting with others in ways that have greater potential for positive and negative consequences.

Advocacy for youth has to be taught. It is a complex package of skills that includes an interest in and ability to identify with youth, education about the problems facing young people and about what would make a difference, and a strong commitment to fight for individual adolescents and, on a larger scale, for the entire age group.

Parenting adolescents also requires special skills, which can be learned. Understanding adolescent risk-taking is one of the most important lessons. Recognizing that it is a complex process, not just hormones playing themselves out, is a first step. Perhaps equally important is an ability to examine your own risk-taking, or lack thereof, and share what you learn with teenagers. Risk-taking characterizes adolescence, but it continues to play an important role throughout life. Parents need to talk with their teens about risk-taking, helping them to acquire knowledge from the process and to identify when they're stuck in an unhealthy or even dangerous pattern. If a teen is stuck, as the stories in this book show, it really is never too late to help.

It is vital for parents to remember that adolescents have to take risks. In the end, parents must promote opportunities for their adolescents to undertake positive challenges, not simply as an alternative to more dangerous risks but because of their intrinsic value in contributing to the development of healthy, confident adults.

Notes

Introduction

1. Carnegie Council on Adolescent Development, *Great Transitions: Preparing Adolescents for a New Century* (New York: Carnegie Corporation of New York, 1995).

2. G. Stanley Hall, *Adolescence and Its Relation to Psychology, Anthropology, Sociology, Sex, Crime, Religion, and Education,* vols. 1–2 (New York: Appleton-Century-Crofts, 1904). This classic work on adolescence, written in Victorian prose, captures the imagination and leaves the reader questioning much of what Hall had to say. It is important to understand exactly how Hall's perspective influenced Sigmund Freud and Ernest Jones directly, and other followers of Freud more indirectly, by promoting the idea that adolescence is a time of unavoidably intense turmoil.

3. Aaron Esman, "G. Stanley Hall and the Invention of Adolescence," *Williams College Alumni Review* (Fall 1992): 28–32. Esman is both a psychoanalyst and a historian who has chronicled the field of adolescent psychiatry. This article is informative and extremely easy to read.

4. Ernest Jones, *Some Problems of Adolescence: Papers on Psychoanalysis* (London: Balliere, Tindall, and Cox, 1922; republished by Balliere, Tindall, and Cox, 1948). Jones did not see many adolescents in his clinical practice, and one has to question how much this paper was informed by theory rather than clinical observation.

5. Erik H. Erikson, *Childhood and Society* (New York: Norton, 1950); *Identity and the Life Cycle* (New York: International Universities Press, 1959). Erikson's works are classics in the fields of adolescence and childhood. He is a clear writer and a careful thinker, and his work is a pleasure to read.

6. Anna Freud, "Adolescence," *Psychoanalytic Study of the Child* 13 (1958): 255–78.

7. In Erikson's concept of the "mandatory crisis" of an adolescent's identity formation, for instance, the very word *crisis* implies turbulence — an association with adolescence that, again, is not well established by research. Several concepts of Erikson's have been better substantiated by later research. The concept of identity formation is extremely valuable and provides language for describing the process of adolescent development. Erikson also introduced the idea that experimenting with testing and trying on new roles in adolescence is common and part of the process whereby young people explore and develop their identities. It is not too great a leap to see Erikson's theories about the process of experimentation as a direct antecedent to our current understanding of risk-taking.

8. Peter Blos, "The Concept of Acting-Out in Relation to the Adolescent Process," in C. N. Negarded, ed., *A Developmental Approach to Problems of Acting-Out: A Symposium*, Monograms of the *Journal of the American Academy of Psychiatry*, no. 1 (New York: International Universities Press, 1966), 108–43. In *On Adolescence* (New York: Free Press, 1962), Blos emphasizes the resurgence of childhood feelings (both pre-oedipal and oedipal) in adolescence as part of the reworking of childhood before an adolescent enters adulthood. This concept follows Sigmund Freud's view that adolescence is a developmental period wherein these earlier feelings must be reworked. This theoretical perspective is not well established, however, and shifts the focus of our understanding of adolescence back toward childhood instead of forward toward adulthood.

9. Daniel Offer and K. Schonert-Reichl, "Debunking the Myths of Adolescence," *Journal of the American Academy of Child and Adolescent Psychiatry* 31, no. 6 (1992): 1003–14.

10. Charles Irwin, "Risk-taking Behavior in the Adolescent Patient: Are They Impulsive?" *Pediatric Annals* 18, no. 2 (1989): 122–33. Irwin also believes that most of adolescent development, even risk-taking, is "normal." His conceptualization of risk-taking as a complex process in which things could go in either a positive or a negative direction is important; it includes the idea that adult guidance and adolescent education can be important parts of this process.

11. Ibid., 122–24.

12. Ralph DiClemente and Lynn E. Ponton, "HIV-Related Risk Behaviors Among Psychiatrically Hospitalized Adolescents and School-Based Adolescents," *American Journal of Psychiatry* 150, no. 2 (1993): 324–26.

13. Ralph J. DiClemente, Lynn E. Ponton, and William B. Hansen, "New Directions for Adolescent Risk Prevention and Health Promotion Research and Intervention," in Ralph J. DiClemente, William B. Hansen, and Lynn E. Ponton, eds., *Handbook of Adolescent Health Risk Behavior* (New York: Plenum, 1996), 413–20. This summary chapter illustrates the scope of the topic while simultaneously encouraging a "hands-on" approach. It also summarizes directions for future research.

Chapter One

1. R. Schwectenberg, *1990 Rainbow Guide* (San Francisco: Alternative Press Syndicate, 1990). The annual *Rainbow Guide* is a wealth of information about this alternative lifestyle group that attracts so many teenagers. It points to one important fact to keep in mind when consulting these references or looking for other sources — information about adolescents is scattered throughout our culture.

2. Mary Jane Rotheram-Borus, M. Parra, C. Cantwell, and M. Gwadz, "Runaway and Homeless Youths," in Ralph J. DiClemente, William B. Hansen, and Lynn E. Ponton, eds., *Handbook of Adolescent Health Risk Behavior* (New York: Plenum, 1996), 369–93. This chapter, although largely academic in nature, is extremely readable, highlights prevention strategies for homeless youth, and provides basic epidemiological data.

3. G. C. Luna, "HIV and Homeless Youth," *Focus: A Review of AIDS Research* 2, no. 3 (1987): 10. This article, which reports some rather unconventional methods to obtain statistics on San Francisco youth, highlights homeless youth in urban cities.

4. Rotheram-Borus, Parra, Cantwell, and Gwadz, "Runaway and Homeless Youths."

5. M. J. Robertson, "Alcohol Use and Abuse Among Homeless Adolescents in Hollywood," *Contemporary Drug Problems* 16 (1989): 415–52. This article highlights the Hollywood runaway "scene," another attraction to the nation's troubled youth.

6. Mary Jane Rotheram-Borus, C. Koopman, and A. A. Ehrhardt, "Homeless Youths and HIV Infection," *American Psychologist* 46, no. 11 (1991): 1188–97. Rotheram-Borus is one of the most important researchers and writers in the field of homeless youth. As she points out, homeless youth are much more vulnerable to all types of adolescent risk behaviors, including, not surprisingly, those associated with HIV/AIDS.

7. R. Jessor, "Risk Behavior in Adolescence: A Psychosocial Framework for Understanding," in D. Rogers and E. Ginzberg, eds., *Adolescents at Risk: Medical and Social Perspectives* (San Francisco: Westview, 1990). Jessor is one of the major theoreticians in the field of adolescent risk-taking and risk behavior.

8. Erik H. Erikson, *Childhood and Society*, 2d ed. (New York: Norton, 1963).

9. Lynn E. Ponton, "The Many Roles of the Child and Adolescent Psychiatrists After a Disaster" [abstract], *Proceedings of the 1995 Meeting of the American Academy of Child and Adolescent Psychiatry*, New Orleans, 24 October 1995. This paper also discusses prevention strategies.

10. V. V. Yacoubian and F. J. Hacker, "Reactions to Disaster at a Distance," *Bulletin of the Menninger Clinic* 53 (1989): 331–39.

Chapter Two

1. Lynn Ponton, "Issues Unique to Psychotherapy with Adolescent Girls," *American Journal of Psychotherapy* 47, no. 3 (1993): 353–73.

2. Enid Gruber, "Adolescent Risk-taking Behavior and Psychopathology: A Review" (unpublished, 1994). In this comprehensive review of adolescent risk-taking and mental problems, Gruber stresses the importance of ruling out psychological problems when adolescent risk-taking develops into the more serious variant of risk behavior. Although I emphasize in this book that most risk-taking is not pathological and actually benefits an adolescent's development, it is important to keep in mind the possibility that an underlying condition may be affecting a teen's behavior in harmful ways.

3. Lenore Terr, "Chowchilla Revisited: The Effects of Psychic Trauma Four Years After a School-Bus Kidnapping," *American Journal of Psychiatry* 140, no. 12 (1983): 1543–50. Terr examines 23 children from the small town of Chowchilla, California, who were kidnapped while riding their school bus and their psychological adaptations to the trauma.

4. Lenore Terr, *Too Scared to Cry* (New York: Basic Books, 1993). This well-known book was written for the lay public. In a highly readable, often spell-binding style, it covers most of the material presented in "Chowchilla Revisited" and alerts us to the many ways a child's life can be affected by trauma.

5. Ibid.

6. E. D. Schwarz and B. D. Perry, "The Post-traumatic Response in Children and Adolescents," *Psychiatric Clinics of North America* 17, no. 2 (1994): 311–26. This excellent overview of the topic of trauma in children and adolescents includes an in-depth discussion of the biology of trauma and its developmental considerations.

7. D. Gelman, "A Much Riskier Passage," *Newsweek* [special issue: *The New Teens*] (Summer–Fall 1990): 10–16. Gelman makes the point that the combination of increased accessibility as the world becomes smaller and increased speed as the world becomes faster have affected risk-taking. As teens have much easier access to dangerous experiences, the stakes can run a lot higher.

8. Diana Baumrind, "Early Socialization and Adolescent Competence," in S. Dragastin and G. H. Elder, eds., *Adolescence in the Life Cycle* (New York: Wiley, 1975). Baumrind is one of the most accomplished research investigators in the field of adolescence. In this chapter she explores the impact that parental style has on guiding and determining an adolescent's lifestyle choices and values.

9. F. Cline and J. Fay, *Parenting Teens with Love and Logic* (New York: Pinon Press, 1993). This book underscores the point that parents have to modify their parenting strategies when their children become teenagers.

Chapter Three

1. Lynn E. Ponton, "Disordered Eating," in Ralph J. DiClemente, William B. Hansen, and Lynn E. Ponton, eds., *Handbook of Adolescent Health Risk Behavior* (New York: Plenum, 1996), 83–114. This chapter is an extensive review of the field of disordered eating as it pertains to adolescents. It covers aspects of definition and diagnosis, epidemiology, treatment, and prevention and identifies eating problems as risk behaviors. Although lengthy, many parents have told me they found it informative and helpful.

2. Lynn E. Ponton, "A Review of Eating Disorders in Adolescent Girls," in R. C. Marohn, ed., *Adolescent Psychiatry: Annals of the American Society for Adolescent Psychiatry* 20 (New York: Analytic Press, 1994), 267–85. This chapter is a more succinct version of "Disordered Eating."

3. Lynn E. Ponton, "Issues Unique to Psychotherapy with Adolescent Girls," *American Journal of Psychotherapy* 47, no. 3 (1993): 353–73. This article discusses different psychotherapeutic strategies and includes a review of development.

4. Carol Gilligan, *In a Different Voice: Psychological Theory and Women's Development* (Cambridge, Mass.: Harvard University Press, 1982). This seminal volume introduced the issue of how choices diminish for girls in early adolescence.

5. Ponton, "Disordered Eating."

6. G. Stanley Hall, *Adolescence: Its Psychology and Its Relations to Physiology, Anthropology, Sociology, Sex, Crime, Religion, and Education*, vols. 1–2 (New York: Appleton-Century-Crofts, 1904); Anna Freud, "Adolescence," *Psychoanalytic Study of the Child* 13 (1958): 255–78.

7. Daniel Offer, *The Psychological World of the Teenager: A Study of Normal Adolescent Boys* (New York: Basic Books, 1969); Daniel Offer and J. Offer, *From Teenage to Young Manhood: A Psychological Study* (New York: Basic Books, 1975). These are just two of the many works by Daniel Offer that seek to debunk the widely held myth that adolescence is a universally turbulent period and instead suggest that there are alternative pathways.

8. Ponton, "Eating Disorders."

9. D. A. Blyth, R. G. Simmons, R. Bulcroft, D. Felt, E. F. Van Cleave, and D. M. Bush, "The Effects of Physical Development on Self-Image and Satisfaction with Body Image for Early Adolescent Males," in R. G. Simmons, ed., *Research in Community and Mental Health*, vol. 2 (Greenwich, Conn.: JAI Press, 1981), 43–73. This chapter underscores the role that fitness rather than appearance plays in shaping a boy's body image.

10. Aaron Esman, "G. Stanley Hall and the Invention of Adolescence," *Williams College Alumni Review* (Fall 1992): 28–31. Esman convincingly describes how difficult it has been to lay to rest the myth of the universally turbulent adolescent. The article describes the relationship between Hall and Sigmund Freud, underscoring its longitudinal importance to both men's work.

11. C. E. Irwin and M. Shafer, "Somatic Growth and Development During Adolescence," in A. Rudolph, ed., *Pediatrics*, 19th ed. (Norwalk, Conn.: Appleton and Lang, 1991), 39–40. Irwin and Shafer, codirectors of the Adolescent Medicine Clinic at the University of California, San Francisco, are prominent researchers and clinicians in the area of adolescent risk-taking.

12. M. Rosenberg, "Self-concept from Middle Childhood Through Adolescence," in J. Suls and A. G. Greenwald, eds., *Psychological Perspective on the Self* (Hillsdale, N.J.: Lawrence Erlbaum, 1986), 182–205. Longitudinal studies reveal gradual and systematic improvement in self-esteem for adolescent boys between grades 7 and 12. Findings also suggest that for both boys and girls self-esteem begins to decline at age eleven and reaches its low point between the ages of twelve and thirteen. One has to examine closely, then, why the self-esteem of girls is not rebuilt during adolescence as it is for boys. It is also important to note that girls who mature physically and enter puberty earlier have more problems with self-esteem than girls who develop later. Early development, combined with the nadir of self-esteem at age eleven, seems to be a kind of double whammy for such girls.

13. Alexander R. Lucas, "The Eating Disorder 'Epidemic': More Apparent than Real," *Pediatric Annals* 21, no. 11 (1992): 746–51. Lucas's careful epidemiological work helps to identify generalized populations at greater risk—in this case, younger adolescents—and at the same time dispel myths about the "widespread" growth of disordered eating and eating disorders.

Chapter Four

1. L. Brown, "Adolescent Pregnancy," Institute on Child and Adolescent Sexuality, 1995 annual meeting of the American Academy of Child and Adolescent Psychiatry, New Orleans, 22 October 1995. Brown charac-

terizes teenage pregnancy as the result of both general adolescent risk-taking and its negative partner—adolescent risk behavior. He underscores the importance of pregnant adolescent girls being able to obtain counseling when they are struggling with decisions.

2. Selma Fraiberg, E. Adelson, and V. Shapiro, "Ghosts in the Nursery: A Psychoanalytic Approach to the Problems of Impaired Infant-Mother Relationships," *Clinical Studies in Infant Mental Health* 3, no. 3 (1980): 164–96. The work of the first author of this classic article, Selma Fraiberg, and her associates has helped to promote and develop treatment opportunities for parents of infants and toddlers across the nation. Fraiberg underscored the importance of understanding and working with a parent's conflicts and parenting deficiencies. This perspective is particularly important in working with teenage parents.

3. Alayne Yates, "Normal Sexual Development: Current Perspectives," Institute on Child and Adolescent Sexuality, annual meeting of the American Academy of Child and Adolescent Psychiatry, New Orleans, 22 October 1995. Yates, a professor of child and adolescent psychiatry at the University of Hawaii, is one of the most articulate and knowledgeable speakers on the topic of adolescent sexuality.

4. Ibid., 1.

5. M. A. Shafer and C. E. Irwin, "The Adolescent Patient," in A. Rudolph, ed., *Pediatrics*, 19th ed. (Norwalk, Conn.: Appleton & Lang, 1991). The authors remind us that the increasingly earlier age at which girls are experiencing the onset of menstruation requires that we provide young people with comprehensive, understandable sex education at earlier ages. Girls need opportunities not only to hear biological facts but to role-play possible sexual situations and determine how they will deal with them.

6. G. M. Wingood and Ralph J. DiClemente, "Cultural and Psychosocial Factors Influencing HIV Preventive Behaviors of Afro-American Females," *Ethnicity and Disease* 2, no. 2 (1996): 381–88.

7. N. Adler, S. M. Kegeles, C. E. Irwin, and C. Wibblesman, "Adolescent Contraceptive Behavior: An Assessment of Decision Processes," *Journal of Pediatrics* 116 (1990): 463–71. Decision-making around risk-taking is itself a very complex process; this article, a complex but valuable read, looks at it from several perspectives.

Chapter Five

1. L. Steinberg, "The Impact of Puberty on Family Relations: Effects of Pubertal Status and Pubertal Timing," *Developmental Psychology* 23 (1987): 451–60. I refer to this article, which examines the possible family dyads, in chapters 5–9 because it provides information about and perspective on these important constellations.

2. Helene Deutsch, *The Psychology of Women*, vols. 1–2 (New York: Grune & Stratton, 1945). This analytic classic was one of the first volumes to develop and expand on the topic of mother-daughter conflict. Although many of Deutsch's ideas have been questioned, this book remains a thoughtful and thought-provoking read.

3. Carol Gilligan, *In a Different Voice: Psychological Theory and Women's Development* (Cambridge, Mass.: Harvard University Press, 1982). This classic work on how girls change in adolescence has been challenged because of Gilligan's research design and theoretical perspective. Her ideas, however, are fascinating, and this book deserves attention.

4. Ibid.

5. Elizabeth Debold, M. Wilson, and I. Malone, *The Mother-Daughter Revolution: From Betrayal to Power* (Reading, Mass.: Addison-Wesley, 1993). This volume, authored by followers of Carol Gilligan and Gloria Steinem, has been criticized because it presents opinion as fact (Z. Luria, [book review of *The Mother-Daughter Revolution*], *Women and Health* 22, no. 3 [1995]: 88–91) and has an overabundance of rhetoric. It is not easy to read but offers many interesting ideas.

6. Terri Apter, *Altered Loves: Mothers and Daughters During Adolescence* (New York: Fawcett Columbine, 1990). Apter also points out that many daughters use the struggle with their mother as a testing ground before they try their skills in the world. Apter's developmental perspective makes this book easy to understand, and the information easier to bear.

Chapter Six

1. Lynn E. Ponton, "Adolescent Dreams: An Examination of Their Sexuality," *Dialogues: Journal of Psychoanalytic Perspective* 8 (1990): 49–56. David's dreams are described in much more extensive detail in this article.

2. Peter Blos, *On Adolescence* (New York: Free Press, 1962).

3. Diana Baumrind, "The Influence of Parenting Style on Adolescent Competence and Problem Behavior," paper presented at the American Psychological Association meetings, New Orleans, August 1989.

4. Ponton, "Adolescent Dreams," 53.

5. Kyle Pruett, *The Nurturing Father: Journey Toward the Complete Man* (New York: Warner, 1987).

Chapter Seven

1. American Medical Association, *1996 Report Card: Violence in America* (Washington, D.C.: American Medical Association Press, 1996). The AMA's overall assessment of violence in the United States is dismal, suggesting that the country is a war zone, with women and children on the front lines.

2. Olga Silverstein and B. Rashbaum, *The Courage to Raise Good Men* (New York: Viking, 1994). This popular book coauthored by Olga Silverstein, a long-standing member of the family therapy movement, is a valuable addition to any library. It focuses on the relationship between mothers and sons, detailing the role that society has played in pushing them apart.

3. H. Steiner, "Stemming the Tide of Youth Violence: How Child Psychiatrists Can Get Involved," *American Academy of Child and Adolescent Psychiatry News* 1, no. 6 (November-December 1995): 9, 31. Steiner, the chairperson of the American Academy of Child and Adolescent Psychiatry's Task Force on Violence, outlines strategies for health professionals working with violent children and adolescents, underscoring the importance of building a team effort in light of how difficult violent behavior is to treat.

4. M. Mandel, P. Magnusson, J. Ellis, and G. de George, "The Economics of Crime," *Business Week* (December 13, 1993): 72–80.

5. Steiner, "Stemming the Tide," 13.

6. T. Beall, "Domestic Violence Reporting Law: A Hazard or a Help to Patients/Victims?" *California Physician* 13, no. 8 (1996): 26–34.

7. M. Straus and R. Gelles, "Social Change and Change in Family Violence from 1971 to 1985 as Revealed by Two National Surveys," *Journal of Marriage and Family Therapy* 48 (1986): 465–79.

8. Lenore E. Walker, *The Battered Woman Syndrome* (New York: Springer, 1984). Walker is one of the most articulate spokespeople on the topic of domestic violence. She has written extensively over the past twenty years, both academically and for the lay reader. Although this popular book is an early work, it is highly readable and provides a basic education in the subject.

Chapter Eight

1. A. R. Favazza, "Why Patients Mutilate Themselves," *Hospital and Community Psychiatry* 40 (1989): 137–45.

2. M. Strong, "A Bright Red Scream," *San Francisco Focus* (November 1993): 58ff. I highly recommend this well-written article, which covers the nature of self-mutilation and its treatment and prevention.

3. Ralph J. DiClemente, Lynn Ponton, and D. Hartley, "Prevalence and Correlates of Cutting Behavior: Risk for HIV Transmission," *Journal of the American Academy of Child and Adolescent Psychiatry* 30, no. 5 (1991): 735–39. This article, which underscores the connection between self-mutilation and a history of sexual abuse, was the first to point out the risk of HIV infection associated with this behavior.

4. Strong, "A Bright Red Scream," 58.

5. Favazza, "Why Patients Mutilate Themselves," 137.

6. American Psychiatric Association, *Diagnostic and Statistical Manual of Mental Disorders*, 4th ed. (Washington, D.C.: American Psychiatric Association Press, 1994). This standard psychiatric diagnostic manual has become increasingly valuable with each new edition as the research and writing have improved.

7. Peter Kramer, *Listening to Prozac* (New York: Viking, 1993). This well-written book for both lay and professional audiences makes depression and its treatment with both medication and psychotherapy more understandable and more humane. It also raises provocative questions about the role of psychopharmacology in modifying personality.

8. Ibid.

9. P. Gjerde, "The Interpersonal Structure of Family Interaction Settings: Parent-Adolescent Relations in Dyads and Triads," *Developmental Psychology* 22 (1986): 297–304. This article was one of the first to examine parent-adolescent dyads. See also L. Steinberg, "The Impact of Puberty on Family Relations: Effects of Pubertal Status and Pubertal Timing," *Developmental Psychology* 23 (1987): 451–60. Steinberg, a clear writer and thinker and one of the recognized experts on adolescents' relationships with their families, focuses here on the role puberty plays in parent-child relationships and points out that the timing of puberty can affect both the parent-child relationship and risk-taking.

10. L. Steinberg, "Autonomy, Conflict, and Harmony in the Family Relationship," in S. W. Feldman and G. Elliott, eds., *At the Threshold* (Cambridge, Mass.: Harvard University Press, 1990), 255–77.

11. Carol Gilligan, *In a Different Voice: Psychological Theory and Women's Development* (Cambridge, Mass.: Harvard University Press, 1982); Carol Gilligan, N. Lyons, and T. Hamner, *Making Connections: The Relational Worlds of Adolescent Girls at Emma Willard School* (Cambridge, Mass.: Harvard University Press, 1990). This more recent volume focuses on adolescent girls at a particular private school, but the authors' conclusions have widespread application to adolescent girls across our society.

12. Gilligan, *In a Different Voice*; Lawrence Kohlberg and Carol Gilligan, "The Adolescent as Philosopher: The Discovery of the Self in a Post-Conventional World," *Daedalus* 100 (1971): 1051–86. It is a little-known fact that Carol Gilligan originally worked with Lawrence Kohlberg studying adolescent moral development. This early paper offers a very different perspective from that of her later work.

13. Lawrence Kohlberg, *The Philosophy of Moral Development* (New York: Harper & Row, 1981). This book on the moral development of boys is a classic.

14. K. McDonald and J. K. Thompson, "Eating Disturbance, Body Image Dissatisfaction, and Reasons for Exercising: Gender Differences and Correlational Findings," *International Journal of Eating Disorders* 11, no. 3 (1992): 289–92. This article stresses the importance of looking at girls'

underlying motivations for exercising. Disordered eating and poor body concepts are less prevalent among those exercising for health. If they are exercising to be thin—sometimes even identified as being "fit"—then exercise can become an insidious component of a damaged perspective on eating and body and sometimes even its own risk behavior. Parents need to listen carefully to what their daughters say about why they exercise and discuss the issues as they arise.

Chapter Nine

1. Diana Baumrind, "Early Socialization and Adolescent Competence," in S. Dragastin and G. H. Elder, eds., *Adolescence in the Life Cycle* (New York: Wiley, 1975), 117–43.

2. Lynn E. Ponton, "When Should a Child of Divorce Be in Psychotherapy?" *Family Advocate* 15, no. 3 (1993): 15–16.

3. R. E. Emery, *Marriage, Divorce, and Children's Adjustment* (Beverly Hills, Calif.: Sage, 1988). This readable volume neatly chronicles the cycles that parents, children, and families undergo pre- and postdivorce.

4. C. H. Sanders, "When You Suspect the Worst: False Issues," *Family Advocate* 15, no. 3 (1993): 54–58. This article describes the worst postdivorce scenarios—for example, parental alienation syndrome and false allegations of child abuse—and offers some commonsense suggestions.

5. Donald W. Winnicott, "Ego Distortions in Terms of True and False Self," in *The Maturational Processes and the Facilitating Environment* (New York: International Universities Press, 1965), 140–52.

6. Judith Wallerstein and S. Blakeslee, *Second Chances: Men, Women, and Children a Decade After Divorce* (New York: Ticknor and Fields, 1989). This well-written best-seller gives the long-range perspective on families and divorce. It is painful to read but extremely valuable, and a must for divorcing or divorced parents.

Chapter Ten

1. P. Trenton, *Independent Spirits* (Berkeley: University of California Press, 1995). This volume focuses on how the American West has been portrayed in history and the mythology that has developed around it.

2. R. Hyman, "The Social Construction of the Latchkey Children," *Sociological Studies of Child Development* 3 (1990): 163–74.

3. C. W. Sells and R. W. Blum, "Current Trends in Adolescent Health," in Ralph J. DiClemente, William B. Hansen, Lynn E. Ponton, eds., *Handbook of Adolescent Health Risk Behavior* (New York: Plenum, 1996), 5–35. This chapter examines broad patterns of adolescent risk-taking and makes predictions about the future—not necessarily an easy read.

4. D. Nutbeam, L. Aaar, and J. Catford, "Understanding Children's

Health Behavior: The Implications for Health Promotion for Young People," *Social Science Medicine* 29 (1989): 317–25.

5. M. Windle, J. T. Shope, and O. Bukstein, "Alcohol Use," in Di-Clemente, Hansen, and Ponton, *Handbook of Adolescent Health Risk Behavior*, 115–61. This chapter provides a tremendous amount of valuable information about adolescent alcoholism, much of it quite accessible to lay readers.

6. I. Lescohier and S. G. Gallagher, "Unintentional Injury," in Di-Clemente, Hansen, and Ponton, *Handbook of Adolescent Health Risk Behavior*, 225–59. This chapter is also quite accessible.

7. A. Schlegel and H. Barry, *Adolescence: An Anthropological Inquiry* (New York: Free Press, 1991). This is a fascinating sociological reference work on adolescence.

8. M. Pipher, *The Shelter of Each Other* (New York: Grosset/Putnam, 1996). This popular volume has many interesting clinical vignettes, but with no notes, it is difficult to decipher what is fact and what is the opinion of the author.

9. Ibid.

10. G. Fine, J. Mortimer, and D. Roberts, "Leisure, Work, and the Mass Media," in S. W. Feldman and G. Elliott, eds., *At the Threshold* (Cambridge, Mass.: Harvard University Press, 1990), 225–54. There are many myths about the role the media play in adolescents' lives. This chapter points out that more research is needed in this important area. In summary, blanket statements about the media and adolescents should be avoided in favor of examining the role of media in the lives of individual adolescents.

11. B. S. Greenberg, "Mass Media and Adolescents: A Review of Research Reported from 1980 to 1987" (manuscript prepared for the Carnegie Council on Adolescent Development, Department of Communication, Michigan State University, 1988).

12. Fine, Mortimer, and Roberts, "Leisure, Work, and the Mass Media," 248.

13. A. Bandura, *Social Functions of Thought and Action: A Social Cognitive Theory* (Englewood Cliffs, N.J.: Prentice-Hall, 1986), 225.

Chapter Eleven

1. Lynn E. Ponton, "Psychotherapy with Asian Adolescents," paper presented at the annual meeting of the American Society for Adolescent Psychiatry, Sante Fe, 13 October 1991. This paper, available upon request, details the psychotherapies of five Asian adolescents from different cultural backgrounds and presents both a literature review and successful clinical strategies for working with this group.

2. Erik H. Erikson, *Identity: Youth and Crisis* (New York: Norton, 1968).

This is one of five volumes on adolescence by Erikson I would recommend, but it does have some problems, including Erikson's attitudes
about the formation of female adolescent identity. For example, noting
that an adolescent girl's physical "design harbors an 'inner space' destined to bear the offspring of chosen men, and, with it, a biological, psychological, and ethical commitment to take care of human infancy"
(p. 266), he further asserts that ". . . much of a young woman's identity
is already defined in her kind of attractiveness and in the selective
nature of her search for the man or men by whom she wishes to be
sought" (p. 283). This book does set the stage, however, for looking at
adolescent risk-taking, both positive and negative, as tools used by the
adolescent to discover and define his or her identity.

3. Mary Jane Rotheram-Borus, "Ethnic Differences in Adolescent Identity Status and Associated Behavior Problems," *Journal of Adolescence* 12
(1989): 361–74. This article, which focuses on the pathology of behavioral symptoms, outlines the process of searching for identity particularly for adolescent ethnic minorities.

4. J. Streitmatter, "Ethnicity as a Mediating Variable of Early Adolescent
Identity Development," *Journal of Adolescence* 11 (1988): 335–46; J. S.
Phinney and L. L. Alipuria, "Ethnic Identity in College Students from
Four Ethnic Groups," *Journal of Adolescence* 13 (1990): 171–83.

5. S. N. Eisenstadt, *From Generation to Generation* (New York: Free Press,
1956); J. S. Coleman, *The Adolescent Society* (New York: Free Press,
1961); P. Goodman, "A Social Critic on 'Moral Youth in an Immoral
Society,'" in *The Young Americans* (New York: Times Books, 1966),
18–19. These authors use case examples of adolescent groups from the
1950s and early 1960s; limited research and clinical material are provided. Perhaps most important, however, each of these works fur-
thered the misconception that adolescents are a unified group locked
into a hostile struggle with adults, especially parents.

6. J. B. Brooks, *The Process of Parenting* (Mountain View, Calif.: Mayfield,
1991). This is one of the best books about parenting children of all
ages, including adolescents. Brooks has a strong interest in the role that
parents can play and provides helpful suggestions backed up by the advice of clinicians and researchers.

7. B. B. Brown, M. J. Lohr, and E. L. McClenan, "Adolescents' Perceptions of Peer Pressure," *Journal of Early Adolescence* 6 (1986), 139–54.

8. A. Schlegel and H. Barry, *Adolescence: An Anthropological Inquiry* (New
York: Free Press, 1991). This volume, written by two sociologists, examines how groups of adolescents work together and are influenced by
adults. Some of the most interesting information is about the very limited amount of time that adults spend with adolescents, especially boys.

9. Brown, Lohr, and McClenan, "Adolescents' Perceptions of Peer Pressure," 139.

10. Nan D. Stein, "Sexual Harassment in K–12 Schools: The Public Performance of Gendered Violence," *Harvard Educational Review, Special Issue on Violence and Youth* 65, no. 2 (1995): 145–62. Dr. Nan Stein, of the Center for Research on Women at Wellesley College, has studied sexual harassment of children and adolescents for decades, and reports that such experiences are extremely common, affecting girls more than boys, and often go unrecognized by parents and schools. Only recently has the government's memo on sexual harassment of children and adolescents been issued. See U.S. Department of Education Office for Civil Rights, *Sexual Harassment Guidance: Harassment of Students by School Employees, Other Students, or Third Parties, Federal Register* 62, no. 49 (17 March 1997): 12034–51.

11. Lynn E. Ponton, "Sexual Harassment of Children and Adolescent Girls," in D. Shrier, ed., *Sexual Harassment in the Workplace and Academia* (Washington, D.C.: American Psychiatric Press, 1996), 181–201. This comprehensive article discusses how harassment occurs most frequently in this age group, as well as treatment and forensic issues.

Chapter Twelve

1. L. Crocket, M. Lasoff, and A. C. Petersen, "Perceptions of the Peer Group and Friendship in Early Adolescence," *Journal of Early Adolescence* 4 (1984): 155–81. This article chronicles the history of cliques across adolescence. Middle-school years are rife with not only cliques but their companion activity, scapegoating.

2. M. Schwartz, "Negative Impact of Sexual Abuse on Adult Male Gender: Issues and Strategies of Intervention," *Child and Adolescent Social Work Journal* 3 (7 June 1994): 179–94. Both long unrecognized and believed to occur less frequently, abuse of males has long been ignored — in large part because boys are reluctant to report abuse because it is considered unmanly and makes them appear weak. This article underscores the importance of hidden abuse.

3. S. O'Malley, "Girls 'n the Hood," *Harper's Bazaar* (October 1993): 239–43, 281–82.

4. D. L. Hussey, G. Strom, and M. I. Singer, "Male Victims of Sexual Abuse," *Child and Adolescent Social Work Journal* 9, no. 6 (1992): 491–503. This article details the problems that boys can be left with as a result of sexual abuse.

5. Mark Lodico, Enid Gruber, and Ralph J. DiClemente, "Childhood Sexual Abuse and Coercive Sex Among School-Based Adolescents in a Midwestern State" (unpublished manuscript, 1995). The consequences of sexual abuse in children and adolescents are extremely serious. Increased involvement in forced sex, either as a victim or as an abuser, is one of the most serious. This study underscores the importance of de-

tecting and treating sexual abuse in boys, who are at significantly higher risk to participate in ongoing abuse, whether as perpetrator or victim, than their nonabused counterparts.

6. Ralph J. DiClemente, Lynn E. Ponton, and D. Hartley, "Prevalence and Correlates of Cutting Behavior: Risk for HIV Transmission," *Journal of the American Academy of Child and Adolescent Psychiatry* 30, no. 5 (1991): 735–40.

7. A. Schlegel and H. Barry III, "Peer Groups and Community Participation," in A. Schlegel & H. Barry III, eds., *Adolescence* (New York: Free Press, 1991), 67–92. This well-written overview of adolescence emphasizes the limited involvement of adults in the lives of adolescent boys.

8. B. B. Brown, M. J. Lohr, and C. M. Trujillo, "Multiple Crowds and Multiple Lifestyles: Adolescents' Perceptions of Peer Group Characteristics," in R. E. Muuss, ed., *Adolescent Behavior and Society: A Book of Readings* (New York: Random House, 1990), 30–36.

Chapter Thirteen

1. Norman Garmezy, "Resilience in Children's Adaptation to Negative Life Events and Stressed Environments," *Pediatric Annals* 20, no. 9 (September 1991): 466. Garmezy has, over several decades, written numerous articles on resiliency. This article, one of the more recent, encompasses many of his earlier ideas.

2. Michael Rutter, "Protective Factors in Children's Responses to Stress and Disadvantage," in M. W. Kent and J. E. Rolf, eds., *Primary Prevention of Psychopathology*, vol. 3, *Social Competence in Children* (Hanover, N.H.: University Press of New England, 1979), 49–74; Rutter, like Garmezy, is one of the most articulate investigators in the field of children and resiliency. See also P. A. Gribble, E. L. Cowen, P. A. Wyman, W. C. Work, M. Wannon, and A. Raoof, "Parent and Child Views of Parent-Child Relationship Qualities and Resilient Outcomes Among Urban Children," *Journal of Child Psychology and Psychiatry and Allied Disciplines* 34, no. 4 (May 1993): 507–19.

3. Suniya Luthar, "Vulnerability and Resilience: A Study of High-Risk Adolescents," *Child Development* 62, no. 3 (1991): 600–616. Luthar is a member of the newer generation of researchers in the field of resiliency. This particularly fascinating study of high-risk youth from a slum describes the burden that resilient teens carry with them throughout their lives.

4. T. H. Ogden, *The Matrix of the Mind: Object Relations and the Psychoanalytic Dialogue* (Northvale, N.J.: Jason Aronson, 1986).

5. B. Neighbors, R. Forehand, and D. McVicar, "Resilient Adolescents and Interpersonal Conflict," *American Journal of Orthopsychiatry* 63, no. 3 (July 1993): 462–71.

Index